FOREWORD BY

SHOCK
OF THE
NEW

THE CHALLENGE
AND PROMISE
OF EMERGING
TECHNOLOGY

CHAD UDELL AND
GARY WOODILL

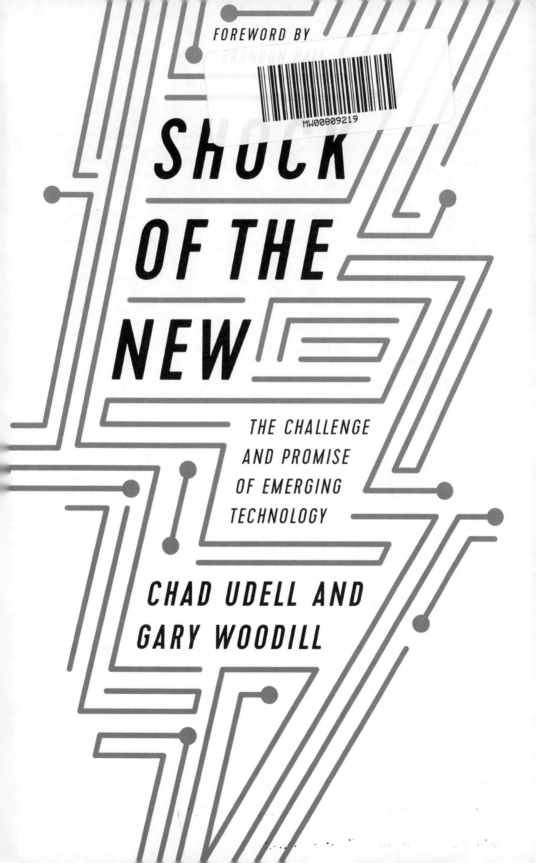

ATD Press is an internationally renowned source of insightful and practical information on talent development, training, and professional development.

ATD Press
1640 King Street
Alexandria, VA 22314 USA

Ordering information: Books published by ATD Press can be purchased by visiting ATD's website at www.td.org/books or by calling 800.628.2783 or 703.683.8100.

Library of Congress Control Number: 2019933796

ISBN-10: 1-947308-80-7
ISBN-13: 978-1-947308-80-0
e-ISBN: 978-1-947308-81-7

ATD Press Editorial Staff
Director: Kristine Luecker
Manager: Melissa Jones
Community of Practice Manager, Management: Ryan Changcoco
Developmental Editor: Kathryn Stafford
Text Design: Michelle Jose and Shirley E.M. Raybuck
Cover Design: Faceout Studio, Spencer Fuller

Printed by Versa Press, East Peoria, IL

CONTENTS

FOREWORD

*I*f you're involved with technology for learning and development, you're facing ever-increasing challenges with the selection and use of technology. This book will give you a multiyear look-ahead of the massive innovations and cool tools you may be asked to learn about and implement over the next five to 10 years.

Here's the thing: Every few months, technology becomes more complex, more interconnected, and more embedded in your organization's internal systems. The BUILDS framework presented here will provide you with a broad perspective you can use to evaluate the predicted as well as the largely unforeseen consequences of a new technology for your organization. You will learn to be a systems thinker; someone who is able to watch out for the concerns of the enterprise as well as those of individual learners—before unintended consequences appear.

How did you first get involved with technology for learning and talent?

I don't know your route, but I'll tell you mine. In the early 1980s, stories about Steve Jobs and the personal computer captured everyone's attention. A cultural shift was happening and I wanted to be part of it. It was time to "Go West, young man," so I picked up and moved to Silicon Valley. I soon bought my first computer, an Apple II. Oh, and then I bought $3,000 of stock in a little-known company named Intel. More on that later.

Besides my early connection with technology, I want you to know what I learned in my first Silicon Valley job with Wilson Learning Corporation. The company's founder, Larry Wilson, was a great teacher and futurist, and he espoused beliefs that were very much related to the book you are holding. He got many of his ideas from another powerful source of the day: Alvin Toffler's *Future Shock*. As a reminder, future shock is what happens when change is coming so fast that people are left confused and stressed, and normal decision making is no longer sufficient to deal with the complexities presented. Sound familiar?

That last part is key: normal decision making is no longer sufficient to deal with the complexities presented. And that's the focus of this book. *Shock of the New* provides a framework for you to use to be mindful of the known and unknown implications—the unintended consequences—of new technology in your organization. This framework will help you become aware of more of the issues, make better decisions, and reduce your organization's future shock, the shock of the new.

I am not aware of any other resources that will guide you in keeping the broader issues of technology selection in mind. You'll find a 30-question scoring system for evaluating the selection of new technologies, which has been organized into six categories. The categories make up the authors' BUILDS framework. You'll then see this framework applied to six different emerging learning technologies, revealing the implications of technologies you'll likely be dealing with soon.

It turns out that every new technology has far-reaching and often novel implications. The BUILDS framework uncovers an entire landscape of these implications and impacts that result from the technology choices you and your colleagues make today and will make tomorrow. It is to your advantage to look at these potential impacts from the broadest possible perspective. You need a way to see the bigger picture, and to be aware of unanticipated outcomes.

My friend and trusted colleague Gary Woodill and his co-author Chad Udell know more about current and future learning and development technologies than anyone else I know. Few people are as tech-savvy, future-aware, and broadly informed as Gary. He has the academic research rigor and persistence to gather all the relevant information to help you understand the topic at hand. His primary objective, for as long as I have known him, is to stay abreast of all the current and emerging trends in technology for learning. He is a technology futurist, and research-based at that. He knows what he is talking about.

Chad is cut from similar cloth. He's unique in combining experience and training in design with one of the most innovative minds in technology. He's truly on the leading edge of technology development, and deeply understands innovative software. As a side project, Chad designed and led a team to develop a smartphone app for people with visual impairments using computer vision, in a project funded by Google. He knows the future of technology and is developing learning apps using both augmented reality and virtual reality.

Future shock is not going away. Not only are bigger changes coming, but the rate, breadth, and magnitude of change is accelerating. And there's no end in sight. There's no future predicted for our lifetime where innovation will slow down and we'll have a chance to get caught up, sort it all out, and fix all the problems. So, use the information in this book to help you and your organization deal with what is coming at you.

To bring this full circle, I spoke earlier of Steve Jobs. As you may know, Jobs started playing with computers while he was still in high school, where he met Steve Wozniak. Until a few years ago, I lived across the street from the house where Steve Wozniak grew up and where he tinkered with circuit boards in his garage. That house is gone, and Steve Jobs has passed on, leaving his mark. Today each of us carries the world's knowledge in our pocket and life will never be the same for any of us, or our children.

Change continues. By the way, I sold that Intel stock after only a year. Today, as near as I can tell, it would be worth somewhere north of $10 million. (Sigh.)

You are one of the influencers for the best use of technology in your organization. Best of luck as you help reduce the shock of the new.

Brandon Hall, PhD
Executive Coach
Founder, Brandon Hall Group

PREFACE

*T*oday, we all are immersed in the flow of nonstop technological change. But, as the currents of change sweep around, over, and by us, we may be so caught up in efforts to keep up with the next new thing, we're hardly aware of how much change has actually happened just during our lifetimes.

The two of us have been collaborating on new technologies and thinking about their meaning for nearly a decade, yet our paths to this common point could not have been more different.

For Gary, an awareness that a shift from an analog to a digital world was under way dawned in 1966 with his first part-time, post–high school job—shelving and checking out books at the York University Library in Toronto, Canada. In the back of each book was a card full of little rectangular holes. To check a book in or out, you stuck the card into a machine that read the information and sent a message to the mainframe computer housed in the basement of the library. The rest was a mystery.

The possibility that computers could be used as teaching tools occurred to Gary in 1974 when his graduate school supervisor at Memorial University in St. John's, Newfoundland and Labrador, Canada, invited him to attend a demonstration of the PLATO computer-based learning system, running on the university's mainframe computer, which was located somewhere on campus (but who knew where?). This led to an interest in building educational content for the Telidon videotext trials at TVOntario in Toronto, and using something called a "personal computer," a Commodore PET, housed in the library of the college where he was teaching. When he started his doctorate in education in 1980 at the University of Toronto, Gary took his first programming courses, and over the next four-year period witnessed the introduction of email on a VAX minicomputer, and the arrival of the Apple II, the MacIntosh LISA, and the IBM PC Junior microcomputers, all used in educational computing contexts.

In 1983 he was surprised and impressed to learn that his new friend, Karen Anderson, had a terminal in her apartment hooked up to the university's VAX computer using an acoustic modem. It was love at first sight, and they were married a year later. They acquired their first computer shortly after—a 26-pound metal-encased Kaypro II running the CPM operating system. A year later, they replaced the Kaypro with one of the first laptops in the world—a Radio Shack Model 100, with 24 Kb of memory. There was a real sense at the time that everything was on the cusp of immense change, brought about by the advent of personal computers, but no one really knew just how much change would happen over the next 35 years.

Meanwhile, young Chad was in first grade and nurturing a love of technology of his own. From the Christmas that brought an Atari 2600 and a few games to the school computer cart (yes, one computer for an entire school!) with the Apple II, Chad was immersed in understanding how games and programming worked. By the age of eight, he signed up for a summer program to learn Basic. He ended up teaching his teachers how to program Logo and write simple text-based applications. As he grew and his love of technology, creativity, and art also grew, he taught himself Illustrator and Photoshop, and then Hypercard, inspired by the now classic 3-D adventure game Myst. He also introduced desktop publishing to the yearbook at his high school.

After going on to Bradley University, spending his nights hacking his PowerMac 7100/66 with ResEdit, and building his first websites for Mosaic in 1995 with SimpleText and GifBuilder, Chad was hooked! He simply had to continue the journey of melding design and the latest technology. After graduation, he got a job designing music websites in Chicago and built Flash games, skins for mp3 players, and lots of other fun digital bits— always at the cutting edge of the web, digital design, and high-tech. Soon, his evenings and weekends were filled with teaching classes on the tools of the trade. He loved sharing his knowledge with others just starting their own journeys.

Later, Chad joined a digital agency closer to his college home and began working on innovative interactive installations featuring gestural controls, Wi-Fi controlled robots, and lots of interactive rich-media and mashups. His exploration of mobile devices started around this time, too, captivating his imagination and pointing to the possibilities of a new age of the untethered computer, one more powerful than its predecessors due to its unique capabilities. He joined his alma mater's interactive media department as an adjunct instructor, lending his expertise to the next generation of technical designers and developers.

In 2010, Chad co-founded Float Mobile Learning, a custom software development company in Morton, Illinois. Float has been an innovator, winning awards for its app design and development, research in xAPI, and groundbreaking work in augmented reality and computer vision. At industry events, the Float team would both showcase their work and help others learn about emerging technologies.

In this new venture, Chad and the team scoured the web looking for new talent to join their team. After Chad reviewed Gary's 2010 book, *The Mobile Learning Edge,* he invited him to join an event Float was planning—a symposium on mobile learning at Bradley University. Gary and Chad hit it off instantly. The bond? New and emerging technology, of course!

We've been working together ever since—on three book projects, including this one, blogs, whitepapers, and conference presentations for Float. Our clients have kept us on the leading edge of change for the past decade. Clients demand innovation to create competitive advantages using the latest technologies. But, as we've learned, achieving a competitive advantage for our clients is not as simple as just using the latest technologies. Every innovation must be assessed in the context of each client's situation, and the pros and cons of the affordances of the new technology.

This book is our effort to raise awareness of technological changes that may be coming your way, to give you the tools to assess emerging learning technologies and their relevance to your enterprise. It's the culmination of our collaboration—and it wouldn't have been possible without countless conversations at conferences, online in our personal learning networks, and, of course, in our close relationships with our co-workers and colleagues. On behalf of both of us, please enjoy *Shock of the New.*

Chad Udell and Gary Woodill
Metamora, Illinois, and
Belleville, Ontario
April 2019

INTRODUCTION

*T*here have been so many new learning technologies over the past decade, it tends to make your head spin. Each year we are confronted by the latest and greatest technologies at conference sessions, in keynotes, and in industry publications. Given that the pace of change is accelerating, how do talent development and learning professionals keep up with what is new? How do we judge what is important for our organizations? How will we know something is not just a fad but will change the way the world works forever? How can we plan for the near future in a world of constant change?

Learning is still critical for companies to remain competitive, to keep up with innovation, and to win in the world of business. This means learning leaders need to ditch old ideas of being mostly experts and sources of information for the more exciting challenges of guiding individuals and teams into a "new normal" that uses technologies to support the company, helps build relevant collective shared knowledge and a "learning culture," and reignites enthusiasm for accomplishing goals that meet real human needs. To do this, learning professionals need to understand the workings and implications of the new technologies, recognizing that workplace learning is critically different than classroom-based learning and is just as important as any other function of a business. Many varieties of learning are going to be called for, from memorization of mission-critical safety and security protocols to experiences with vision-busting simulations in virtual reality, and everything in between.

Emerging technologies are those that have already been invented but are not well known or widely distributed. They are defined as technologies "currently being developed and holding a realistic potential to not only become reality, but to become socially and economically relevant within the foreseeable future" (Stahl, Timmermans, and Flick 2017). Emerging technologies are often unpredictable, changing things in ways we could not have foreseen. As for relevancy in the next five years for learning and development, some of the most commonly discussed emerging technologies include 3-D printing, artificial intelligence (AI), augmented reality (AR), big data and analytics, cloud computing, the Internet of Things (IoT), mobile learning, personalization algorithms, robotics, virtual reality (VR), and wearables. Other information and communications technologies (ICT) that are emerging over a 10- to 20-year timeframe and will likely impact learning in the longer term include affective computing, ambient intelligence, bioelectronics, a redesigned Internet, human-machine symbiosis, neuroelectronics, and quantum computing.

To say that we are living through a period of rapid change is already a cliché. The reaction to the new will be different for each individual, depending on the impact of the change on one's life, one's tolerance for change, and one's ability to cope. Many of us welcome change and new technologies, and thrive in the novelty and wonder of what is coming next. Others experience turmoil, loss of jobs, precarious work, and a feeling of being overwhelmed with the requirements of managing all the new technologies that show up each year. Learning professionals are no different than anyone else; they will have a variety of reactions to the disruptive times we are going through.

When we began our research, we assumed that learning technology evaluation frameworks or rubrics that we could work from already existed. But after an extensive search, we found none that could actually assist us in evaluating recent emerging learning technologies for the workplace. The few evaluation frameworks that were available were well over 10 years old, making their examples almost irrelevant in terms of today's technologies (for example, Oliver 1998). Consider that 10 years ago the iPhone had just been invented, augmented reality was largely confined to lab environments, and the iPad simply did not exist. (However, we did find some of the evaluation criteria in these frameworks were still useful—for example, Geisler 1999).

While we were able to locate many examples of evaluation frameworks for *educational* technologies (Heinecke et al. 1999; Oliver 2000; Johnston and Barker 2002; Noeth and Volkov 2004; Ozkan and McKenzie 2006; Calinger and Howard 2008; Lee and Cherner 2015), we felt that they were not representative of trends and contextual variables in non-educational organizations, such as companies, the military, governments, or the nonprofit sector (collectively referred to as *enterprise* learning). As we argue later, the evaluation of learning technologies for workplaces has to be quite different than for school or university-based classrooms.

That said, we were unable to find an evaluation approach that both reflected the realities of changing workplaces and considered all the new technologies that have arrived since 2000. A few writers focused on evaluation frameworks for specific technologies and workplace learning (such as Ramstad's [2009] "developmental framework for innovation and learning networks" and Hsu and Ching's [2015] review of "models and frameworks for designing mobile learning"), but there is no overall framework for the evaluation of emerging learning technologies. Perhaps the closest attempt to develop a framework for the evaluation of emerging enterprise learning technologies is the one based on the business-oriented Balanced Scorecard (BSC) approach developed at Tehran University in Iran (Kaplan and Norton 1992). "E-learning BSC contains four original perspectives: (1) financial perspective (2) e-learner perspective (3) internal process perspective (4) learning and growth perspective" (Momeni et al. 2013). While we find these four perspectives supportive of our thinking, they don't go far enough.

Welcome to the BUILDS Framework

So, we developed our own framework, with lots of help from the research and writing of others in the enterprise learning field. Our work has been a genuine collaborative effort, with weekly phone calls; sharing of articles, journals, and books; exchanges of many drafts; and the melding of more than 60 years' combined experience in the field of learning. In this age of complexity, collaboration is the only way to overcome the "ingenuity gap" that humans now face (Homer-Dixon 2000).

We particularly wanted to take a broader view of evaluating learning technologies, one that went beyond "the workplace" to include the wider world. This was important to us because we are now living in a highly connected networked society, and the technologies we use have larger implications for our society as a whole.

In thinking about the evaluation of learning technologies, we worked and reworked different ways to critically describe the current and emerging situation in enterprises in Western societies. We recognize that while we are both technophiles with biases for the use of technologies (rather than seeing them as inherently dangerous), critics of technology are out there. We take their concerns seriously and address the fact that all technologies have bright and dark sides (Holland and Bardoel 2016; Foer 2017).

For our framework, we've picked six evaluative perspectives:

- Business
- User experiences
- Impact
- Learning
- Dependencies
- Signals.

The first letter of each of these six perspectives form the acronym BUILDS, which adds a positive spin (as we noted, we do have a bias in favor of technology!). To apply the framework, we've created a rubric of 30 questions—five per perspective—that you should consider when evaluating any emerging learning technology.

While we recognize we could be missing something or have failed to recognize an implication of adopting a technology that may show up in the next few years, that's the nature of the emergence of "complex adaptive systems" (Holland 2012). As such, changes in enterprises and learning technologies are inherently unpredictable. At best, we can map out likely scenarios for the next five to 10 years. Beyond that, all bets are off.

About This Book

Our purpose in *Shock of the New* is to both offer answers to some of the questions we posed at the beginning of this introduction and to provide you, as learning and talent development professionals, a framework for making judgments about the importance of emerging technologies that can affect you and your organization.

In chapter 1, "The Digital Transformation of Enterprise Learning," we look at the last 20 years of disruption within the learning and talent development field, caused by the introduction of digital technologies. We outline what is driving the growth of digital technologies, especially those that are important for the learning and talent development industry. But, we also caution against the idea that disruption is *automatically* happening within specific industries. While disruption theory suggests that the old collapses and the new takes over, this is often not the case (Christensen, Raynor, and McDonald 2015). There are both incremental changes and disruptive changes happening at any given time in all industries.

Whenever change happens within an industry, it engenders a feeling of turmoil. But eventually things level out and we experience a "new normal"—a pattern known in evolutionary theory as "punctuated equilibrium," borrowed from evolutionary biology where bursts of change and abrupt speciation are interjected between relatively stable periods of stasis. The same concept can be applied to technology as well, where many devices, services, and other products emerge abruptly, followed by some level of percolating calm.

In addition, not all technologies are successful or useful, or capable of sustained success (Cochrane 2012). There are numerous examples where a specific technology has been hyped and investments made and some growth occurred, only to recede and disappear a few years later. A good example is the growth and decline of the simulation platform Second Life as an educational environment (Mark 2014). While it had 5.5 million users in 2016, that had dropped to less than half a million users a year later. We don't know anyone in the learning and talent development industries who is still on the platform, which is now described as a "digital ghost town," with residents and businesses "fleeing for more popular social networks long ago" (Veix 2018).

How can we know if this is likely to happen to other technologies? And, even if a technology grows and thrives, is it the right technology for you as a learning professional? Will it help you accomplish your mission in your organization? It's important we get a realistic view of what the new normal is likely to be so we can be prepared for it.

The heart of the book, chapters 2 to 7, presents the six perspectives of our BUILDS framework for evaluating emerging learning technologies. Chapter 2, "Business Needs for Learning Technologies," shows how to evaluate a technology's impact on your business's bottom line. Learning and development departments can sometimes overlook this key area of technology assessment by placing a premium on learning; business stakeholders, on the other hand, have no difficulty placing a premium on bottom-line numbers. If impact on the bottom line is not the first consideration, it may be hard to get funding for the implementation of any new technology.

In chapter 3, "User Experiences of Learning Technologies," we explain how to evaluate technologies in terms of end user experience (UX) and identify their key affordances. There are many ways to design the implementation of any technology, as each new technology has a set of "affordances" or features that allow something to be done with that technology. Indeed, understanding the value of the design to the user by uncovering the users' true needs and goals is vital to determining if a new technology is worth using in your business.

When it is introduced to the world, every technology has both intended and unintended consequences. Chapter 4, "The Wider Impacts of Learning Technologies," describes a new technology's three levels of impact—the micro-level impact on individuals and small teams, the meso-level or organizational impact, and the macro-level impact at regional, national, and global levels. We briefly look at how to evaluate the impact of emerging learning technologies for individuals, organizations, and the planet to remind us that we are all interconnected. Learning usually takes place within a "complex adaptive system" (Holland 2012), which includes a designated learning environment as well as networked connections for all employees. Learning and talent development is only one part of the functioning of any organization, but we need to play our part in making each enterprise sustainable in the future.

One of the main purposes of any learning technology is to facilitate learning. However, as we'll see in chapter 5, "Learning With Emerging Technologies," there are many different types of learning, and some technologies better support one type over another. For the purposes of discussion in this book, we emphasize workplace learning over learning that takes place in educational settings such as schools and universities. This is an important distinction, as we all have grown up in an educational system and tend to have a bias toward its methods of teaching and assessment.

In chapter 6, "Dependencies of Learning Technologies," we discuss those aspects of the environment and other technologies that need to be in place to have a successful implementation of a learning technology. Dependencies can range from having proper policies in place to receiving support from upper echelon executives or key employees, getting impeccable security, and ensuring that the right infrastructure, hardware, and software are available to company employees. There is a dark side to dependencies as well, due to the secondary definition of the word, which we also cover. Dependency is often a topic that is ignored or neglected when evaluating new learning technologies.

Chapter 7, "Signals of the Future," examines the final category of the BUILDS framework—those signs of where a technology is going next and what to expect in the near future. Here we take a five- to 10-year perspective because it is almost impossible to predict the state of technology and the world beyond that. At the same time, we recognize most of the technology that's coming within the next five years has already been started somewhere in the world, either as a proposal or a prototype. Here we reveal our sources and methods for predicting the (near) future of emerging learning technologies.

In Chapter 8, "Crafting Strategies for Emerging Learning Technologies," we look at what is needed to manage the changes that are inevitable when new technologies are introduced into an organization. How will a new technology affect jobs and the organization chart? Does your group have a change management strategy in place? If not, this chapter points the way to developing such a strategy. Given that emerging digital technologies are usually disruptive and can leave the executives and staff of an enterprise behind, what are the skill sets necessary for successful learning and talent managers in the digital age? What is digital literacy for a corporate or government talent development leader?

In addition to a glossary, the appendix features the BUILDS framework in its entirety, along with six samples of the framework applied to specific emerging technologies.

We see this as an optimistic book. While it is true that your roles as learning and talent development professionals are rapidly changing, you can look forward to important new missions in the evaluation, selection, implementation, and operation of a host of new learning technologies. In reading and using the guidelines and suggestions we make, we hope that you will gain a new perspective on what is coming next, and what you can do to get ready for the changes on the horizon. Most of all, we hope that you find *Shock of the New* useful, both at the higher-order levels of help in planning, strategy, and change management, and at the day-to-day level facing the challenges of implementing a specific learning technology in your workplace, wherever it may be.

CHAPTER 1

The Digital Transformation of Enterprise Learning

Marshall McLuhan (1966), the communications guru of the 1960s, once remarked that he didn't know who discovered water, but he was sure that it wasn't a fish. Of course, a fish will notice when it is taken out of water, because this disruption is life-threatening and highly unusual. Today, we humans are metaphorically swimming in a vast sea of electromagnetic signals, electronic devices, complex software, and highly interconnected infrastructure. It's everywhere, so like the fish in water we tend not to notice it as we go about our daily lives.

Unless, of course, something happens to disrupt our daily living with digital devices. People panic when they can't find their mobile phone. They know when the Internet goes down and fret about lack of access until it is back up. If the electric grid goes down, we notice the absence of the technologies we take for granted. But, it doesn't take long for a newly introduced technology to be normalized and become an essential part of our taken-for-granted world, even if it didn't exist a few years earlier. We have become that fish.

The Fourth Industrial Revolution

In the years following World War II, most people in the West were still in the "third industrial revolution" of desktop or larger computers, magnetic storage disks, local company servers, and large IT departments to manage it all. (The first and second industrial revolutions were those based on steam power and then electricity and assembly lines.) The "fourth industrial revolution" describes the "exponential changes to the way we live, work and relate to one another due to the adoption of cyber-physical systems, the Internet of Things and the Internet of Systems" (Marr 2018a). It's based on global networking, sensors, mobility, distributed cloud-based storage of information, and the use of algorithms and machine learning. Klaus Schwab (2017), founder and chairman of the World Economic Forum, contends that the fourth industrial revolution is "fundamentally changing the way we live, work, and relate to one another. In its scale, scope and complexity, what I consider to be the fourth industrial revolution is unlike anything humankind has experienced before." He adds, "We have yet to grasp fully the speed and breadth of this new revolution."

There are now so many distinct changes in how the world is organized, and therefore how we live, that there are too many to track. In *The Inevitable: Understanding the 12 Technological Forces That Will Shape Our Future*, futurist Kevin Kelly (2016) lists some major changes we are currently experiencing (and there are many more):

- **Becoming.** We are all newbies in the changes that are coming, some of which are unpredictable.
- **Cognifying.** While artificial intelligence has been in development for many decades, true AI is only happening now with the new global mind being constructed through the networking of billions of electronic devices.
- **Flowing.** Welcome to the world of the "liquid enterprise," where the expectation of stability has gone out the window.
- **Screening.** Everything is a potential display and screens are everywhere.
- **Accessing.** Ownership of property is disappearing as we move into a world of real on-time demand for objects and services we need at the moment.
- **Sharing.** Free, open, and user-generated content that can be shared by anyone is becoming the norm. A side benefit is the development of a sense of community through the act of sharing and collaboration.
- **Filtering.** Curating and recommendation engines have become

necessary in a world where there is too much to know and a superabundance of choices.

- **Remixing.** Content now has many new forms, and recombinant innovation is the most common form of innovation of old and new forms, while fans produce their own sequels and illustrations of stories.
- **Interacting.** It used to be that interacting meant clicking on a button. Now we have the added information of augmented reality and the deeply immersive experiences of realistic virtual reality to stimulate our senses. Simulated worlds, populated with the avatars of other people, draw millions of people online each day.
- **Tracking.** Inexpensive wearable devices mean that almost all aspects of life can be monitored and recorded. Sensors linked together in the emerging "Internet of Things" (IoT) will generate immense amounts of data stored in the cloud for later access and analysis.
- **Questioning.** Certainty about the nature of truth has decreased, while the search for answers has increased. The emergence of a new level of organization based on large-scale collaboration and real-time social interaction is changing the game and making questioning absolutely necessary. At the same time, technologies for building trust are emerging.
- **Beginning.** We are at the beginning stages of building a global brain with a collaborative interface accessed through mostly mobile devices. As we use this new invention it is learning about us as individuals and as collectivities all the time.

To be successful in the future, we need to pay attention to new organizing principles that realign how we deal with the world. These include the ideas of dynamic emergence instead of static authority; pulling information when we need it instead of it being pushed to us; using digital compasses and GPS instead of paper maps to guide us through the new landscape; taking risks instead of staying safe; disobeying rules when appropriate instead of automatically complying; learning from practice rather than theory; looking for diversity instead of expertise; valuing resilience over strength; and living with non-linear complex systems containing feedback loops instead of static objects that never change. In fact, we are probably dealing with nested relationships where individual components of a system may themselves be complex systems (Ito and Howe 2016). For example, a typical smartphone is sort of a "Trojan horse" made up of more than 30 distinct technologies. This new world is not circumscribed by the boundaries of an organization or a department, but is affected by inputs from and outputs to the larger environment. Understanding what is happening requires a whole new analysis of the world as well as our own little corner of it (Gibson and Ifenthaler 2017).

How did it come to this in such a short period of time? One of the first people to recognize the immense changes that we are going through was the founder of the MIT MediaLab, Nicholas Negroponte. In his 1995 book, *Being Digital,* Negroponte argues that the key change was the shift from the concrete analog world of atoms to the ephemeral construction of a new form of reality made of bits of pure information. As he explains:

> World trade has traditionally consisted of exchanging atoms. . . . You go through customs you declare your atoms, not your bits. . . . This is changing rapidly. The methodical movement of recorded music as pieces of plastic, like the slow human handling of most information in the form of books, magazines, newspapers, and videocassettes, is about to become the instantaneous and inexpensive transfer of electronic data that move at the speed of light. In this form, the information can become universally accessible... The change from atoms to bits is irrevocable and unstoppable.

It is much easier to trash and then rebuild something made out of bits than to get rid of and reconstruct an item made of atoms. This is why software pioneer and investor Marc Andreessen (2011) argues that "software is eating the world." He adds, "Six decades into the computer revolution, four decades since the invention of the microprocessor, and two decades into the rise of the modern Internet, all of the technology required to transform industries through software finally works and can be widely delivered at global scale." So, while the new infrastructure that is being built is absolutely necessary for digital transformation to occur, it is the development of software that makes it all happen.

Digital computers that use binary programming were first developed by German engineers around 1939, and have grown in number and power ever since. German computing was countered by the primitive computers and programs developed by Alan Turing and his colleagues in the United Kingdom for breaking Nazi codes during World War II (Dyson 2012).

Digitization is a unique form of representation, where some aspect of reality is broken into discrete units, which are then represented by two or more "digits." We tend to think of digitization as a new phenomenon, but as Berlinski (2000, 14) points out, the idea is present in the ideas of 17th-century philosopher and mathematician Gottfried von Leibniz:

> Ultimately, Leibniz argued, there are only two absolutely simple concepts - God and Nothingness. From these, all other concepts may be constructed, the world, and everything with it, arising from some primordial argument between the deity and nothing whatsoever. And then, by some inscrutable incandescent insight, Leibniz came to see that what is crucial in what he had written is the alternation between God and Nothingness. And for this, the numbers 0 and 1 suffice.

The code used in 19th-century electrical telegraph systems (which were preceded by sophisticated non-electrical visual telegraph systems) was a digital, binary code (Eschner 2017). Combinations of dots and dashes were used to represent the letters of the alphabet, numbers, and punctuation marks, forming a scheme like the ASCII code developed for computer displays in 1963 (Pushman 2003).

But the true power of digitization is not in binary coding or its ability to transmit information. The electric telegraph could do both. Rather, it is in the ability of electronic computers to break analog phenomena into discrete pieces; represent those pieces as digits; store this data in memory or permanent media or both; manipulate the digits to transform them into something else according to instructions in stored programs; and then output the results either in another digital form for later use or transmission to other computers, or in the form of analog (re)constructions that are then available to humans through their senses. The digital computer and related high-speed networks are new representational, transformational, and distribution technologies that, together, "change everything" (Parrish 2017).

What was once science fiction has become real. How do things go from idea to execution? Innovation starts at the fringes, in the science fairs and poster sessions where eager graduate students reveal their latest ideas and projects. Eventually, the best of those ideas may become commercialized— made into products and widely distributed.

Disruption often comes in the form of something new and unanticipated. Suddenly, we notice a technology we have never seen before and wonder how it will change our world. We tend to think of it as having just arrived, when in fact most new and emerging technologies have been in development for several decades.

Take mobile learning, for example. Mobile phones have been dreamed about and written about in science fiction since the beginning of the 20th century. The first example of "mobile learning" that we can find was based on a radio receiver used by groups of patrons of the Stedelijk Museum in Amsterdam in 1952 as they moved from painting to painting listening to descriptions of the piece of art they were viewing (Tallon 2008). Mobile learning emerged from the complex interactions of many people and technologies, developing slowly from the 1950s to the present.

Yet for many people, mobile learning began just over a dozen years ago with the development of the Apple iPhone in 2007, when the term gained popularity in the learning and talent development industry. It's just that most people don't see an emergence coming until it becomes a commercial product. Whenever it happens for you, the awareness of something radically different in your world can trigger "the shock of the new." It is actually an involuntary bodily reaction we have to radical change, argues Goldin and Kutarna (2016) in their book, *Age of Discovery:*

It seems every day we wake up to a new shock. And shock itself is the most compelling evidence that this age is very different, because it's data that comes from within. Shock is our own personal proof of historic change—a psychic collision of reality and expectations—and it has been the relentless theme of all our lives. It agitates and animates us. It will continue to do so.

Change is especially a problem if there is little space between the introduction of one new technology and the next. Similar to perceiving a movie as a whole even though it is actually made up of rapidly presented still pictures, when change comes too fast, we may perceive it as continuous.

Sometimes a new technology goes through periods of growth and rapid adoption only to then face equally rapid decline as newer and better technologies take over. A good example is the rapid rise and slow decline of CD-ROMs, as streaming media took over the music, video, and gaming industries (Lynskey 2015). Sometimes new technologies are simply transitional, a signal that an even more impactful technology is on its way, like the laserdisc was to the DVD, for example. It is also a reminder that it is easy to fixate on one technology as "the next big thing" and to be unaware that in the background many different technologies are being developed and will eventually emerge as a whole new phenomenon.

Mobile devices are only one of more than a dozen new and emerging technologies that have recently influenced or will shortly affect the world of learning and talent development. Augmented reality, virtual reality, 3-D printing, big data and analytics, machine learning, wearables, robotics, sensors, cloud-based services, and the Internet of Things (IoT) are some of the new and emerging technologies that will need to be evaluated by learning and development leaders over the next few years. New "cognitive services" from large companies such as Microsoft and IBM offer easy ways to upgrade existing technology so that they are "smart," by adding functionality such as computer vision, semantic search, adaptive computing, personalized recommendations, natural language processing, speech recognition, and live translation to everyday learning applications. Of course, computer processing power will only increase and networking will become more densely connected as full digital transformation takes place.

While it is beyond the scope of this book to discuss all the changes in our society caused by the fourth industrial revolution, we use the BUILDS framework to examine the impact of key emerging technologies on the function of learning and talent development in enterprise-level organizations. We conclude with strategies for dealing with changes happening in the near future. These changes pose both threats and opportunities; learning leaders will be challenged to evaluate promising emerging learning technologies and develop effective strategies to leverage the best among those technologies and avoid high product and company failure rates.

Impact on Learning and Talent Development

As an important part of large enterprises, learning and talent development departments will continue to be affected by the digital transformations of the fourth industrial revolution. John Hagel (2017) contends that "training programs have become more and more marginal to learning. By the time you've managed to document processes and procedures, create training materials, and deliver them, the world has already moved forward." Josh Bersin (2017b) notes, "the corporate L&D market has been through wrenching change over the last decade. In only 15 years we've come from long, page-turning courses to a wide variety of videos, small micro-learning experiences, mobile apps, and intelligent, adaptive learning platforms." In our opinion, many more "wrenching changes" will occur over the next decade. *Buckle up!*

Learning technology expert Jane Hart takes the discussion a step further tweeting: "what would happen if there were no Training/L&D department?" The dominant point made in several of the replies to her tweet is that "the responsibility for learning would coalesce around individuals and teams, empowered as they now were to access content and learning tools online." The conclusion? "It seemed there was consensus that learning and development at work were necessary and desirable, even if the L&D profession was dispensable" (quoted in D. Taylor 2017).

When you're in the middle of a period of rapid technological change, such as now, with no anchor points to hang onto in sight, it can seem never ending. In reality, the perception of change is highly variable. For some, change often occurs slowly, sometimes even imperceptibly, and is only apparent after a long period of time. At other times, though, change can be rapid and disorienting, even shocking. But eventually things settle down into new patterns. We then experience the new patterns as a period where things seem "normal," followed by a new period of rapid change, in turn followed by a new normal, where things settle down once again into a new taken-for-granted reality.

As previously mentioned, punctuated equilibrium is a useful concept for thinking about the changes that have taken place in learning technologies and in the talent development industry over the last 75 years. Classrooms are a familiar way of delivering instruction—the modern version of classroom teaching has been around for about 250 years. This started to slowly change when e-learning technologies, introduced as early as 1960 with the PLATO mainframe learning system (Dear 2017), were designed to follow the same course-based model onscreen—the presentation of materials followed by periodic assessments of learner achievement, reflected in a final grade or score at the end of the course.

The classroom metaphor for e-learning has persisted into the present, based on commercial learning management systems (LMSs) and learning content management systems (LCMSs), which allow online courses to be authored, launched, tracked, assessed, and reported on by learning and development departments. Most of the technological change we've seen since then, up until the widespread smartphone revolution that began with the iPhone, was just a simple path of maturation of this technology. Sure, the mainframe has given way to the cloud, but after an awkward adolescent phase of CD-ROMs, we were back to accessing learning content delivered by a server.

The mobile technology that would eventually disrupt the seemingly entrenched classroom delivery of information pattern began with the invention of the transistor in December 1947 (just over 70 years ago). The transistor led to the miniaturization of electronics, shrinking devices from large boxes to handheld mobile phones and even smaller sensors that could be deployed everywhere. It is the growth of mobile technology—and the accompanying rapid rise in the power of computers, the global spread of computer networking, the distribution of content through cloud-based storage, and the increasing sophistication of machine learning algorithms—that is now (finally!) disrupting the classroom course model in the learning and talent development industry.

As we write today, we are deep into a transition period of disruption in the learning and talent development industry. It is similar to what happened when the Blackberry 900 was first released in 1996 and stimulated a startling growth in the use of mobile communications devices. Today things have settled down to a new normal where billions of people are constantly checking their phones, and where changes in the use of mobile devices are now seen as incremental rather than disruptive. Texts, social networks, searches, and e-books are just some of the ways we're learning today on these amazing devices.

In the same way, a number of familiar practices in talent development and learning are currently being disrupted by several new learning technologies. In a few years, these new ways of learning will be commonplace—taken for granted as the usual way things are done. Classroom and course-based training will mostly give way to learning that takes place anywhere, any time, and as needed. Because of the capacity of mobile devices to receive input from almost any location and source, on-demand microlearning, based on the modularization of information into small chunks, will become the norm. The shifts that we believe will take place over the next few years are shown in Table 1-1.

Annual performance reviews will give way to continuous assessments as sensors are tied to workflows feeding information to personalized dashboards. According to Tim O'Reilly (2017), in *WTF?: What's the Future and Why It's Up to Us,* artificial intelligence and chatbots will soon outperform humans as experts and instructors, and the role of humans will be to manage the artificial intelligence behind the software that will develop content for employees and be made available where, when, and however they need it.

Table 1-1. 10 Shifts From the Familiar in Learning and Talent Development to a "New Normal"

The Familiar	Technology Disruptors	The Coming "New Normal"
Classroom and course-based training; learning taken out of context	Mobile devices and modularization of content; open learning resources	Learning everywhere, any time, any place; self-service learning; learning in context often based on user location
Proprietary text and still image–based content, often in books or binders	Streaming video and audio; podcasts and live-casting events	A rich mixture of live, still, and streaming media; content embedded in work tools
Assessments by superiors and summative testing	Performance tracking and support; games and gamification	Notifications; microlearning as needed; rewards and badges
Annual performance reviews	Sensors tied to workflows; IoT	Continuous assessment with personalized dashboards for performance support
Humans as experts	Artificial intelligence and chatbots; peer networks and social media	Humans as managers of AI; sharing by peers and mentors
Scarcity of learning content	Information explosion with smart search; new types of content including AR and VR	Personalized delivery of appropriate content as needed in multiple formats
Storage of learning content on drives and servers	Cloud computing	Little need to own or keep any content locally
Annual upgrades of LMS and learning software	Move from closed applications to connected platforms	Continuous development and content change
Collection of course tracking and assessment data	Software for collecting sensor and keystroke data	Collection of big data, use in learning analytics, and personalization of content
Emphasis on individual learning	Collaborative platforms, trust assurance, and social media	Shift to much more collective learning and organizational culture

The old requirement that human instructors present information as experts in their subjects to students seated in classrooms assumed that the specific content (knowledge) contained in a curriculum is both essential and scarce. In this model, experts are repositories of this knowledge, which they impart to others by giving presentations in the classroom and at conferences. The earliest classroom-based style of e-learning simply gave experts another platform to present their material.

But, as we now know, the information explosion means that there is way more content (information) than any one individual can possibly deal with (Weinberger 2014). Instead, new jobs will be created for those who can find and curate the best content, and their work will be augmented by highly intelligent and efficient search and recommendation engines. At the same time, any enterprise function that can be automated will be.

Cloud computing means that the storage of all information is essentially limitless, which will remove the scenario where essential information is stored on local drives that are jealously controlled within company silos. Knowledge flow will improve within organizations, but there will also be information spillover among organizations and countries.

Assessments, currently achieved through testing or by observation, will be replaced by performance tracking and support, along with the automatic evaluation of employees through gamification. In the soon-to-arrive new normal, assessment algorithms using big data will feed personalized dashboards. Learning management systems, which are often closed, cathedral-like applications, are giving way to open platforms that create a learning ecosystem connected to many sources, and function through links and application programming interfaces (APIs). And, because we are all linked together in the global mind that is developing, watch for a shift from an emphasis on individual learning to collective learning and the importance of having a robust organizational learning culture.

There is no doubt that the roles of L&D professionals are changing. There is pressure to get more done faster (often with fewer people), and the amount of new information that is available can be overwhelming. We are living in an age of big data, and soon the amount of recorded knowledge in the world is predicted to double every 12 hours (Schilling 2013), especially as the Internet of Things becomes more widespread. Whether we like it or not, we need digital technologies to help us cope, and assist in making data-driven decisions.

But, not *everything* needs to change. In their exploration of digital tools for identifying new talent, organizational psychologist Chamorro-Premuzic and his colleagues (2016) note that sometimes the new-fangled innovations are "largely technologically enhanced versions of traditional methods." As a learning and talent management professional, you will need to evaluate each and every technology that is available to stay ahead of the curve.

Looking Ahead

The first steps in any workable strategy are to assess and diagnose the situation you find yourself in, develop a guiding policy for dealing with the issues you face, and carry out a set of coherent actions to effectively address the situation (Rumelt 2011). Because the learning and talent development function takes place within enterprise-level organizations, we'll start with an analysis of how new learning technologies can support and add value to the business functions of any large organization.

CHAPTER 2

Business Needs for Learning Technologies

usiness and learning professionals have long had a problematic, yet productive partnership. For the most part things work out when they collaborate. But conflicting views and goals and differences of opinions can result in loss of time, productivity, and success. Learning and talent development and business units like operations, sales, and even management don't always see eye to eye on key priorities.

This conflict may result in learning and development technology projects that ship late, have poor uptake or low usage, or even end up shelved or neglected. This is because while the efforts of learning professionals may meet certain learning objectives, they fall short of management goals to add business value or achieve meaningful organizational performance improvement. Not all learning technologies are created equal, after all.

However, it doesn't have to be this way. In our opinion, learning and development departments are often the cause of the problem, thanks to their diehard adherence to core principles and dogmatic views on what constitutes "learning." Yet, change is happening; more learning professionals are linking their efforts to business results, spurred on by thoughtful practitioners and such books as *The Six Disciplines of Breakthrough Learning: How to Turn Learning and Development into Business Results* (Pollock, Jefferson, and Wick 2015) and Elaine Biech's 2018 book *ATD's Foundations of Talent Development*. The reality of today's fast-paced business world is that learning professionals must continue adapting their approach to align with the goals of their business partners to produce successful outcomes for the enterprise.

Peter Drucker (1974), father of modern management theory and creator of the term *knowledge worker,* framed it this way:

> Management must always, in every decision and action, put economic performance first. It can only justify its existence and its authority by the economic results it produces. There may be great non-economic results: the happiness of the members of the enterprise, the contribution to the welfare or culture of the community, etc. Yet management has failed if it fails to produce economic results. . .It has failed if it does not improve, or at least maintain, the wealth-producing capacity of the economic resources entrusted to it.

Align to Business, Adapt, Mirror Change

To counteract past failure and chart a path going forward with emerging technologies, it is vital that learning and development teams understand and articulate the business value of any given learning technology. What does it help us achieve? How does it further the overall goal of providing value for customers? To create value for the business, L&D must be able to clearly understand the business's goals, key revenue streams, and vital relationships, as well as any partnerships and channels those goals and revenue streams require. Learning in and of itself is not the ultimate goal; the ultimate goal is achieving business success. We cannot forget that.

Business value itself is often an elusive term for those who have come from an academic or learning science background. In learning and talent development, we simply haven't been trained to think that way. In business, the bottom line doesn't refer to course attendance, e-learning launches, test scores, or even establishing competency models and "sticking to them." Business value is established by enabling the business to execute its business plan, create sustainable business success, and extend its reach to enable future growth according to the overall business strategies. Alignment of these success metrics is necessary before embarking on new technology research and delivery. David Sward (2006) sees four indicators of the business value of information technology (IT):

- direct contribution to the corporation's market position or revenue
- deliverables and results that support solving customer business needs and challenges
- financial improvements derived from customer cost savings or benefits
- examples of technology investment that advance the industry.

In *The Art of Business Value*, Mark Schwartz (2016) notes that a "core principle of Agile and Lean theory is that software development projects should seek to maximize business value. Projects should be judged not on their adherence to cost and schedule milestones, but on their delivery of value to the enterprise." Now, Schwartz is primarily discussing traditional IT projects, but the fundamentals for learning technologies should follow the same path.

Since the 1960s—when training departments first became corporate universities (McDonald's Hamburger University formed in 1961) and, later, centers of excellence—the business value proposition most corporate L&D organizations articulated was that they create "experts," bringing knowledge to employees in a lifelong learner model. This value proposition is clear from the use of the term *university*. After all, universities are places of higher learning with a mandate to fill student's heads with information. However, this value proposition is not only outmoded, it is poorly adapted to the modern business climate (Bersin 2007). It also denies the fact that most work is a collective, not an individual undertaking; it's an effort by the entire firm, done in concert and through collaboration among colleagues. Learning and development must adapt its value proposition to focus on the basics of the new change-driven economy—social, informal, high velocity, augmented, hyper-connected, and constantly flowing and upgrading (Kelly 2016).

We propose that learning and development professionals restructure their value propositions around delivering access to knowledge through open information channels and cognitive services in as low friction a manner as possible. This reformed model, centered around access and cognitive services for learning, mirrors the change in the business climate to cloud (access) and AI/machine learning ("cognitive services" such as those provided by IBM's Watson, Amazon's Lex, Microsoft's Azure, and so on). This is a more adaptive and flexible strategy, which meets learners where they are, providing tools and services that more closely mimic how people learn when they are not at work. The move away from formal course structures and historical learning practices offers the advantage of empowering smaller organizations that lack large learning infrastructures. It's well known that "the smaller the firm the less likely it is to be engaged in training, and a sizeable proportion of small firms undertake no training at all" (Stone 2012).

Create a "Starter Kit" to Evaluate New Technologies

When we add this up, it's clear that the move to global business and cognitive services, APIs for learning services, and self-directed learning activities has raised many questions and created uncertainties in an area that hasn't shifted significantly since the birth of the LMS and e-learning programs (Chandok, Chheda, and Rosendahl 2018). How can we see if the new tools, technologies, and processes are effective?

To assist in understanding the effectiveness of a technology in creating business value, we have created a "starter kit" of five steps with questions you and your team should ask when evaluating new learning technologies for your business. The questions are similar to a SWOT process, but with an added dimension centered around finding and examining examples in business that help illustrate your suggested use of a proposed technology.

- **Find the strengths:** What can this technology be used for?
- **Identify the problems:** Where can this go wrong? What are the possible detriments to using this technology?
- **Explore the opportunities:** What new opportunities does this technology enable?
- **Identify risks:** If things go badly, what might happen? If we skip this step, what are we missing?

- **Find examples:** Who else is using this technology in business? Are they being successful with it?

What Are the Strengths of a New Technology?

Traditional or established learning delivery methods have certain strengths—things they are good at—and new or emerging learning technologies are no different. A classroom setting is great for advancing dialogue (if the instructor welcomes it) and pointing to what learners should study, but not so great at providing hands-on or in-context learning. An emerging technology like augmented reality is great for providing just-in-time information in context, but would probably be a distraction or at best an unnecessary prop in a classroom.

So, the core question here might be, "Does the technology fit the task?" (Liang et al. 2007). The technology should feel like a natural match; it shouldn't have to be shoehorned into a process or event. In the case of emerging technologies, the bar is even higher; the technology should not only fill an obvious gap, but it should do it better than the technology or process it replaces. If it doesn't do something better, introduces new risks or higher costs, and lacks clear business value, why would you use it in a full deployment? Certainly, undertaking a prototype or proof of concept are exceptions to this rule, but a full deployment across the enterprise must catapult you ahead of your current level of development or that of the competition.

In determining strengths, reading past research and current analyst views can help you identify in broad terms what a technology offers. But getting to the core of what it means for your business is an entirely different proposition. Interviewing internal stakeholders, providing time for thoughtful, deep research and discovery, and discussing the technologies with potential users are all good places to start. As we detail in the next chapter, a good understanding of the affordances of the proposed technology will greatly facilitate its evaluation.

Good questions to ask at the evaluation stage center around understanding the use cases the technology was originally created to address (Brandenburg 2018). If you are in a different field than the one for which the technology was originally developed, ask questions focused on how the technology can be used to great effect in your industry or market. What use cases can you find in your organization that share characteristics that support the transfer of this technology throughout your enterprise?

What Are Its Problems?

At its core, technology is neither good nor bad. Its faults and strengths are determined by how it is implemented and used. So, while a technology may have clear strengths when used in one setting, it also very likely has problems that may impede its usefulness or even create detrimental side effects in another.

Much has been written on the distraction caused by mobile devices and the app culture in which we currently live. In addition to the myopic view that mobile devices and apps cause dependence on social networks, games, and their associated dopamine rushes, there are other dangers such as cyber bullying, trolling, and a tidal wave of fake news and bot accounts. Would we trade the access to our friends around the globe and the many connections made to go back to pre-digital social networks simply because of these detriments? Some say yes, with lots of people leaving some of the larger networks because of the high levels of harassment and abuse (Hsu 2018; Shane 2018).

A similar conversation will have to take place in your organization when you consider emerging technologies for use in the enterprise. For example, if you plan to rely on blockchain technology to aid recording, validating, and tracking learning experiences and working activities, you must be prepared to deal with the immutable nature of the data and the significant computing and electricity resources it takes to create and validate the data. It will be more difficult to go back and retroactively mark superior officers in your business as "compliant" in terms of completing their annual training just because they said, "I'm too busy to get to it right now; I'll get back to it after these deadlines on these projects." You will no longer be able to fudge things as easily. This may seem a net positive, but it will also require change management and communications inside your business to make sure that everyone understands the pluses and minuses.

Many of these emerging technologies rely on trust and the ability to access information on demand. Obfuscating data or creating fiefdoms to centralize power and control of knowledge are counterproductive to adoption and use of new technologies. The business value isn't always immediately evident, and it can take time to develop. Your business must be willing to wait for key pieces to fall into place. We'll cover more on that in chapter 6 when we discuss the concepts of dependencies.

It will be up to you and your team to uncover the downsides of adopting new technologies. Apply a healthy dose of skepticism when you look at these recent technologies and consider aspects of each that could introduce negative effects if adopted.

Are There Opportunities?

The definition we cited for emerging technologies—briefly, those technologies currently in early stages of development with significant, wide-reaching potential—illustrates our views about how a technology must not only provide an advancement in capabilities, but also open up new avenues for innovation. Moving from flip phones to smartphones created an entirely new ecosystem of apps, communication methods, and so forth. Increasing the screen size of smartphones, on the other hand, merely enhanced the things we could already do. These enhancements just made materials easier to read. The user wasn't granted additional powers or capabilities beyond improved image clarity or size.

But, from a learning and performance perspective, the use of smartphones to provide business information and training materials to a user in situ created the ideal vehicle for almost instant performance support, something that will increase business value. The affordances offered by new technologies should always refer to the business objectives and strategies that L&D is chartered to support and improve.

With an emerging technology like augmented reality, the new opportunities it brings to your workforce for improving performance were not possible with traditional performance support tools like printed job aids, or even, more recently, with standard mobile apps. What does a new technology unlock that was science fiction for your business just a couple years ago? How does it begin to bridge the gap between learning and performance to truly create business value? These questions should be explored with respect to any new technology you are contemplating bringing into your business.

What Are the Risks?

Consider a risk management and risk mitigation chart, the bane of many a project manager's existence. You know what these are—a matrix grid view of everything that could go wrong and the potential impact of what happens when they do. These are difficult enough to complete when you have a good grasp of the technologies at hand. If you've already created and deployed similar projects during your tenure at your company, you know what can go wrong and how to mitigate those risks to emerge successfully on the other side.

However, when you add in variables of unknown technologies, things can get murky. How long will this project take? How might this technology fail or not meet our needs as planned? It can be easy to fall into a Chicken Little, "The sky is falling!" scenario. Calm heads must prevail if you want stakeholders and management to sign on. Take a bit of extra time to read up on case studies, news articles, and perhaps even academic journals so that you have a good grasp on failure points that have happened in other implementations. In software, the way you start to plan for risks requires "gaming" out the scenarios; this can also take time.

The flip side of not proceeding with a new technology—taking a wait and see approach or skipping it altogether—may also pose a significant risk to your business. You might lose the opportunity for a competitive advantage: being perceived as a first mover or leading-edge by customers. You may later get shut down due to trademarks, patents, or other intellectual property issues. You may enable smaller, nimbler companies to pick away at your market share. You may lose employees who want to work for innovative, fast movers. You may lose respect or the ability to advance in your business because you weren't able to figure out how to leverage an advanced technology and articulate avenues to benefit your company.

The history of learning technology is littered with failed products, platforms, and technologies. What makes you think you can avoid making choices that will also fail? The answer is that you can never completely remove risk from your choices and situation. You can only reduce or mitigate it through planning, limiting your efforts to doable tests, and adjusting for future iterations by learning from your (hopefully) small mistakes.

The key to reducing risks is to make plans and stick to them. Make specific plans for the maximum amount of investment or loss you are willing to take on with a test or proof of concept. Make deliberate decisions about how many people you will engage in this effort to contain it. Determine the maximum amount of time you are willing to spend. Put a stake in the ground for the minimum amount of return or success that is needed to deem the technology worthwhile. Yes, this all sounds like scope, schedule, and budget, which are the basics of planning any technology implementation.

What Do Your Examples Show?

Case studies are a vital part of any organization's decision to buy software and services. Buyers want to see a track record of success before they jump into any new area of technology (Moore 2014). This works well when you are talking about mature marketplaces, such as Software as a Service (SaaS) web hosting providers, mobile device manufacturers, and learning management systems. When you attempt to use this tool on an emerging technology, it can be particularly difficult to find examples that map to your use case, much less your vertical market or industry. If you are blazing trails, who is out ahead of you?

This requires more critical analysis of what it is you are seeking to achieve with a case study. A simple 1:1 comparison isn't going to be possible. Start by comparing the business problem or gap you are trying to solve and then identify case studies centered around that problem. Don't start the search centered around the technology and certainly don't rely on finding case studies in your specific industry. After all, if you are truly doing something leading-edge you are unlikely to find a touchstone that's a perfect fit.

You may have to look outside the learning industry altogether; for example, you may want to start with trade magazines, technology journals, websites, academic publications, research reports, and Department of Defense documentation. Allot a significant amount of research time for the business gap or problem and start to curate a bookmark list or portfolio of sites, services, and groups that post frequent research papers. Then, when business problems arise, you'll have a list of sources to search and share with your colleagues. Because the case studies may require some amount of abstraction and analysis, it's probably wise not to send them on as simple emails forwarded to your business colleagues. Instead you should explain what problems or gaps they fill and then relay that view to the stakeholders, drawing your story together by illustrating the similarities.

If this all seems too obtuse, take a little time to consider an emerging technology that many in learning and talent development have their eye on: big data and learning analytics. In the corporate learning space, big data is still something of a curiosity, largely because learning departments often have very little good data to serve as a foundation for a big data approach or the data they have is mostly compliance driven, which isn't helpful in illuminating behavioral patterns for learning activities or work endeavors.

But, having a massive data set is not the problem for the U.S. Department of Defense, which publishes dozens of data-rich research projects annually. The DoD has a large number of users doing mission-critical work and many scientists and researchers to propose, study, and report on ground-breaking technologies. Most businesses, and especially their learning departments, do not have access to such rich data sets.

Lack of data is also not the problem for operational groups like sales teams in high-performing organizations where software like Salesforce (a giant data acquisition platform used by the entire team) is capable of providing insights into the correlations between those salespeople who use specific tools and those who close deals. After all, these operational and mission-critical departments drive the business forward and have little or no problem in articulating strengths, identifying opportunities, recognizing risks, and creating examples for the entire business. The types of data that sales groups gather are usually a lot more in-depth and pervasive than simple course launches and grades on multiple-choice quizzes, the kind of data usually available from an LMS.

This means that you may need to step outside your industry and find examples that, while may not exactly fit, are based on significant data points to make your case that big data and analytics might be useful in your field. You should also be aware that many levels of government produce open data sets that anyone can download and use for experimentation with this emerging technology. What is often needed is the courage and motivation to move forward with the immense resources that are already available to you. For example, if you want to try working with an accessible data set, try playing with Google's digitization of the full text of more than 5 million books using its free and easy to use Ngram Viewer application. You can use a similar approach of experimentation or pilot studies for demonstrating the value of other emerging technologies.

Evaluating Technologies for Your Business

Business is key to the BUILDS framework, because budgets and strategies are decided on by owners, stakeholders, and executives. At a minimum, they want to know the business value of any new technology that you're planning to adopt. Without the support of the decision makers in your organization at best you'll have to adopt any new technology "under the radar"; that's not the most strategic move.

All this is to say that any new technology you want to introduce must fit with your organization's business needs. This is why it's important to develop local criteria for evaluating any new technology, because there may be organization-specific requirements that, unless met, will stop implementation dead in its tracks. And, while the hype around a new technology may make it seem fantastic and exciting, as part of your evaluation you must identify both the benefits and any problems that could arise if it's adopted.

To convince decision makers that adopting an emerging technology is a good idea, you need to do several things. One is to identify any new opportunities that the technology will bring to your company, especially opportunities that will be of interest to the company's decision makers.

Another is to honestly assess any risks, and have a plan addressing how those risks can be mitigated.

Finally, any CEO worth their salt will want to know who else in their industry has adopted this technology. Having case studies at hand will give comfort to CEOs who are cautious and pragmatic about leaping ahead with new technologies. While you may be the kind of person (like we are!) who gets excited about new technologies, executives tend to be tougher when it comes to what Geoffrey Moore (2014) has identified as "crossing the chasm." This refers to the gap between early adopters and technophiles falling in love with a technology and a CEO or other high-level executive deciding to fund its implementation. The chasm is where a lot of new technology adoption gets stalled.

You can still be a technology leader without case studies to back you up, it's just a lot harder to get sign-off on a project if no one else is out there ahead of you. At the same time, it is important to recognize that some of the biggest winners who have spawned billion-dollar companies are those who experiment and take big risks, learning how to fail fast and then move on until they find a winning formula (Shirky 2008; Galloway 2017).

While there are many other important issues to consider when evaluating an emerging technology, in our opinion, supporting business objectives is the most important. They are reflected in the first set of questions for the rubric we developed for the BUILDS framework:

1. Have you conducted a value proposition analysis for adopting this new technology? Does the new technology fit your business needs?

2. Have you identified any problems in adopting this new technology?

3. Does adopting this emerging technology open up new opportunities for your organization? Have you assessed these opportunities?

4. Will you have a risk management plan in place when these technologies are adopted?

5. Have you gathered case studies of other companies in your industry that have adopted this technology that you can present to your executive team?

Looking Ahead

Many learning and talent development departments have some work to do to come to the table with a good understanding of the value new technologies can bring to the business at large, while others are barreling ahead with new learning technologies that improve business value. Change cannot happen until a department has determined its long-term vision of the value proposition for learning for the larger organization. The task at hand is daunting, but once you realize that you may simply need to venture outside your comfort zone to identify, understand, and test these technologies, it can be done. This is more about creating a flexible view that adapts over time than it is about creating a rigid structure that is the final authoritative answer.

If you're willing to look, the information may already be at the fringes of your business (what are called *edge cases*), or readily available as open-source data sets with which you can experiment. Maybe the technology you are interested in is being used in government installations. Maybe other vertical industries are seeing success, or perhaps even other departments in your business are reaping the benefits of using these amazing new tools.

It's time to look around and see what is happening at the leading technological edges of your industry. The place to start is discovering the experiences other users have had with the latest tools to find out what works or doesn't work. This step is absolutely necessary before designing or adopting a new application for your workplace. We turn to this issue next.

CHAPTER 3

User Experiences of Learning Technologies

As vital as good design is to virtually every aspect of our lives—the design of dwellings, food supply chains, water delivery and infrastructure, telecommunications, transportation, and other products or services we depend on—we don't give it much thought in developing enterprise software. Good design is not necessarily woven into the products and services that e-learning vendors bring to L&D audiences; think about learning management systems, e-learning courses, and an entire litany of digital products intended to help the workforce learn. Many of them, but not all, are difficult to use, cumbersome, and derivative. Why is this? It's not because vendors of these products want to produce hard to use, obtuse, or arcane solutions. Is producing well-designed products and services really that hard?

At our company, we've been designing learning technology solutions since the beginning of this century in the form of presentation media, e-learning programs, and educational kiosks. And, we were right at the beginning of the mobile revolution—building apps, small learning tools and utilities, calculators, widgets, and whole host of point solutions focused on enabling workers while on the go. We've never been too hung up on determining if something we produced was "creating learning," or simply enabling performance. What we really focused on, and the reason we tend to gravitate immediately to new technologies as they emerge, is that we care; we empathize with the user. When we say "user," in this instance, we are specifically referring to the learner—you know, the person for whom you are producing content and pathways to knowledge.

A user-centered design approach may seem like rudimentary thinking for those involved in the design and creation of consumer-focused apps and websites. Using this type of thinking for that market has clear competitive advantages. It sells products and creates more satisfied customers. But it's rare to find a user-centered approach in companies that develop software for other businesses.

There is a very important difference in the two types of industries we are discussing: business to consumer (B2C) marketing and communications versus business to business (B2B) learning and development tools and platforms. The B2C creators clearly know their audience. It may be a buyer on an ecommerce site, a subscriber to a social network, or maybe the owner of a specific brand of vehicle visiting the manufacturer's website. It is clear that most B2C vendors have observed, researched, prototyped, and tested their products with their intended markets.

For the developers of learning tools—from authoring environments to learning management systems and everything in between—it's never been that clear. Is the product maker aiming to provide a great user experience (UX) for the technology team responsible for implementing the system, the content author creating learning materials, the business problem owner creating reports and dashboards, or end users of their offerings? Maybe it's all of them.

The actual learner is, unfortunately, often the last to be considered. The true consumer of learning content often gets UX design as an afterthought, not as a key driver or a defining success metric. And good luck creating positive learning experiences for an organization when it seems that the processes are hell-bent on creating tools for the corporate purchasing departments, IT system administrators, and business managers rather than the real end users of the content in the system. When no one understands or values the end user, no one can possibly understand how to value the role that user experience plays in the design of learning activities.

Four Factors Favoring the User Experience

Emerging technologies offer a way to correct these historical wrongs. How is this possible? What makes a new technology different from previous generations of what were once emerging (but now widespread) technologies? A variety of things contribute to this trend, from new product development practices such as the use of ethnographic observation methods, to improved adoption rates, better distribution channels, and falling distribution costs. These factors and more make developing user-centric products and services more attractive all the time.

New Product Development Practices Are Fast and Lean

Technology design and development processes have gone agile. Lean, fast development cycles that result in new offerings and an ever-quickening upgrade path are now the norm. The times are changing, and with them our ability to acquire the latest and greatest is changing too. We now get new apps, software, and even hardware products quarterly, sometimes monthly. New generations of products are released with the ability to add new capabilities through software and firmware updates even after they launch. This allows product developers to work more quickly, iterating and experimenting with features that they wouldn't have been able to in previous product generations.

Computers, phones, smart thermostats, and even durable consumer goods like appliances and vehicles now have the ability to get upgrades (Musk 2018). This creates a culture of innovation and encourages people to buy products early in the product life cycle. This practice also allows vendors to add emerging technologies to devices and operating systems without expecting the entire audience to discard their older devices. Apple and Google, for example, have all enhanced and increased capabilities for their users through updates to their AI/intelligent agents and augmented reality platforms well after the original products shipped. These technologies are user-centric and highly contextual, placing the users in control of their mobile computing needs in ways that were purely science fiction only a decade ago.

Technology Adoption Rates Continue to Accelerate

The fourth industrial revolution has been driven in part by software and hardware development practices, but also by consumer demand and widespread, rapid adoption of product technologies that provide value and offer user-centric approaches to reducing friction of day to day tasks. Electronic payment systems like Venmo, Apple Pay, and Google Wallet burst onto the scene in 2013, and now more than a quarter of all smartphone users regularly utilize an electronic wallet (for more on this trend, see www.pymnts.com). What led to this rapid growth of mobile payments? It's very, very easy to use, that's for sure. It works on almost all smartphones, most retail chains accept it, and for those who regularly forget their wallet on a short trip uptown, it may offer the only way to fill up their car.

We are in the midst of a rapid transformation of the traditional 20th-century growth models for technologies like telecommunication, transportation, and commerce. The home telephone took 60 years to reach ubiquitous status in America; the smartphone did it in eight (DeGusta 2012; McGrath 2013). A major contributing factor is that these technologies are portable, easy to use, and affordable. Emerging technologies like AI, bots, cloud computing, AR, and VR are also easy to use and affordable, and they consistently outperform the previous technologies they extend or make obsolete in terms of adoption rates.

Distribution Channels Are Growing

Who sells the product or service you are seeking? Once upon a time, that question might have been tough to answer. Now, almost everything is a Google or Apple Spotlight search away. E-commerce giants, digital app stores, software as a service (SaaS), platform as a service (PaaS), and infrastructure as a service (IaaS) have all knocked traditional brick and mortar retailers back on their heels. While it's playing out nastily in the malls and shopping centers of the world, there have never been easier, faster ways for consumers to get the products and services they want when they want them. If you hear about the newest AR app or blockchain currency while out with friends, you can simply pull out your phone and buy or download it right then. Need that new VR system for your office or living room? Go online and have it delivered to your home in two hours or less. Heck, if you have an idea for the next killer app yourself, you can continue enjoying your café latte, log into your Amazon Web Services (AWS) account, spin up a Lambda server instance, and start coding without even leaving the coffee shop. It's a world of instant availability and access, and this shift from ownership to access is reshaping people's buying decisions, habits, and usage patterns.

These changes all signal that user-friendly technologies are taking over from the previous structures that dramatically favored the seller—centralized markets and distribution channels, one-size-fits-all products, and closed ecosystems. AI, blockchain, big data for learning, and most of the technologies covered in this book are available for instant purchase; some don't even require ownership for you to take advantage of them. The SaaS marketplace for emerging technologies is growing quickly and provides access for a fraction of the cost of ownership, making experimentation easy for a relatively a small investment. That's user friendly!

Deployment Costs Are Dropping

With more channels, more devices, and more software platforms out there every day, it should be no surprise that the cost to get technologies into user hands is dropping rapidly. Smartphone costs have dropped, of course, with some carriers even offering "free" handsets or other incentives in exchange for longer-term contracts. The more interesting comparisons are those in the emerging technology sectors like smart glasses, AI processing, and augmented reality. Google Glass launched in 2014 as an experiment—and a fairly pricey one at that. It required a parked smartphone (approximately $600, depending on make and model) and an initial purchase of $1,500 for the prototype device. Fast forward to 2018, and for about half that cost you can get a stereoscopic (compared with Glass's monocular view) pair of decently operable smart glasses for about $1,000. That's a 50 percent price drop in just four years for a far more capable device. In the meantime, Google Glass has moved from being a failed consumer product to providing real performance support applications on the factory floor; there is a second life for some technologies (Levy 2017).

AI processing for machine learning deployments is a CPU (central processing unit; the "brains" of a computer) intensive process. Just a few months ago (the dark ages of early 2018), it would have taken 12 hours or more to train a model for a computer vision project on a Mac to be used on iOS devices. Other faster options required costly GPUs (graphic processing units; a fast, specialized processor made for many simultaneous calculations done in parallel) or less convenient cloud-based services. A mere 10 months later, thanks to recently released changes to the development tools and upgrades to the operating systems, that same machine learning model can be trained in minutes. If you don't care about owning the hardware on which your AI training occurs, you can utilize a Google TPU (tensor processing unit; a cloud-based server optimized for machine learning) for less than $2 per hour. Spin it up when you need it, turn it off when you don't. That's a lot less money than maintaining a server yourself, which would require buying a computer, choosing and configuring a powerful GPU for neural networks, and maintaining it. Buying such a beast could cost the same amount as running a server for years.

Putting People First (For Now) Makes Sense

We are on the precipice of a massive shift in usage of the web, connected technologies, and digital business processes and tools. In 2017, approximately 48 percent of all web traffic was generated by people. The rest was bots, scripts, and other agents. The percentage of web traffic generated by humans is projected to drop rapidly as more IoT devices, bots, and AI agents come online over the next decade. At some point, putting humans first in your design decisions, without considering the requirements of various non-human agents, may not make the best choice for your business. Simply designing tools and processes only for use by humans may cost more in the long run, and it will do nothing but temporarily maintain a status quo until the industry or the way we do online and offline training is disrupted. We need to anticipate how the shift to automation in training is going to affect our business strategy in the next few years. While we are naturally biased to favor humans over robots, we should not be ignoring the implications of the digital transformation that is taking place.

With that transformation, a shift in who does the work of today's knowledge worker will also occur. As that shift happens, design priorities will also shift—perhaps favoring machine readability and data portability over human usability, but until then, planning for and creating human-friendly UI and UX makes for a good approach to creating business value. In simple terms, if people can't easily use an emerging technology, they probably won't use it.

This has serious implications as AI enters the learning and development space. As content is generated, written, and curated by machines, how will we know if that content is non-biased, meant for our consumption, and intended to help our fellow human employees? A specific, eye-opening example from a recent study illustrated how gender bias and other biases exist in words and images embedded in Google search results, news, and other information retrieved from the web (Otterbacher 2016). We see this in clarifications attached to words that have longstanding gender biases in professional occupations, such as *male* nurse or *female* quarterback. It's not a stretch to foresee a future where the bots we interact with may incorrectly assume that a participant is of a specific gender and have some types of ableism due to the training used to create the simulation, interactions, or experiences for which they are created. In 2016, Microsoft's bot, Tay, was horribly manipulated by users into spouting racist tweets within about 24 hours. Tay had to be taken offline to prevent more cyber bullying (Vincent 2016).

In order to design for humans, one must understand them. The term *design thinking* or *user-centered design* gets tossed around quite a bit, but there is something deeper missing from the design processes of many learning and development tool and platform developers. In-depth ethnographic research must be a priority as emerging technologies become more common in learning and talent development. As sociologist and UX researcher Sam Ladner wrote in her 2014 book, *Practical Ethnography:*

A Guide to Doing Ethnography in the Private Sector, an anthropological approach must be taken to truly understand one's users. An observational approach is needed; a simple interview will not do. She also discusses how common methodologies used in big business, such as Lean and Six Sigma, incorrectly start with the company's business goals, not with the end user.

So, if not for bots (which are the majority of the traffic on the web now) and if not for companies (which many corporate policies dictate), why would you consider designing learning for your humans with emerging technologies?

The fact is that humans talk. A lot. To each other. And now, they talk to each other, a lot, online. This content is always available, searchable, and often tagged, cross-referenced, and fully indexed for easy retrieval. These types of social and informal interactions drive us toward a collective mindset. When implemented as a repository for your organization, you are essentially re-creating and digitizing the institutional knowledge base from the ground up. This may require more human interaction initially to get the network effect started, of course, but each person can do just a little bit to add value to the overall network and create new collaboration methods and value chains (McAfee 2009). This can happen through commenting, rating, and tagging—all of which spin the flywheel of big data and provide more fodder for the nascent workforce of AIs. As long as people are making the calls, signing the contracts, and buying the products, it's probably wise to keep them talking, learning, and performing. After all, they are acting as teachers for the bots that will come next. Good-quality human interactions on digital networks provide a balanced breakfast for the baby bots chewing on the knowledge bases of today.

Quality Matters More Than Ever

With competitive markets, it is becoming clear that users value quality, not only for consumer technologies but enterprise and government purchasing agents are seeing this shift as well. The days of battleship gray applications and one-size-fits-all approaches to service design are behind us. Job posting and placements for UI/UX roles are up more than 15 percent since the great recession of 2008 (Burrow 2017). The UI/UX focused website Dribble has seen its traffic and paid accounts grow to become a top 1,000 trafficked website with virtually no advertising in roughly the same time period. UI/UX is hot, hot, hot.

This attention to detail is more than just decoration. Integrated product feedback loops, active beta testing programs, and multivariate A/B testing all illustrate this move to user-centric design and a humanistic approach to delighting one's customers. Users expect high-quality UX and bug-free operations. Comments and reviews of new apps in Apple's App Store can be vicious. The app tracker service Kahuna reports that apps with a four star or better rating get 540 percent more conversions than those rated two stars (Kahuna.com 2015). Brutal. You want people to use your stuff? It better be good.

People will not put up with inferior experiences just because the technology is "cool" or "cutting edge." Not only must the technology be valuable, but it also has to be easier to use than the tech it replaces or the process it makes obsolete.

Designing for Personalization Drives Business Value

The learning and development industry has been slow to adopt personalization and adaptive technologies for use by learners. This is surprising given the amount of talks at conferences and the number of people who advocate for the effectiveness of creating personalized learning plans, research on adaptive learning tools, and tailored instruction. Contrast this with the larger web design industry and it's even more surprising that personalization isn't everywhere in L&D.

Chad's first professional position out of design school was working for a company that built and maintained some of the most popular music websites in existence, including Tunes.com, Rollingstone.com, DownBeat.com, theSource.com. Even in 2000, there were robust personalization tools in place for customizing search results for end users. With just a few clicks, visitors could choose their favorite genres, artists, albums, and songs. This all enabled a personalization engine that tailored the user's newsfeed, on-site listening preferences, and concert updates, among other things. This had to be done to remain competitive, relevant, and useful. That was nearly 20 years ago!

Why has it taken this long for the L&D department to join in? The simplest answer it seems is lack of competition. There are dozens of music sites out there, so it's of great importance that a site provides an engaging, useful experience for the visitor. Considering this, how many L&D departments do you have in your company? How many channels for learning content? How many LMSs and learning portals with competing information or different user experiences? When there is no competition, there is no compelling reason to improve products or user experiences.

The interesting thing about the emerging technologies we are discussing is that most of these technologies are gaining a lot of consumer traction, with rapid adoption cycles and huge uptake. This is a good thing for learning and development. It gives us the chance to take advantage of the design choices the technology platforms are making for the larger marketplace.

Designing for Accessibility Is Just Good Business

Part of designing for humans is designing for usability. Usability requires inclusivity. Part of inclusivity is accessibility for persons with a disability. In addition, designing for persons with disability should be designing for everyone, a concept known as *universal design* (Schwab 2018).

Usable systems are tested for acceptance, functionality, and other factors like efficiency and effectiveness. The W3C, an international community focused on making the web a more human-friendly place by recommending and studying design standards, has a great section on its website devoted to the intersection of these topics. This is relevant to businesses because a system or product must reach certain levels of accessibility to be used by government agencies and nonprofit organizations. In some cases, universities and publicly traded companies have been shamed, sued, or at least embarrassed by their lack of usability, accessibility, and inclusivity. These have led to boycotts, lost time in courts, and of course millions of dollars in settlements. EdX, the MOOC system founded by Harvard and MIT in 2012, was the focal point of a 2015 lawsuit filed by the National Association for the Deaf for not providing closed captioning in its online content systems (LaGrow 2017). This was based around the well-known but often-misunderstood Section 508 of the Rehabilitation Act of 1973, which requires accessibility, and the often-overlooked Section 504, which requires accommodation.

The amazing part of all of this is that making your emerging technology solutions accessible for humans likely opens them up to be accessible to bots and AI, because the same sorts of underpinning technologies power the recognition of words such as speech to text, text to speech, optical character recognition (OCR), and natural language processing.

If you design for accessibility and accommodate through inclusivity you will likely end up with a more usable system. This will bring better user acceptance ratings and with it, likability.

As you evaluate new technologies for a potential place in your learning ecosystem, make sure you bring your accessibility teams into the evaluation process and put the technologies you evaluate through their paces.

Don't Sacrifice Security for Power, Ease, or Utility

Smart home devices do make things easier for us—we can use our phones to adjust the temperature of our house before we return from vacation, check on the kids sleeping in the bed upstairs, verify the garage door has been closed, and turn on the lights in the living room. Not only are they easy, but they are useful. But they are also insecure.

As we are seeing on the evening news and in technology security bulletins, emerging technologies make for emerging security challenges. The expenditure on security for IoT devices is estimated at more than $1.5 billion, according to Gartner (2018), a leading technology analysis firm. Why is this? With the rapid increase in adding IoT devices to factory floors, logistics, supply chains, and many other aspects of modern business has come a rapid rise in attacks on these often poorly secured devices and systems. The 2016 Mirai Botnet targeted millions of IoT devices—everything from routers to smart home hubs and baby monitors—to create an army of distributed denial of service (DDoS) soldiers to attack Barclay's Bank and Lloyds of London in the United Kingdom, among many other Internet accounts (Bursztein 2017). This attack spread rapidly, mutating when the source code was released into the wild. The out-of-control blitz on IoT devices crippled financial networks and made a number of high-traffic websites inaccessible, including Reddit, Twitter, and Airbnb. Rutgers University was also crippled by an outbreak of the attack, and it is believed that it even knocked the entire nation of Liberia offline. The originators of the Rutgers outbreak of the virus were sentenced to five years of probation, 2,500 hours community service, and forced to pay $127,000 in restitution.

Many of the emerging technologies for learning—AR, VR, IoT, and blockchain—are also convenient, easy to use, and, possibly, insecure. It's vital that as we assess the new products entering our work environments we always perform a security or threat assessment to determine if they are ready for prime time. In the case of Mirai, the botnet was able to thrive because designated system admins (in this case, often just homeowners or consumers) neglected to change the default passwords that came with their new technologies.

Cost isn't the only thing holding up massive adoption of smart glasses and other AR products (it will come down), it's also the fact that they don't often have the same provisioning or security hooks in place as smartphones or tablets, which are already ubiquitous on company networks. Until we get a more balanced approach to where the utility and usefulness matches or exceeds the risks posed by adding them to existing networks, we are not going to see massive uptake by many companies. The benefits must outweigh the detriments.

Evaluating User Experiences of Emerging Technologies

Without users, in this case learners, new learning technologies will go nowhere. But, you would be surprised by how often new applications are developed without anyone having real end users try them out. Instead, some developers rely on how they imagine a "learner" would *probably* use the new technology, based on their own experience of how they learned when they were involved in corporate training or school. Or, alternatively, developers rely on experienced subject matter experts to tell them how a learner would act, or to predict how a learner would feel about using the new software.

If the new learning software is based on traditional or known models of instruction, then a case can be made that there is already evidence for how the user will react to a new application. For example, if an onscreen application is based on an interview situation, then developers might assume that the user's experience will be similar to interviewing in a physical room. There are several reasons why this assumption is likely wrong.

First, the experience of interacting onscreen with someone is quite different than working with a person in the same physical space. Most people have a sense of presence when they are with someone in the same place, which is lacking when interacting with people online. The lack of presence is one reason people are less inhibited online, often being more rude or forward than they might act in person (Adams 2011; Suler 2015).

Second, designing online environments to replicate situations and settings as if they were identical to a known physical world, an approach known as *skeuomorphism*, may help a user by giving them a familiar scene to work in, but it also limits many other ways of designing the user experience that may improve learning. By only using familiar metaphors and literal renderings of objects, we opt for a very safe (and often limited) way of designing software.

The only way around this is to recognize that technologies have many affordances, including those that are not based on the physical world with which we are familiar. The affordances of emerging technologies may solve problems in unique ways or they may allow learning experiences never before possible. A thorough inventory of possible affordances can lead to innovations by using them in new ways, or by recombining them to produce entirely fresh applications that may change the world.

No amount of imagination or subject matter expertise will substitute for actual observations of real users trying out new applications. Observational studies of how users react to new applications require a level of care and expertise in observing and recording that requires training and patience.

So, if you are a learning technology developer, get out of the office and go to a place where your potential users work or learn; then use practical ethnographic observation techniques to learn about them in depth (Ladner 2014). If you are making a major software or hardware purchase from a vendor, ask if you can observe users interacting with their product at one of their customer's sites. At the very least, ask if they can show you video of end users interacting with the technology.

One mistake that is often made is to assume there's only one primary user for a piece of software. However, the use case analysis technique tells us otherwise. There usually are several kinds of users for a learning program, including learners, instructors, administrators, clerical personnel, IT staff, and even a variety of computer programs (yes, in use case analysis, a user can be another computer program or system, such as a database or a learning analytics program). Each kind of user needs to be considered in your evaluation of the new product.

Increasingly, user experiences are personalized. This personalization is based on data gathered as each user works through learning software, which in turn collects data about all sorts of parameters, some as fine-grained as recording every keystroke. In addition, users often enter their own data indicating their preferences and interests, and generate feedback on the experience they've had with a given program. These data are all useful for algorithms that do the work of personalization.

Finally, people are used to highly polished and incredibly well-designed software experiences when they purchase games, utilities, productivity programs, personal fitness trackers, and other items from the consumer technologies market. Is the software you're developing or planning to buy up to these standards? If not, it may not be widely accepted by your target users.

Here are five questions for you to think about when evaluating user experience within the BUILDS framework:

1. Do you have a thorough analysis of the affordances of this technology? What new capabilities does it offer your users?

2. Has your company carried out an observational (ethnographic) study of how users would employ this technology?

3. Has your team carried out a use case analysis for your company for this technology? Who are the primary, secondary, and tertiary users, and how would each category of users employ this technology?
4. Does this technology collect enough data to allow it to be personalized for each user? Have you gathered feedback from users on how this technology can be iterated and improved?
5. Is the technology supplying a high-polish end user experience comparable to consumer technologies that they may be familiar with and use at home?

Looking Ahead

The world of technology in the consumer realm has exploded, and with it, people's expectations of the quality, usability, and user experience of those technologies has also grown. When evaluating new and emerging technologies for use in your learning and development department endeavors, it's vital that you take a critical eye to see if the technology's user experience meets your audience's expectations. Is it easy to use and secure? Is it accessible and widely deployable? Does it put humans first and allow them to personalize their user experience?

After answering these questions, we need to move beyond the individual user experience to assess the overall impact any emerging learning technology we are working with has on non-users, the organization, and the world we live in. We turn to those considerations next.

CHAPTER 4

•————————————•

The Wider Impacts of Learning Technologies

*W*hile business objectives and user experiences are key considerations in the evaluation of any learning technology, there are wider impacts to consider in any evaluation of an emerging technology. In this chapter we go beyond business considerations and individual user experiences to consider how to evaluate those impacts.

No technology exists in isolation from the rest of society, and its adoption can have short-, medium-, and long-term internal and external consequences for any organization. A technology's impact can be felt in its effects on other technologies, social organizations, economic systems, and even politics (Gibbons and Voyer 1974). One of the future roles of learning and talent development departments will be to design workplace learning to consider these broader issues.

As jobs become more precarious and less stable, as brick and mortar offices decline in importance, and as employees become part of diverse connected systems and decentralized teams, learning leaders will become a critical part of developing collaborative networks that bring together disparate types of workers in a virtual setting. At the same time, greater flexibility and agility will be required from everyone to make such a system work. In the near future, we will all have to become learning designers or at least be prepared to engage in design thinking.

The objectives, techniques, and processes that allow users to act as co-designers is known as *meta-design*. Learning technologies are examples of socio-technical systems (STSs) that can be analyzed using meta-design methods. Meta-design "does not provide fixed solutions but a framework within which all stakeholders (designers and users) can contribute to the development of technical functionality and the evolution of the social side such as organizational change, knowledge construction, and continuous learning" (Fischer and Herrmann 2015). Using a meta-design approach allows us to develop technologies that empower users to be more than just consumers of experiences that have been created for them. It requires engagement at broader levels than a focus on individual user experiences (although optimal user experiences remain critically important). Because design must always be changing to meet the needs of new users, emerging technologies, and not-yet-invented processes, meta-design is vital to facilitating the redesign of older designs.

In this chapter we propose evaluation criteria for judging the impact of emerging learning technologies at individual, organizational, and global levels. Our objective is to make sure that any learning technologies of the future are life-affirming tools that allow users to infuse their own world with meaning and to use these tools for the purposes they have chosen themselves (Fischer 2003a). At the same time, we need to recognize that most technologies are networked and interdependent, creating a dynamic and complex social-ecological system that requires multiple perspectives to understand. And, while it is well beyond our scope in this publication to do a full in-depth evaluation of all the issues accompanying the use of emerging learning technologies (or technology in general), you should review these three levels to see if they are relevant to the decisions about whether to use a particular learning technology in your workplace.

Impact on Individuals

In chapter 3 we looked at individuals as *users* to evaluate their experiences with a specific learning technology. But technologies can have other kinds of impacts on individuals beyond the specific user experiences that apply to the learning technologies they encounter. For example, there are non-users (including other computer systems that employ data generated by a new platform) within an organization who may be *indirectly* affected by the introduction of a new technology: The adoption of a sales enablement platform will have the most impact on a firm's sales staff, but will also have implications for marketing staff, designers of the company's brand image, the IT department, C-suite executives, and the computer systems that manage both accounting and customer relationships. Technologies can have a positive or negative impact, depending on whose interests are being served.

Here are some possible positive impacts of emerging digital technologies for employees:

- Positive work changes. New work experiences may be less boring and repetitive than many industrial forms of work. For example, mobile devices that allow people to work from anywhere at any time and retrieve information at the time of need might be more compatible with the demands of their home life.
- Connectivity. Keep in touch with family, friends, and peers worldwide, and meet new people at almost no cost to the individual.
- Information sharing. Share medical, safety, and other valuable information almost instantly.
- Trust building. Use peer recommendations and new technologies like blockchain to help build trusting relationships.
- Democratization of content creation. Anyone can make user-created content available.
- Health and fitness monitoring. Track the status of your body through self-tracking (also known as the quantified self).
- Coordination and collaboration. Communicate with others through social media to make it easier to work together at a distance and to organize for collective action.
- "Sousveillance." Offer protection from oppressive authority by making their actions visible.
- Lower costs. Save money through access to wider markets and price comparison.
- Save time. Perform online tasks that would normally require travel and queuing.

- Entertainment. Pursue hobbies and interests, and view an immense amount of video content.
- Learning. Expand knowledge and skills through online courses, educational materials, and search. Learn at the time of need or as a by-product of being online.

But, all technologies have a dark side and negative impacts may include:

- Negative work changes. Work may become more intense with expectations of being available and performing 24 hours a day.
- Too much information or connectedness overload can cause stress and anxiety.
- Internet platforms are often designed to be addictive to increase profitability.
- Open systems without regulation may contribute to polarization around issues.
- Computational thinking may put limitations on human creativity and the range of thinking.
- Biases in the default settings of forms, standard responses, and algorithms can lead to exclusion and lack of diversity. This has led to the design of software that can allow and even facilitate harassment and abuse.
- Digital technologies may reduce face-to-face interactions, directly speaking to people, and the sense of presence of others. This may lead to a shallowness of engagement in life with little time or motivation for reflection and concentration.
- There are obvious threats to privacy and a danger of others controlling individuals, especially vulnerable populations. May require employees to wear devices that track their every movement.
- Rapidly developing conspiracy theories, fake news, and other breaches of trust is problematic.
- Negative social pathologies, trolling, bullying, and anonymous defacement of digital properties have occurred.
- Questions arise about the authority and accuracy of information that is presented and issues of how to make rational judgments about the information we receive.

- Issues of ownership of information and the channels or platforms through which it is transmitted can lead to a digital divide, whereby a few wealthy people have immense control, while most people become more impoverished and less powerful.
- Barriers to accessibility to technology may work against specific groups and can also lead to a digital divide, whereby one group has access to learning materials while another does not.
- Use of digital devices often raises ethical issues in the workplace.

Computational Thinking

One of the dangers raised by critics of digital technologies is that we start to think like computers and accept the information presented by technologies as more real than our own thinking. As James Bridle (2018) notes, "we have come to live inside computation," and it often has become the foundation of our thought. He adds, "As computation and its products increasingly surround us, are assigned power and the ability to generate truth, and step in to take over more and more cognitive tasks, so reality itself takes on the appearance of a computer; and our modes of thought follow suit. . . . That which is possible becomes that which is computable."

The expression *user experience*, and how we design for it, often assumes a passive role for users, where UX designers make decisions based on their observations and intuitions about how a piece of hardware or software will be used by individuals. But, human beings are naturally creative, and often want to modify or extend the tools they use, adapting them to address problems they face. A movement for end user development, led by Gerhard Fischer at the University of Colorado, develops technologies that empower people to be more than just users or consumers, and to invest technology with their own meanings and purposes (Fischer 2003b; Fischer and Giaccardi 2006). This movement builds open, evolvable systems that put users in charge by "under designing" programs to allow for design elaboration at the time of use (Fischer and Scharff 2000; Fischer, Fogli, and Piccinno 2017).

Biases

For the most part, our digital technologies have been developed by white males, with a notable lack of representation from women or people of color. In *Technically Wrong: Sexist Apps, Biased Algorithms, and Other Threats of Toxic Tech,* Sara Wachter-Boettcher (2017) ably documents the many biases found in digital technologies. Such biases can be found in learning content, forms that need to be filled out, canned responses to questions and actions in interactive software, and in the stereotypes deep in programming algorithms that drive many types of software. Even robots have gender stereotypes attached to their design; for example, "research shows that users tend to like a male voice when an authoritative presence is needed and a female voice when receiving helpful guidance," and this is often reflected in robot design (Simon 2018). Sometimes, there is pressure on programmers to build in biases for a client's product to meet the requirements of a contract (Sourour 2016).

These biases seem to be an inherent part of tech culture, which originated from the libertarian ideas of maximum freedom and individual eccentricity. Meredith Broussard (2018), in *Artificial Unintelligence: How Computers Misunderstand the World,* summarizes the situation:

> We have a small, elite group of men who tend to overestimate their mathematical abilities, who have systematically excluded women and people of color in favor of machines for centuries, who tend to want to make science-fiction real with little regard for social convention, who don't believe that social norms or rules applied to them, who have unused piles of government money sitting around, and who have adopted the ideological rhetoric of far-right libertarian anarcho-capitalists. What could possibly go wrong?

One of the things that has gone wrong is the astounding amount of harassment and abuse that takes place among users of online platforms such as Twitter and Facebook. Some of the ways that social media can lead to harassment in the workplace include (Farrell 2012):

- **virtual harassment:** harassment through a social media site, for example, friending a co-worker on Facebook and then sending offensive messages (or repeated requests for a date)
- **textual harassment:** harassing, intimidating, or sending inappropriate text messages
- **sexting:** sending sexually explicit or offensive photos or videos through electronic media
- **cyberstalking:** harassing employees by following them on blogs, posts, and social websites.

Recently, executives responsible for these platforms have tried to clean up their content by removing the most offensive material, reducing the influence of bots, eliminating fake accounts, hiring content moderators, and using AI to help police their platforms. But they still have a long way to go (Nieva and Hautala 2018).

Privacy and Control

Facial recognition software has become so accurate that artificial intelligence algorithms are able to recognize and track people as they move around their world. In a 2018 article about China, Paul Mozur of *The New York Times* reports, "Beijing is embracing technologies like facial recognition and artificial intelligence to identify and track 1.4 billion people. It wants to assemble a vast and unprecedented national surveillance system, with crucial help from its thriving technology industry." Already, at least 18 countries have purchased this software from China to monitor their citizens (Freedom House 2018). "It's like Christmas for repressive regimes," says Sophie Richardson, China director at Human Rights Watch (CBC 2018). As facial recognition software becomes more readily available, other governments, large multinational corporations, and many more organizations will use this type of software as a matter of course, unless it is regulated.

One danger inherent in workplace learning software is that companies will monitor employees in order to control them, or to detect when they are stepping out of alignment with company policy. As Douglas Heaven

(2017) writes in his anthology of *New Scientist* articles on AI, "Start to slack off or show signs of going rogue, and an algorithm could tattle to your boss. . . . The idea is that it could detect when someone might pose a security risk by stepping outside their usual behavioural patterns."

This has already started at large corporations such as Uber and Amazon, which use forms of control software. Uber's issues with the ethical treatment of its drivers are well known, including tolerance of sexual harassment of female drivers, sexist promotions, not paying minimum wage or benefits, and many other scandals and controversies involving its drivers, executives, and the treatment of its customers (K. Taylor 2017). Across Europe, Amazon workers have complained about "timed toilet breaks and strict targets, with many falling asleep on the warehouse floor" (The Week 2018). In his book *New Dark Age: Technology and the End of the Future*, James Bridle (2018) describes conditions for Amazon workers in the UK that are facilitated by new tracking technologies:

> The handheld devices carried by Amazon's workers and mandated by its logistics are also tracking devices, recording their every movement and keeping score of their efficiency. Workers are docked points—meaning money—for failing to keep up with the machine, for toilet breaks, for late arrival from home or meals, while constant movement prevents association with fellow employees. They have nothing to do but follow the instructions on the screen, pack and carry. They are intended to act like robots, impersonating machines while remaining, for now, slightly cheaper than them. Reducing workers to meat algorithms, useful only for their ability to move and follow orders, makes them easier to hire, fire, and abuse.

Another interesting impact we are seeing play out with Uber and Lyft (or really anything in the gig economy; Airbnb and VRBO are two other examples) is rating inflation. For example, a rating given by a patron of less than five stars is seen as a hostile rebuke of the service provider. (Basically, it's supposed to be like third-period health class in high school—show up and you'll get an A.) This type of artificial control by crowdsourcing and the redirection of a reward to one of punitive implications is another dark side of this social technology.

The Ethics of Learning Technologies

In general, ethics is about what people *should* do in specific situations based on accepted community norms. Ethics includes the fair resolution of conflicts of interest based on accepted community-shared principles. Community norms can involve social influence on others; political pressure; support for cultural, linguistic, and bodily diversity; and etiquette—how people treat one another while interacting through their digital devices.

Concerns over the ethics of using digital devices have been expressed for several decades. In a 1986 article for *MIS Quarterly,* Richard O. Mason, then a professor of management sciences at Southern Methodist University, identified four ethical issues of the information age:

- **privacy:** which information can be withheld and which cannot, under what conditions and with what safeguards
- **accuracy:** the authenticity and fidelity of stored information
- **ownership:** both of the information and the channels through which it is transmitted
- **accessibility:** what information does a person or an organization have a right or privilege to obtain, under what conditions, and with what safeguards?

Many more ethical issues with learning technologies have been identified since then. In 2006, Lin and Kolb wrote about "ethical issues experienced by learning technology practitioners in design and training situations." They noted, "A laundry list of such ethical issues includes, but is not limited to, digital copyright infringement, violation of online private information, and misuse of learning technologies in learning situations." Ashman and colleagues (2014) zeroed in on ethical issues with personalization technologies used in e-learning, and list privacy compromise, lack of control, reduced individual capability, and the commodification of education as some of their concerns. Mayes, Natividad, and Spector (2015) add that as educational technologies "continue to evolve, ethical issues such as equal access to resources become imperative." Pardo and Siemens (2014) include trust, accountability, transparency, and data ownership and access to their ethical issues for learning analytics.

In particular, workers and trainees in settings with populations of vulnerable people, such as hospitals, schools, day care centers, prisons, rehabilitation centers, and professional offices, need to ensure proper informed consent and maintenance of privacy before recording, photographing, or videotaping individuals or groups in these settings. The casual creation of digital data or materials for professional or personal purposes and how they are used, raises issues of power, accountability, and vulnerability.

For example, employees of prisons, hospitals, and psychiatric facilities are in the position of being able to take advantage of those in their care through the recording and distribution of personally embarrassing or compromising materials that are potentially harmful. Preethi Shivayogi (2013), a doctor serving on an ethics committee in Bangalore, India, says organizations serving vulnerable populations need to have solid safety monitoring plans in place with data safety monitoring committee supervision and, wherever applicable, observational study monitoring boards. A framework developed by Asif and colleagues (2013) for an integrated management system for corporate social responsibility includes a case study of how the nonprofit organization Truckee Meadows Tomorrow (TMT), in partnership with Charles Schwab Bank, facilitates community responsiveness to the most vulnerable populations in its geographical area.

A big concern, of course, is privacy, but this is also a two-way street. The rise of "sousveillance," whereby ordinary citizens use mobile devices to document and distribute images of abuse by those in positions of power, can counter some of the issues of privacy and use of power that technology also enables (Mann, Nolan, and Wellman 2003). However, this is a complex area that is still in flux and needs further exploration.

With the advent of big data and machine learning, new ethical concerns have come to the forefront, including "the abuse of probabilistic prediction" by emerging artificial intelligence systems (Heaven 2017; Bostrom 2014). AI systems now can push us toward purchases or new behaviors, and will soon be able to predict our future behavior and then try to move us in that direction, or in a direction that reflects the values and biases of those who program or own learning and social platforms. "The trick," writes Heaven (2017), "will be to accept that we cannot know why these choices were made, and to recognize the choices for what they are: recommendations, mathematical possibilities. There is no oracle behind them."

At the most extreme is software that makes decisions without human guidance that end up changing people's lives. For example, AI systems can "decide who gets a bank loan, who gets a job, who counts as a citizen and who should be considered for parole" (Heaven 2017). And, with immutable blockchain technology available to store a person's complete social history, work history, and their successes and failures, AI algorithms will have a much richer source of data with which to work (Ahmed 2018).

Today, for better or worse, these technologies are being introduced gradually through a process known as *nudging* (Thaler and Sunstein 2009). This occurs when people's decisions and actions are manipulated or nudged by the state to reach certain outcomes desired by officials or politicians (Helbing 2015). This tendency toward conformity is also seen in the well-publicized "filter bubble" effect that the AI-driven personalized search results from search engines like Google are known to produce (Pariser 2011).

As this situation moves beyond the control of individuals, there is a call for new forms of governance of these powerful tools. Ian Harris and his colleagues (2011) in the UK have developed a framework called DIODE to assess the ethics involved in the use of specific technologies, including radio frequency identity devices (RFID), smart dust, biometrics, nanotechnology, and robotics. DIODE reflects the five stages of their methodology, namely, definitions, issues, options, decisions, and explanations:

- Define questions. Ensures that the assessor has defined the technology or project to be examined and is, therefore, able to frame the ethical questions.
- Issues analysis. Ensures that all relevant parties who might be affected are considered (and where appropriate consulted) and that the relevant risks and rewards are examined from both teleological and deontological perspectives.

- Options evaluation. Ensures that relevant choices are made. This is not merely a go/no go assessment; often the answer will be to go ahead, with appropriate safeguards or checkpoints along the way.
- Decision determination. Ensures that the assessor can clearly state the ethical decisions made and reasoning behind them. It encourages the assessor to revisit minority interests at the stage before making the decision. The decision should include guidance on the circumstances that would lead the assessor to revisit the problem.
- Explanations dissemination. Ensures that the decisions are communicated appropriately, including public domain publication wherever possible.

More technology will not ensure the ethical behavior of those taking training. Karen Fields (2016) holds that many employees follow the ethics of their senior leadership. She writes that executives need to be "genuinely interested in avoiding ethical breaches, then they need to be proactive in communicating with their management teams to make it clear that they're serious about what is being taught to the rank-and-file."

The Shift to Lifelong Learning

Rapid technological change and the provision of new platforms and forms of content are transforming the learning landscape. For many, the shift from rigid credential-based models to flexible learner-driven ecologies of creativity and collaboration gives hope for the future, as we move toward knowledge-based societies in which lifelong learning is the norm.

It used to be that post-secondary students took courses aimed at a specific field, culminating in a terminal degree that indicated they were ready to join the workforce and (hopefully) find a lifelong career. Now, the average worker changes jobs every 4.4 years, and by 2020, work-related knowledge acquired by college students is expected to have a shelf-life of less than five years (Hagel et al. 2015). The ever-changing nature of jobs and work has been referred to as having a *Protean career* (D. Hall 2004), which now requires continuous learning and development to adapt to changing professional skills, interests, and career identities necessary for working in this new reality. A new report from the National Academies of Sciences, Engineering, and Medicine (2018) suggests that, instead of traditional training, an organization's culture can play a key role in facilitating an employee's development in this new work environment by doing the following:

- Promoting a "big picture" perspective from which employees know what the goals of the organization are. This enables workers to align development with organizational goals.

- Providing assignments that permit people to stretch beyond their job description. In learning organizations, people are assigned tasks that provide opportunities to do new things, learn new skills, and apply what they learn back on the job.

- Fostering a climate where people can learn from their mistakes. In learning organizations mistakes are tolerated, particularly when people are trying new things in the early stages of learning. Research suggests that error-prone practice can enhance learning, so if mistakes are tolerated, they can lead to greater development.

- Making employees accountable for their own development. For example, performance evaluations might include ratings for engaging in autonomous career-related professional development.

The move to lifelong learning is well underway. A 2016 Pew Research Center survey found that 73 percent of American adults agree that the phrase "I think of myself as a lifelong learner" applies "very well" to them and another 20 percent say it applies "somewhat well" (Horrigan 2016). This shift toward lifelong learning started in the late 1960s and early 1970s (R. Harris 1999), but has accelerated in the past decade:

> The Great Recession that began in 2008 was an especially brutal reckoning for many American workers about their place in a changing economy, the reliability of their jobs, the value of their skills and education, their place in the class structure of America, the state of the benefits safety net, and their prospects for retirement. The recession has

> prompted much commentary about the "skill recession" and the role of learning centers both in traditional settings and in cutting-edge digital platforms in helping workers adjust to new economic realities. (Horrigan 2016)

A new ecosystem of learning providers and support technologies is emerging, independent of more traditional providers of workplace learning, such as post-secondary institutions, company-sponsored training, and trade conferences. Some of the innovations at the edges identified by John Hagel and his colleagues (2015) include:

- third-party education programming providers, including MOOCs, microlearning, and boot camps
- learning mobilizers, which facilitate collaboration among not just students, but a diverse array of community members and corporate partners
- creation spaces, which provide locations and tools for students to build things
- open-source communities for people to share skills and knowledge
- agent businesses, which help students strategically navigate through all their learning options
- third-party learning aggregation platforms that gather all learning experiences and recognition of learning together.

It's clear that these new user-centered design approaches and the "What's in it for me?" equations that make these technologies attractive for individuals can also have significant advantages at the organizational and societal levels.

Impact on Organizations

Beyond the impact on individuals, emerging learning technologies can exert a variety of influences on an entire organization. These influences can include:

- changes in the structure of the organization
- shifts in power relationships and politics within an organization
- improved knowledge flow within an organization
- spillover effects from one organization to another.

From Rigid to "Liquid" Organizations

New networked platforms enable collaboration, support communications among members of virtual teams, help increase trust, allow for mobility and working from anywhere at any time, and grant access to immense stores of sharing resources and information. Organizations have moved from being rigidly organized fixed entities to "liquid" ecosystems that can evolve and change rapidly (Bounfour 2016). Change results in fluid knowledge that can be valid one day and invalid the next.

Organization charts have become passé; today, dynamic maps are needed to tell us what is happening within systems. Person-to-person networking has been displaced by virtual networking that stretches around the globe and is not bound by time or place. As the need for speed has increased, there is now more autonomy across business units to be able to respond more quickly to changing conditions.

Workplace Politics and Power Relationships

Much of what we think about learning is based on our own classroom experiences of schools and postsecondary education. New understandings of workplace learning can be obtained by abandoning an educational perspective on learning, because workplaces are often quite different than the reality portrayed by the slowly changing curricula of educational institutions.

Power relations in the workplace are particularly different. Within an organization, internal politics can influence opportunities to learn, and how employees interact with the workplace. As Dutch researchers Doornbos, Bolhuis, and Simons (2004) explain:

> Workplaces can be highly competitive and the opportunities to learn unevenly distributed. . . . Cliques, politics, and power may intentionally or unintentionally influence the distribution of opportunities to learn. Those with more access to power can claim learning opportunities, and they can also deny opportunities for learning, whereas those with less power may find access to what they want difficult.

In contrast, access to learning is assumed to be equal within a formal education setting.

Political behaviors within an organization can have a strong impact on workplace learning as documented by Cacciattolo (2013), who identified political behaviors such as "narcissism," "the new employee considered as a threat," and "bureaucracy." Many of these behaviors do not fit with our models of learning within classrooms, but can occur in a work setting.

External politics, those which stakeholders cannot control, can also influence the provision of workplace learning. Examples of external politics that can affect workplace learning are employment laws, tax policies, trade restrictions, trade reforms, international agreements, environmental regulations, government funding programs, and military spending. Indeed, many of the emerging learning technologies used around the world were first funded by the U.S. Department of Defense, including the Internet, e-learning, and GPS.

Networking and Knowledge Flow

Computer networking has had a tremendous impact on knowledge flow within and among organizations. In the past, traditional bureaucracies hoarded and guarded information, producing the famous silo effect that has often been criticized as contributing to organizational inefficiencies. However, starting with the first email sent in 1971, communication through digital networks has exploded around the world, changing the flow of knowledge within and beyond organizations.

Within organizations, networking has vastly improved internal communications and the sharing of company knowledge. In addition, knowledge is flowing out of organizations through the same networks, causing spillover effects because knowledge cannot be contained within the walls of a single organization. The movement of internal information to outside entities became even more pronounced with the popularity of mobile phones equipped with cameras, Internet connections, and a variety of messaging apps.

Because of the rapid spread of connectivity around the world, new approaches to evaluation frameworks for innovation and learning networks have been developed. Elise Ramstad (2009) saw this coming a decade ago when she wrote, "new types of broader networks that aim to achieve widespread effects in the working life have emerged. These are typically based on an interactive innovation approach, where knowledge is created jointly together with diverse players. At the moment, the challenge is how to evaluate these complex networks and learning processes." Her solution is an evaluation framework with three elements: "the micro level of the work organization, the meso level of the innovation infrastructure and the macro level of innovation policy and broader society." Learning is not something that only happens within individuals; it is a group phenomenon that involves employees and workplaces, research and development units, and policymakers all working and sharing together.

Impact at a Global Level

Based on the libertarian ideals of many of the original founders of the Internet, global networking has been seen as a commons to be used by everyone. Electronic technologies were originally seen as technologies of freedom that would give a voice to all and usher in a new age of peace, love, and understanding (de Sola Pool 1983). Unfortunately, it hasn't quite turned out that way.

Control of these emerging digital technologies is critical because some will attempt to use them to gain great power and wealth at the expense of others. All these new technologies have the potential to hijack our minds and steal our attention away from more important things in life, argues Tristan Harris (2016), founder of the Center for Humane Technology and the "Time Well Spent" movement. In his work as a design ethicist, Harris shows how a few hundred people, using principles of behavioral psychology, can influence and manipulate billions of people to buy more or to act against their own interests.

With the rapid growth of e-commerce and the building of "walled gardens" by a few giant platforms that aggregate users and collect data from them, the Internet has mostly become a commercial space governed by the rules of the market. While users treat the offerings of digital providers as public spaces, in reality, these providers are, for the most part, businesses dedicated to maximizing profits for their shareholders. Companies like Amazon, Apple, Facebook, Microsoft, and Google control the vast majority of transactions on the Internet, and make immense amounts of money doing so. They do this by using the data they collect to manipulate us into buying even more goods, so they can make even more money (Galloway 2017). Beyond using our data for increasing their own business revenue, these large Internet companies sell large quantities of our data to other companies. For these Internet giants, we have become the product.

We are at a crossroads as to how the Internet will be governed in the future. The United States continues its market-centric approach with light or no regulations, which allows innovation to grow rapidly. Americans have done this by exempting the big platforms like Facebook, Google, and Twitter from liability for content posted by their users. While this has promoted rapid growth, it is also led to many of the abuses that we now see on these platforms.

Some countries, such as China and others ruled by dictatorships, see the need for "cyber-sovereignty," the desire to control all computer networking within their national borders, and to project their influence around the world (Segal 2018). On the other hand, India has developed a new inclusive network, where the government has built open systems as public goods (Nilekani 2018). The Europeans took a third approach and introduced the General Data Protection Regulation (GDPR), a new set of rules that went into effect in May 2018 that greatly strengthens the protection of private data (Dixon 2018). It is not clear at this point which approach will win out in regulating the future of the Internet.

The stakes are high. Emerging information and communications technologies (ICT), are being networked and interconnected to create something that has never existed before—a global "brain" that is open to all and will be connected to the various specialized artificial intelligences we are building. What we don't know is how this new form of intelligence will turn out—some think it might take over and enslave the human race, while others argue that it will be used to solve some of our most intractable problems (Heaven 2017). It is surely a critical question as to who controls and regulates these powerful platforms and the global infrastructure that makes it all possible (Kornbluh 2018).

Perhaps the greatest crisis that humanity has ever faced is the prospect of global warming caused by climate change due to the burning of fossil fuels since the beginning of the first industrial revolution. More than 97 percent of the world's scientists agree that the planet is heating up due to the use of non-renewable fossil fuels, and that the problem may be accelerating faster than we think (Wallace-Wells 2017). Most of the countries in the world (with the notable exception of the United States) have signed on to a global agreement to limit the impact of this threat to life as we know it.

You may be wondering how emerging learning technologies are implicated in this trend. Like all computer-based technologies, they use a lot of electricity, which is currently being generated by the burning of fossil fuels such as coal and oil. According to Bryan Walsh (2013), "the digital economy uses a tenth of the world's electricity—and that share will only increase with serious consequences for the economy and the environment." By 2015, the data centers around the world that make up the "cloud" consumed 3 percent of the world's electrical power; that's the same carbon footprint as the airline industry and it exceeds all the electricity used that year by the United Kingdom. The demand for electricity for data centers is expected to triple in the next 10 years. A study in Japan suggested that the power required for all digital devices and services would outstrip current generating capacity in that country by 2030 (Bridle 2018).

On the other hand, there are valid arguments that the use of computer networking and mobile devices in learning and development is actually good for the environment because it reduces the need for travel to a specific location for training, leading to cost savings in transportation, accommodation, and food necessary to gather employees together. Against that argument, we need to consider the costs for manufacturing, transporting, selling, powering, and maintaining all the equipment and content that goes into online training. We also need to recognize that global networking and online learning platforms may be the best technologies to support the spread of learning worldwide that will be necessary if we are to solve environmental and other major international problems in the near future.

Evaluating the Wider Impact of Emerging Technologies

In the last chapter we focused on different types of users and their experiences with emerging learning technologies. But the impacts of adopting a new technology are wide-ranging and far-reaching. They can affect many people who are not end users; shake up teams, companies, and other types of organizations; and even have a significant influence on regions, nations, and the planet as a whole. While most of us will focus first on local impact for our end users, it is important to evaluate other potential consequences of introducing new technologies into the workplace.

For example, people with a disability may be affected differently than those without one. This may be positive: a new technology can enable new forms of accessibility or augment the abilities that a person with a disability might have. Because innovation often starts at the edges of society, many new devices and uses of new technologies are initially developed for people with disabilities. Examples include text readers, speech recognition software, speech synthesis, electric wheelchairs with navigation using a person's thoughts, exoskeletons, cochlear implants, and the telephone (initially developed for Alexander Graham Bell's wife, who was deaf). At the same time, however, new technologies can also have a negative impact if they introduce a barrier that excludes people with a disability from full participation in society. Barriers can be part of the impact of emerging technologies for other groups, as well, because of biases related to gender, race, or culture. All these impacts on individuals need to be evaluated.

The introduction of new technologies can also affect the work experiences of people within an organization. Instead of slowly learning about a process or a customer from more experienced employees, a great deal of information about what is needed for performing one's job is often available instantly on computer monitors or mobile devices. Similarly, training that was once only available in classrooms can now be offered to each employee on demand through their mobile phone. These are only a few of the effects new technologies can have on work experiences.

Changes in how work is experienced can ultimately affect how a company is organized and managed. When roles change, so does an organization's structure, and how people within that structure relate to one another. This can raise ethical issues such as privacy, control, harassment, and abuse, especially if your organization is working with people with vulnerabilities. Do you at least have a checklist for evaluating these issues?

Finally, you need to be aware that all technologies affect the environment and may or may not be sustainable in the long term. Does the adoption of the technology you are evaluating entail harsh working conditions for people in other countries? For example, some of the rare minerals used in the production of mobile phones come from mines in countries with horrible working conditions or use of child labor. By investigating and evaluating potential issues, you are in a position to make environmentally friendly and sustainable choices, while becoming aware of the working conditions of other people in the supply chain for the technology you are using. In this age of abundant information, it's not difficult to find answers to questions about the ethics of the impact of a technology.

At minimum we recommend asking the following questions about the impact of an emerging learning technology on your employees, organization, and the world in which you live:

1. Is the emerging learning technology accessible for people with a disability? Does it have any obvious biases or barriers for specific groups (for example, groups based on gender, race, or culture)?

2. Would the adoption of this technology introduce new work experiences into your company? Does it allow for mobile learning?

3. How would the adoption of this technology change your company's organizational structure?

4. Does this technology introduce ethical issues or problems (such as at-risk populations, privacy, and control)?

5. Is this emerging technology environmentally friendly and sustainable?

Looking Ahead

In the end, it is a matter of choosing the kind of world in which we want to live, and collectively, as a human community, anticipating the future and deciding how to get there—a concept known as *anticipatory governance*. Helbing (2015) articulates the choices we are facing in light of emerging technologies: "We must decide between a society in which the actions are determined in a top-down way and then implemented by coercion or manipulative technologies (such as personalized ads and nudging) or a society, in which decisions are taken in a free and participatory way and mutually coordinated."

What is needed is nothing less than a revolution in individual and collective learning, whereby humanity solves the problems it is facing rather than surrendering to those who control and own emerging technologies.

A key question for us as learning professionals is whether the use of digital learning technologies is sustainable and effective; that is, does it promote change in a positive way that meets and enhances present and future human needs? We need to be able to show that educational and workplace learning work better with emerging technologies than without them. We turn to that question next.

CHAPTER 5

Learning With Emerging Technologies

At the heart of any evaluation of emerging learning technologies is, of course, the phenomenon of learning. Related to learning are the many activities we call teaching—helping others to learn. While teaching and learning are not the same, they are related. In this chapter we lay out the relationship between learning and learning technologies to develop evaluation criteria for emerging technologies that can support learning, teaching, assessment, and the management of learning activities.

The use of technology in learning dates back to at least the 13th century, when medical lectures were delivered at the University of Bologna, and moves forward to the recent use of brain implants, which can improve memory by up to 30 percent (Bates 2014; Hamzelou 2017). Lecturing (from the Latin, "to read") began as a copying technology. It started with monks reading a single book out loud to other monks who wrote down what they heard to produce additional copies of a manuscript. Although lecturing and reading have persisted until the present day, many new learning technologies present alternative ways to deliver or access information. Just as the invention of reading changed how the human brain functions, the heavy use of digital devices is also changing our brains. This has prompted literacy expert Maryanne Wolf (2018) to call for "biliterate" education for young people, equivalent to learning two languages, where both reading-based and digital-based approaches to thinking are taught in schools. More on that idea later.

There is no question that the field of learning "has become very complex, with different foci, founders and proponents, schools, and disciplinary approaches" (Qvortrup and Wiberg 2013). At the same time, we agree with JD Dillon (2017) that "at no point . . . is L&D expected to throw away everything it's already doing." In one of the first critiques of the impact of computer technology on human knowledge, Dreyfus and Dreyfus (1986) used philosopher Gilbert Ryle's differentiation of "knowing-that" and "knowing-how" to argue that human problem solving and knowledge application depends on context, rather than a process of searching through everything we know for the right answer to a given problem. Biggs and Tang (2011) make the distinction between surface learning (based on memorization) and deep learning (based on understanding). Recently, Frank (2017) argued for the separation of mimetic learning (memorization and recall) from transformative learning (learning to be creative, intuitive, and feeling based), suggesting that digital adaptive tutoring programs strongly favored mimetic learning at the expense of transformative learning. How do we make sense of all these different ways of learning and their interactions with emerging learning technologies?

One way is through rigorous experimentation, which is what Nobel laureate Daniel Kahneman (2011) has done with a lifetime of careful research on human thinking. He reconciles many of the distinctions we've listed with his dual-process theory, confirming that, in terms of how we think, we are two selves in one body. One self is fast thinking, intuitive, and heuristics-based, whereas the other is slow thinking, rational, and analytical. The two systems within one brain shown here are adapted from Canadian philosopher Joseph Heath's 2014 book, *Enlightenment 2.0:*

- System 1. The Experiencing Self: Fast, Intuitive, Heuristic
    - unconscious, automatic
    - rapid, computationally powerful, massively parallel
    - associative
    - pragmatic (contextualizes problems in the light of prior knowledge and beliefs)
    - does not require the resources of central working memory
    - functioning is not related to individual differences in intelligence

- low effort
- prone to biases and errors.
- System 2. The Remembering Self: Slow, Rational, Analytical
  - linked to language and reflective consciousness
  - slow and sequential
  - linked to working memory and general intelligence
  - capable of abstract and hypothetical thinking
  - volitional or controlled—responsive to instructions and stated intentions
  - high effort
  - prone to losing focus due to fatigue or interruption of attention.

The implication of Kahneman's research is that we need to consider both systems when designing instructional technology for workplace learning (or education-based learning). It may turn out that the exciting, stimulating, multimedia approach of augmented and virtual reality works best for training the experiencing self, while a more formal, careful presentation or reading approach (whether online or in a classroom) works best for instructing the remembering self. Kahneman's research may put an end to the controversy over which approach to learning is better, as both approaches will be needed in the future. And, in spite of its detractors, classroom technologies and direct instructional strategies, such as presentations, may provide important scaffolding for the development of rational thinking and memory work appropriate for specific kinds of learning tasks (Wood, Bruner, and Ross 1976; Heath 2014).

For instructional designers, the problem is that the heuristics used by the experiencing self are prone to behavioral biases and systematic errors. So, despite managers acting fast and feeling right, their decisions may need to be supervised by the more rational remembering self. For example, according to Lejarraga (2010), "Entrepreneurs learning from descriptive sources (e.g. market analyses, industry reports, or records of entrepreneurial ventures) about the potential payoff distribution of a given venture make more Type I errors (selecting poor ventures), while those learning from self-experience make more Type II errors (forgoing promising ventures)." Instructional designers need to take this kind of information into account when designing learning materials. Moving forward, learning and talent development departments need to understand and develop instructional strategies for both kinds of thinking (Campbell 2015).

The Rise of Work-Based Learning Technologies

The importance of work-based learning has grown with the ever-increasing pace of technological change. One estimate of the critical importance of continuous and lifelong learning is that "technology skills have to be updated every three years in order to have continued relevance" in today's economy (Grand-Clement 2017). Although a baseline of knowledge is necessary for any job or profession, the need to always know specific information has decreased in importance, while the ability to find information when needed and assess its quality is now a critical skill for adult learning. In this section we offer our views of the process of learning and relate how learning technologies are being used and might soon be used at each stage of the learning process.

Lachman (1997) proposed the following definition of learning: "Learning is the process by which a relatively stable modification in stimulus–response relations is developed as a consequence of functional environmental interaction via the senses . . . rather than as a consequence of mere biological growth and development." We like Lachman's definition for several reasons. Besides emphasizing that learning is a process of relatively stable modifications in response to stimuli, we agree with his emphasis on the fact that learning takes place within a context and necessarily involves the senses. While we elaborate the process of workplace learning in more detail than does Lachman, we think his definition of learning makes for a good starting point in our discussion. At the same time, our concepts of learning are changing. The conventional view of the process of learning that has dominated classroom teaching was articulated by Robert Gagné (1985) more than 35 years ago when he defined learning as "a change in human disposition or capacity that persists over a period of time and is not simply ascribable to processes of growth." He listed these nine steps as "events of instruction" (Gagné, Briggs, and Wager 1992):

1. Gain attention.
2. Orient the learner.
3. Stimulate recall of prior knowledge.
4. Present content material.
5. Provide learner guidance.
6. Elicit performance "practice."
7. Provide informative feedback.
8. Assess if lesson objectives have been learned.
9. Enhance retention and transfer.

While the process outlined by Gagné describes a conventional direct instruction approach, much has changed thanks to the cognitive revolution in psychology and the tremendous advances made in neurology over the past 20 years. A more updated view of processes involved in learning is provided by *How People Learn II: Learners, Context and Cultures,* perhaps the most comprehensive review of the latest research on learning available today. This collaboration of the National Academies of Sciences, Engineering, and Medicine (2018) identifies five learning strategies for which there is good evidence of effectiveness:

- Retrieval practice. The act of retrieving information enhances learning it, and the ability of a learner to retrieve and use knowledge again in the future is enhanced.
- Spaced practice. Spaced practice (compared with massed practice such as cramming) distributes learning events over extended periods of time and shows greater positive effects across learning materials and stimulus formats, for both intentional and incidental learning.
- Interleaved and varied practice. Practicing skills in different ways and mixing different activities in the same learning session promotes better learning.
- Summarizing and drawing. Producing a verbal description that distills the most important information from a set of materials and creating a diagram that portrays important concepts and relationships both enhance learning.

- Constructing explanations. Techniques of elaborative interrogation, self-explanation, and teaching others all have been shown to facilitate learning.

None of the above resembles passive students listening to lectures, but active involvement in the act of learning at all times. While learning involves memory, learned memories are *reconstructed* in our brain each time we remember something (National Academies 2018). Learning is a dynamic and ongoing process of connecting memories and a current problem or context, not simply the storage of information for later wholesale retrieval. But, near verbatim reproduction of presented materials or texts has been the gold standard for success in passing assessments for a very long time.

Marshall McLuhan noted in the 1960s, "We look at the present through a rear-view mirror. We march backwards into the future" (McLuhan and Fiore 1967). It is not surprising, then, that the first vendors of digital learning technologies created standard school-based instructional applications, such as the delivery of textbooks, notetaking, courses, lectures, and assessments, as well as class management procedures, such as taking attendance, daily planning, recording grades, and producing report cards. Learning management systems (LMSs) and learning content management systems (LCMSs) simply bundled most of these functions into one big, and usually expensive, program. Content was presented onscreen in much the same way that a teacher would put content on a blackboard or show an occasional movie. Innovations such as classroom response systems (such as clickers) and presentation software (such as PowerPoint) freshened the classroom experience but did little to change the relationship between learners and instructors.

Before the Association for Talent Development (first known as the American Society for Training Directors and then the American Society for Training & Development) was founded in 1943, most training in industrial settings was either done on the job or close to the job as vestibule training. During and after World War II we saw the beginnings and growth of purpose-specific training classrooms. There, training, usually provided and managed by the human resources department, became more formal and aligned to designated job skills to support specific business units. The end of the 1990s saw the growth of classroom-based and online course–based corporate universities, which were more aligned to wider organizational goals. Instructors followed a stepped curriculum and held the status of workplace learning and performance professionals, usually reporting to a chief learning officer (Abel 2008; Meister 1998). Training also took place in seminars and conferences, which were both extensions of the classroom metaphor for training.

But with the arrival of mobile and immersive technologies, learning could take place anytime, anywhere (Udell 2012). Since the beginning of the new millennium, learning departments, talent development programs, and corporate universities have scrambled to catch up to the implications of the newest technologies. The change is best summarized by Prieto, Dimitriadis, and Asensio-Pérez (2014) who observed that learning environments (including classrooms), "are becoming messy, complex socio-technical ecosystems of resources."

Given this latest shift to learning within "complex socio-technical" environments, traditional methods for evaluating learning technologies must also change. From the 19th century to the 1960s, the gold standard of scientific research methods has been *experimental evaluation,* with an emphasis on control through double-blind studies, a random selection of subjects, and the use of rigorous statistical procedures to come to conclusions with a specified degree of confidence (usually 5 percent or 1 percent). Since World War II we have also seen the rise of *ethnographic evaluation,* with participant observation, careful recording of both behaviors and contexts, and "thick description" of results (Geertz 1973). Starting in the 1980s, the emerging wave of evaluation methods has been *environmental evaluation* based on network analysis, ecological interdependencies, complexity theory, and emergence. On the horizon (and already here in a few instances) are *algorithmic evaluations* by computers using big data, machine learning, and artificial intelligence for pattern recognition and correlation of connected variables. While examples of all four approaches can be found in the latest research on work-based learning, it is clear that a more complex and ecological view of the meaning of enterprise learning and its new technologies is pushing us to rethink how we approach the evaluation of learning technologies.

Faced with constant change, an explosion of available information, and myriad resources, the instructor in an enterprise has moved from being principally a source and presenter of knowledge to a guide and curator for individual and group learning. At the organizational level, the instructor has become a conductor who orchestrates teams to learn to operate in the most optimal way for a business (Prieto et al. 2011; Dillenbourg 2013). Further complicating the matter, employees are increasingly moving toward "self-regulated workplace learning," reducing the roles of learning professionals altogether (Siadaty et al. 2012).

Clearly, we are in a transition period between two approaches to delivering training to employees. While new technologies are now used in the corporate world to support self-directed learning, it is still the case that "passive learning . . . consisting largely of sitting down and then consuming pre-packaged content in bulk that's presented formally by an educator" remains the norm (Hinchcliffe 2017). In our opinion, this is about to change. Workplace learning is increasingly being facilitated through new teaching strategies, including "modelling, coaching, questioning, scenario building, organizing and sequencing of workplace experiences, encouraging interpersonal interactions, helping to identify learning conditions, and teaching in the use of learning strategies" (Snoeren, Niessen, and Abma 2015). Emerging learning technologies are having effects that are only going to accelerate.

What has changed in workplace learning is the realization that going digital allows for possibilities that have never existed before, and that some of these new opportunities improve the competitiveness of a business. In the design world, "affordances" are the qualities or features of an object or an environment that allow an individual to perform an action (Norman 1988). The new affordances of digital technologies allow for many other possibilities to support teaching and learning than those found in a traditional classroom. As vendors learn to innovate and the learning and development market accepts possibilities beyond the usual "tell and test" procedures common in the era of in-class instructors and three-ring binders, new features have gradually been introduced to emerging learning technologies, such as:

- mobility, making anytime learning possible from any location with access to the Internet
- networking to anywhere in the world allowing access to vast amounts of information
- social media that allows peer-to-peer commentary on user-created content
- collaboration tools that support working with others
- location-based (using GPS) applications that permit algorithms to understand and use contextual cues
- games and gamification techniques that improve motivation
- sophisticated search software that supports do-it-yourself learning
- cloud computing that allows content to be retrieved from any location
- self-tracking and immediate feedback
- sensors to collect and store massive amounts of data on individuals and groups
- artificial intelligence and data to personalize content and interactions with software.

As a society, we are only now realizing the new possibilities that the abilities of digital devices can bring to the design of learning technologies. Few of these affordances were possible in the classroom, and all are still in early stages of development. And, they all interact together, creating a new reality for learning leaders called *intertwingularity* (Nelson 1974). The term refers to the complexity of the interrelations of human knowledge whereby the cross-connections among topics cannot be easily divided into simple categories. Thus, learning technologies are *intertwingled,* and cannot be treated as separate, unrelated technologies for learning. The skill set needed to operate in this new environment requires managers and instructional designers to step up their game in terms of their own personal learning and collaboration with others (Woodill, Udell, and Stead 2014).

At the same time, there is lots of resistance to change, and vendors never want to get too far ahead of the market in their offerings. Despite what learning and development departments or vendors want, many employees, especially younger ones, have discovered these new affordances and often bypass official channels to use them. This trend is only going to accelerate as the capabilities of digital devices, especially smartphones and global networking, rapidly improve, and the working populations shift to include even more new entrants.

The Workplace Learning Process

Williams (2010) describes three key elements of work-based learning that distinguish it from learning in an educational setting:

- learning is acquired in the midst of action and dedicated to the task at hand
- knowledge creation and utilization are collective activities where learning becomes everyone's job
- learners demonstrate a learning-to-learn aptitude, which frees them to question the underlying assumptions of practice.

For these reasons, a workplace learning experience is often more innovative and variable than a school-based learning experience.

At the same time, we need to recognize that, for many employees, workplace learning is tacit, undocumented, rooted in repetitive body movements and "muscle memory," and often not spoken about explicitly. It is just something that happens as we work and absorb job procedures from the environment and those around us, and continually practice them. It is a social and collective process where knowledge is both co-constructed by, and held within, a local group of workers. It is often *tribal*, where the knowledge created holds its value within the tribe, sometimes with little usefulness beyond group boundaries.

If we step back and take a system view of learning, the description of the process for Western culture might look like this: Because human beings exist in the world, all teaching and learning necessarily takes place within a context or environment. The process starts with getting a motivated learner's or learners' attention, followed by a stimulus or experience that, combined with memories, results in a modification to the person's usual response to that stimulus. That modification, which is also stored in memory, can be strengthened through practice, spacing, and other techniques for improving retention. As this happens, data can be collected using a variety of technologies and used to assess whether learning has taken place. These data and assessments can be further examined using the techniques of learning analytics, which can form the basis of reports or feedback and be used to justify the issuance of credentials that attest to the fact that accumulated learning has taken place. That learning is now available to be combined with new contexts, problems, and experiences in an iterative loop (Figure 5-1).

Figure 5-1. Stages of a Learning Process Involving Current Western Cultural Practices

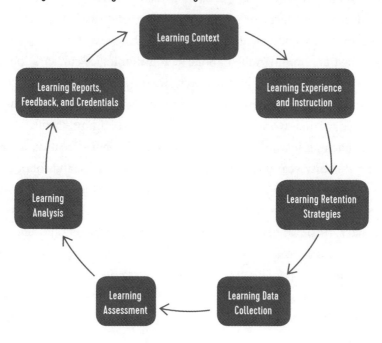

At each stage of the learning process, digital technologies can be introduced to support or take over parts of the process. Some of these technologies are being offered with great fanfare right now, while others are on the horizon and will likely appear and become commonly used in the next five to 10 years. The central question for this book is how do we evaluate these emerging technologies?

One of the most accepted definitions of technology was formulated by sociologist Read Bain in 1937: "Technology includes all tools, machines, utensils, weapons, instruments, housing, clothing, communicating and transporting devices and the skills by which we produce and use them." A learning technology is anything that can be used to support learning, teaching, assessment of learning, or the administration of learning or teaching practices.

Today, by "learning technologies" we mostly mean digital information and communications technologies (ICT), but textbooks, classrooms, blackboards, desks, school buildings, conferences, lecterns, and analog audiovisual equipment also qualify as learning technologies, even if they are not digital. By "emerging learning technologies" we mean mostly digital devices, products, or services that have newly arrived or are on the horizon for likely implementation in the next five years.

The most commonly talked about new technologies currently on offer from commercial vendors and research organizations such as universities and corporate labs include 3-D printing, cloud computing, simulations, 360-degree virtual worlds, enhanced search algorithms, artificial intelligence, machine learning, computer vision, augmented reality, adaptive tutoring systems, wearable devices, the Internet of Things, and robotics. We believe that other, even more exotic or nascent technologies, such as quantum computing and embodied digital devices will be available or coming in the next 10 to 20 years and may also assist in learning. For example, while much work needs to be done to make quantum computing viable for everyday use, it is possible to try out several simple quantum computing apps right now (Captain 2018; Russon 2018). Whatever the changes, the world of learning and talent development will surely look much different 10 years from now.

The Workplace as Context

As embodied human beings living in a specific location, learning always has a context. Sometimes the context is simply the place or time in which we find ourselves, while in other instances we are in a specifically designed learning environment; a place (for example, a learning lab, classroom, or simulated environment) that has been deliberately set up to facilitate learning, and which, therefore should be seen as another learning technology. Sometimes this place is virtual, as in a set of goggles that tries to reproduce the sensations of a realistic locative experience. Other times this place is augmented, with a mixed reality overlay that blends digital media with a physical space or location.

Describing the physical environment as a technology is not the only aspect of context to be considered in any analysis of learning (Hinton 2014). Also relevant are:

- the affordances of the individual physical elements in an environment
- the semiotics of both natural and designed elements including color, space, sounds, and visualizations
- the semantic functions of language as an environment, both as text and spoken words
- the personal context that people bring to their environments including embodiment, identity, situations, interests, and past narratives
- the social dimensions when other people are in an environment
- digital information that is available to augment the immediate information in a specific setting
- mapping systems of meaning by combining these elements.

Understanding and using context to support learning is often called situated or situational learning and can be facilitated in several ways using emerging multimedia technologies (Tretiakov and Kinshuk 2003). Yusoff, Zaman, and Ahmad (2010) describe a mixed reality technology supported by 3-D graphics, animation, text, narration, and music to give biomedical students some exposure to the regenerative concept and in-vitro processes of animal tissue culture, but note that there is little research on the effectiveness of this approach. Batson (2011) argues that adults learn best with "situated learning, a humanistic view of learning that envisions learning in real life occurring constantly, outside of the classroom as well as in the classroom" and advocates for the use of e-portfolios as the best way to document this type of learning. Leinonen and colleagues (2013) use contextual inquiry and participatory design to develop a number of new technology-enhanced techniques for the construction industry, including wearable point of view cameras, RFID tags, and augmented reality headsets—all integrated into the workflow of a job site. These are all examples of setting up a learning technology as a situated environment.

One related emerging technology to watch is "context modelling for learning" (Yin et al. 2015), whereby several standardization efforts have been undertaken to develop learner models and learning objects embedded in a learning context. One example of context modeling is the IMS Global Learning Consortium's (2018) Learner Information Package, which defines the context for ubiquitous learning as the "learner's state," "the educational activity state," "the infrastructure state," and "the environment state." Each state has its own set of variables and its data can be collected for future analysis and used within machine learning algorithms. This approach is an example of how context is being turned into data to be used later in analytics and personalization.

The Learner as Context

Before individual learning can take place, there needs to be a motivated learner willing to learn. Employees are part of the context of a workplace, and each one brings a personal learning orientation, past work and social history, embodied characteristics such as physical abilities and intelligence, and various degrees of motivation to get a job done. Motivation can be supplied through personal interests, a set of goals that orient the learner, fears, desires, or simple enjoyment of learning.

Yet, a 2013 Gallup poll reported that almost 70 percent of Americans who work are "actively disengaged in their work." This lack of engagement costs the U.S. economy billions of dollars annually (Parlavantzas 2015). Technologies like simulations, games, virtual reality, and other attractors are all attempts to re-engage employees to improve productivity and profits. Rollag and Billsberry (2012) contend that improved information technology over the past decade has led to a shift from passive to active learning, where, independent of any developmental or organizational input from an L&D department, employees simply look up the information they need, when they need it. Learning has definitely become more learner-centric, which means that, more than ever, instructional technology designers need to take the characteristics and interests of learners into account when they develop technology-enhanced learning.

With this self-directed approach to learning taking hold, learners have altered the context and inserted their motivations and desires into the conversation. Providing ways for the employees to increase their connection and engagement with the business through easy-to-use learning technologies may unlock performance improvements previously unrealized or neglected.

The Social Context of Workplace Learning

Collective or group learning is not the same as individual learning. In North America, individual learning has traditionally been favored over group learning in workplace learning research and practice. This is a mistake because learning is first and foremost a social enterprise. As noted Russian psychologist Lev Vygotsky (1978) stated, as individuals we always relate to a "shared social world."

Collective workplace learning, also known as organizational learning, often occurs within and among teams, and "involves the exchange of facts and concepts, experimenting with ideas, joint reflection on them, and the collective restructuring and fine-tuning of them" (Andres 2013). Organizational learning is the process of constructing and storing new knowledge within organizations—or reconstructing existing knowledge to improve the functions of individuals within the organization or the organization as a whole—and is embedded in an organization's culture.

Collaborative learning and knowledge building have many different facets, including mutual teaching, exposure to multiple perspectives, division of tasks, pooling results of actions, brainstorming, critiquing, negotiating, compromising, and agreeing (Stahl 2004). In fact, group learning may take precedence over individual learning in that it supplies the cultural background, the motivational support, and the interactive experiences to facilitate individual learning (Stahl 2006).

Workplace climate, especially positive supervision and encouragement from other members of one's workgroup, can influence motivation. It can also change how workers view emerging learning technologies introduced into the workplace. A 2012 study by Cheng and colleagues found that "employees' perceived managerial support and job support had a significant impact on their perceived usefulness of the e-learning system for individual learning, and that perceived organizational support had a significant influence on the perceived usefulness of the e-learning system for social learning."

Varieties of Technology-Enhanced Learning

There are at least four broad ways to learn in a workplace:

- incidental or accidental learning (from everyday experiences that have not specifically been designed for learning)
- self-directed learning
- directed learning or instruction
- collective or social learning.

Let's look at each in terms of how they can be influenced by technology.

Incidental Learning

We are always learning simply by being alive and experiencing the world as we encounter it. Sometimes those experiences are painful and unexpected, but learning still takes place—a process referred to in the literature as "incidental learning." For example, railway engineers can learn from derailments or train collisions even though they are not planned. Of course, the experience is very different if you are involved in such an incident compared with investigating it later or reading about it.

Lukic, Littlejohn, and Margaryan (2012) developed a framework for learning from incidents in the workplace, especially in a health, safety, and environmental context, which can improve organizational safety and productivity. A critical factor in the success of learning from incidents is the level of engagement of employees and their ability to challenge the status quo within the organization. Here, reporting technologies, such as documenting safety concerns by posting digital photos of hazardous conditions online, can improve safety through group learning.

Self-Directed Learning

Methods used by employees for self-directed learning include the development of good search skills; being comfortable linking to a variety of information sources, including audio and video; networking with peers and mentors as an information source and for .collaborative learning; being members of learning communities (also known as communities of practice); self-tracking of body movements and performance measures; and simply following employee interests. Increasingly, digital devices become part of workplace learning processes along with other material elements, a concept referred to as digital materiality (Pink, Ardèvol, and Lanzeni 2016). Embedding digital games for learning along with a manual assembly process for manufacturing is one example. Games can be used for motivation, microlearning, performance support, and simulations for learning teamwork (Cela-Ranilla et al. 2014).

Direct Instruction

Direct instruction refers to the explicit teaching of information, concepts, or skills using presentations or demonstrations of the required learning materials. It includes lectures, tutorials, laboratory sessions, discussion groups, audiovisual presentations, conferences, seminars, workshops, apprenticeships, internships, assigned readings, supervised practice, organized games, simulations, field trips, triggered locative learning, and other forms of arranged learning experiences. Mostly, it uses language in the form of text or narration to convey information, and is usually based on a documented curriculum that is being followed by the person or people who are giving the direct instruction.

Systematic direct instruction may use specific behavioral objectives to facilitate assessment and measurement of results. This approach has been also termed instructionism, and while it can have an impact on learning it is now seen as inadequate for learning in a knowledge economy (Sawyer 2014).

Direct instruction is often driven by measurable behavioral objectives, but much learning cannot be measured quantitatively or even qualitatively, and tacit knowledge can remain hidden until a person is called upon to enact a specific skill or remember a specific piece of information in a particular context. Similarly, direct instruction is often not seen as a way of exciting or motivating learners about content that needs to be learned, which is why it is sometimes referred to pejoratively as just-in-case learning.

Although direct instruction has fallen somewhat out of favor with the movement away from classrooms toward mobile learning, there is substantial empirical evidence supporting its effectiveness, at least for material that needs to be committed to memory, such as emergency instructions or legally binding regulations. A recent meta-analysis of a half-century of research (328 studies) on the effectiveness of direct instruction was very supportive of its effectiveness (Stockard et al. 2018). As noted earlier, direct instruction may be the best way to teach representational language-based knowledge, by supporting and motivating learners to pay attention to material that they otherwise might not learn.

What if a company wants to teach something very specific to their employees? Lots of canned learning programs are offered and sometimes mandated with varying degrees of success. One of the strategies for increasing motivation to follow a specific program of learning is the use of games and gamification techniques to develop employee skill sets and build competence in different tasks. Games are generally immersive, engaging, and motivating—all ingredients for attracting and holding learner attention. Moreover, with most games learners are active and doing something. They usually have a storyline that moves the learner on to completion of a training session.

Games can be a form of direct instruction if they have been specifically designed for learning. According to Karl Kapp (2018): "Learning games provide context, engagement, challenge and the thrill of mastery." Kapp (2013) also writes, "there is solid research and overwhelmingly compelling evidence that games can and do teach a variety of subjects effectively." Also known as serious games, many have shown good results in terms of motivation and knowledge acquisition. For example, the Facebook game FarmVille has been used to teach accounting skills (Krom 2012).

One of the criticisms of direct instruction is that it mostly has been used to teach lower-order thinking by emphasizing the memorization and regurgitation of information. Much work has been done on the development of higher-order cognitive skills through the publication of taxonomies of behavioral objectives, such as Bloom's (1956) taxonomy (more recently revised by Anderson and Krathwohl in 2001). Beyond the higher-order thinking skills has been a rich literature on meta-learning or learning how to learn. Finally, systems thinking allows the widest view of the learning enterprise and how it relates to larger issues (Meadows 2008).

Collective or Social Learning

Collective learning can happen at several levels. At the lowest level, we can all make contributions to a group effort. That group effort can then be coordinated so the group works together without conflict with one another. Beyond that, groups that work together can engage in collaboration as a form of learning. Finally, collective action also can result in social movements that get things done. The results of collective learning can be stored within the memories of individuals in an organization or archived through online storage methods. Collective learning can become part of the culture and social cohesiveness of any organization.

Collective learning is situated within the context and culture in which it occurs (Lave and Wenger 1991). It involves social interaction in the building of a feeling of community, as well as the beliefs and practices that become part of an organization. As newcomers join the organization they start at the edges of what is known and gradually learn how things are done as they become enculturated within the organization. This legitimate peripheral participation is a normal process of becoming part of a group.

E-mail and social media have been cited as examples of learning technologies that support collective learning, but they are mostly based on individual-to-individual communications, or supporting small local groups of friends. We mentioned the nasty side of social media in the last chapter, and large platforms such as Twitter and Facebook are now trying to correct and improve on these unpleasant and dangerous side effects of open, anarchistic communications software without limits.

There are dozens of examples of emerging technologies that seek to improve collective learning and internal communications within organizations, but this market is still in flux, without any clear winners dominating the sector. Commonly used communications, collaboration, and collective learning software include Dropbox, Google Docs, Slack, and Basecamp. But there are many more productivity tools available at a variety of price points, and more are added every month.

Technology-Enhanced Assessment

Even before the hiring process starts, emerging assessment technologies are being used for talent identification and evaluation of the suitability and potential abilities of prospective employees. Chamorro-Premuzic and colleagues (2016) state, "From smartphone profiling apps to workplace big data, the digital revolution has produced a wide range of new tools for making quick and cheap inferences about human potential and predicting future work performance."

Early developers of learning assessment software produced simple tests and quizzes, mostly based on the types of questions typically found in school-based teacher-constructed tests. From the beginning of the use of computers in education and training, vendors have touted the ease with which computers can calculate results for a wide variety of question types. Drag-and-drop, multiple choice, multiple response, numeric, choices on pull-down lists, ranking, text matching, graphic matching, true/false, yes/no, fill in the blank, find a hotspot, and Likert scale items are all ways to measure recall of material. Essay answers and simple explanations can now be "marked" by computer, with about the same reliability as human markers. And, files can be uploaded to instructors for later manual perusal.

Memorization is one of the principal ways that we consider whether something has been learned, and testing for retention in memory is the major form of computer-based assessment. Practice is a technique to move content from short-term sensory memory to working memory, and then to long-term memory. Because of this emphasis on memory, some of the earliest technologies for learning were drill and practice programs, where a computer simply presented examples of content over and over, evaluating answers for correctness based on what was stored in the memory of the computer, and repeating exercises when wrong answers were detected.

More advanced assessment techniques that don't just rely on memory are now available. These assessment techniques can be used to record observations, maintain online portfolios, record pathways and decisions in working through learning materials, trace digital bread crumbs (Schwartz 2010) to show where a learner has been online, track the processes learners follow to solve problems, and embed nonobvious assessments (also known as stealth assessments) in games and simulations. All these techniques and more are possible with current technology.

Procedures such as note-taking and repetitive games were also a favorite of early developers, perhaps because they were relatively easy to program and could be run with the limited capabilities of early computers. While memorization of content has its place in the repertoire of learning processes, learning by doing, inquiry learning, and experiential learning are alternative approaches to learning that have greatly been helped by the improved power of new digital technologies. Assessment technologies for these forms of learning are mostly the provision of methods of recording and recalling performance, such as the use of e-portfolios that can later be assessed and validated by subject matter experts or workplace supervisors.

Coming next are personalized adaptive assessments in which tasks are automatically matched to the real-time performance of individual learners. The focus of the assessment will shift to understanding the current learning situation; this understanding will then be used to provide personalized materials, monitor progress, give performance support, and evaluate ongoing effectiveness. These advances allow on-the-fly adaptation of what is presented to each learner, high-quality feedback for the learner and the instructor, and the gleaning of expert knowledge on common learner errors and misunderstandings. This knowledge can then be used for diagnostics, guidance to the learner, and adaptive tutoring on the areas of difficulty (Masters 2015). In effect, the technologies of assessment become interconnected, forming an ecosystem with different sources of data feeding into the profile of each learner, which is continuously updated whenever the learner is online (Behrens and DiCerbo 2014).

Critics of this approach to assessment describe it as mimetic, designed to encourage the regurgitation of standardized answers. While there is a case to be made for learning specific materials, such as in regulatory compliance training, this use of computer technology is not seen as transformative, whereby the learner becomes more reflective, creative, and thoughtful through the use of adaptive technologies (Frank 2017). But, as we noted at the beginning of this chapter, the choice between memorization and experiential approaches to learning should not be an either/or proposition. Both approaches to training will be needed and used in the future.

Technology for the Management of Workplace Learning

Traditionally, instructors and managers of learning and development departments managed the administration of workplace learning sessions with paper-based methods: records of attendance and participation, assessment results, and content nicely organized in books or binders. Computer-based technology substantially changed all that, starting in 1978, with the development of spreadsheets such as VisiCalc (the first "killer app" for microcomputers) for maintaining records and calculating assessment results. Spreadsheets as workplace learning management tools were followed by virtual learning environments or learning management systems, which were developed in the 1980s and improved throughout the 1990s (for a detailed history of these systems see the Wikipedia article, "History of virtual learning environments"). These systems launched courses, presented learning content, tracked student attendance and participation, administered basic quizzes and tests, and recorded and reported on assessment results. They were often high-priced, cumbersome, and difficult to use, but were seen as necessary for the administration of learning and development.

Learning management systems were not designed to support informal, just-in-time learning. Nor were they designed to gather data on all types of learning activities in real time as those activities happen. Only by tracking the clickstream of online activities and interactions can learning administrators get a good handle on the actual daily learning activities of students or employees. Antonelli (2017) advocates tracking "elements like topics searched and shared socially, time viewing learning videos, engagement with corporate content, and tie these with people analytics from HR systems." Tracking, of course, must be carried out with the informed consent of those being tracked.

In the new organizational and learning analytics approaches, large amounts of data are collected from entire populations, rather than small samples, enabling researchers to make correlations between inputs and outputs in the learning process. Most learning analytics data are gathered automatically, as learners interact with digital tools and information. Learning management for emerging technologies must break out of the browser-based prison and reach out to a wide variety of disparate data sources. The newly minted standard for such collection and tracking, xAPI, does just this, but it is up to learning experience designers and the learning management team to ensure that learning activities are used to provide data for engagement tracking and assessment. This leads us to the next key component in understanding this ecosystem—where to put all this new data.

Data Collection

With the information explosion, the knowledge available in the world today is "too big to know" and the amount of available information is increasing exponentially (Weinberger 2014). In addition, the raw data generated by information technology is overwhelming in terms of sheer quantity. Even experts are unable to use or process all the data available in their own fields.

The collection of data and its use in analytics is an emerging trend in workplace learning. While most learning platforms purport to "do analytics," the term means many different things depending on the kinds of data collected and the applications using the data. Emerging learning analytics platforms can collect data that can be used in six different kinds of analysis (descriptive, inferential, pattern recognition, visual, predictive, or prescriptive) applied at two different levels: individual and organizational.

Analytics can apply to individuals and are generally referred to as learning analytics. Analytics that provide information at organizational levels are called institutional or organizational analytics. Compared with most LMSs, emerging analytics platforms (such as those based on the xAPI protocol) can collect many new data points that can be used for both learning analytics and organizational analytics, thus opening the potential for new big data approaches to organizational analytics, learning analytics, and data-driven decision making. Adaptive learning, personalized recommendations, and AI-driven personal assistants all feed off large data sets and are enhanced immensely by having access to good data. However, to take advantage of these types of emerging technologies, the pumps must be primed, so to speak. We'll cover more on that in the next chapter on dependencies.

As these new platforms record user activities, they also store relevant contextual data, making search results more meaningful to users, as well as enhancing insights for researchers, administrators, and other interested stakeholders. These data points provide a gold mine for analysis by CIOs and other C-suite executives, who can use the data to better understand how to improve learning materials without relying on subjective anecdotal feedback, as well as be used in many other analytical applications. Adding contextual metadata and analytics to the use of content enhances existing resources, encourages collaboration, and provides valuable insight into how learning materials can best be deployed.

Knowledge flow is greatly improved by networking, because newer search engines can find resources from anywhere, including applications like Google Drive, Pinterest, OneNote, OneDrive, Dropbox, training apps, connected repositories, professional learning environments, and learning management systems. Once identified, a persistent link can be maintained to the content that is found without moving or making a copy of it. Newer programs can store the data points that come from the search results, such as names of folders, files, lessons, or metadata tags. This makes every search result easier to use, easier to keep and organize, and easier to share, as well as trackable for future analysis. Data can be visualized immediately using a built-in dashboard.

For data-driven learning systems, all this data and metadata can be available for individual users as well as larger entities (for example, a linked program, a learning object repository, or a database), generating even more data points. If metadata is anonymized and not traceable to a specific user once aggregated, privacy of individual users can be maintained.

Analytics

Generating such a rich set of data points allows for the subsequent use of the mass of data collected for both organizational analytics (providing organizations information to support operational and financial decision making) and learning analytics (providing organizations, teachers, and students with information to support achieving specific learning goals). These data points could also be used as data sets for use by authorized external analytics software or authorized researchers and analysts.

On the organizational analytics side, the data collected can be used by companies to understand learning materials, analyze trends, generate summary statistics, correlate variables, visualize patterns, provide logical explanations of patterns, evaluate system performance, and predict future behaviors of groups. Once sufficient data is collected, various models can be produced that CIOs can use to formulate or evaluate training policies and instructional approaches. Forms of modeling can include user knowledge modeling, user behavior modeling, user experience modeling, and domain modeling, including human ecosystem modeling. Using APIs, emerging analytical platforms can link to many external modeling and analytics systems.

On the learning analytics side, a learning analytics program can be used to identify and track a variety of user interactions, sessions, and the completion of tasks within sessions, as well as record any other learner activity. Data can be used as an early alert system by sensing if an employee is having difficulties, and individual data can be used to personalize advising, recommendations, adaptive learning, and cognitive tutoring. Other uses of data include the application of various machine learning techniques and algorithms for capturing, processing, indexing, storing, analyzing, and visualizing data. Once enough data is collected on the "learning trails" that learners follow (Walker 2006), it can be classified, analyzed in clusters, and used for "attribution modeling" (Deshpande 2017), a form of association rule mining that connects various inputs to outcomes (Borne 2014).

Sometimes, associations can be surprising. For example, when a sales analyst at Walmart looked at associations between products, he found that many customers who bought diapers also bought beer. He realized that it was stressful to raise kids, and parents impulsively decided to purchase beer to relieve their stress. So, he bundled diapers and beer together, and sales of both skyrocketed (Choi 2016).

A learning analytics program can be configured with a set of standard reports or it can be used with other data analytics software and reporting programs through external APIs. It can connect to and cross-reference data with external human resources management systems, align data with standards and objectives, and work with other systems that collect data, such as most learning management systems or learning record stores. Newer learning analytics programs can collect their own data, as well as aggregate and integrate data from other learning platforms and databases or content repositories.

As data scientist and author Thomas Dinsmore (2016) notes, "At a high level, the analytics value chain includes three major components: steps that acquire data, steps that manage data, and steps that deliver insight. Delivering insight to human or machine users is the critical link in the chain; a system that successfully acquires and manages data but does not deliver insight has failed." By delivering such a huge variety and amount of data points, and integrating both internal and external data resources, a learning analytics program enables educational insight in many different ways.

Evaluating Emerging Technologies for Their Support of Learning

By now it should be apparent we don't believe that learning is mostly about the memorization of information or procedures. There are many different ways to learn and many types of learning. We introduced the work of Nobel laureate Daniel Kahneman at the beginning of this chapter, noting that we each have two kinds of selves: the experiencing self that is fast, intuitive, and based on the use of heuristics, and the remembering self that is relatively slow, rational, and analytic. Both need to be considered when we look at how people learn. We believe that new technologies, such as augmented and virtual reality, are effective because they cater to the experiencing self, while at the same time we believe that well-designed e-learning programs may work best for the remembering self.

Of course, from an instructional design point of view, there are many ways to design learning activities using new technologies. But, some technologies are effective for one kind of learning but not another. This is something you'll need to evaluate.

We have emphasized that workplace learning is substantially different from learning that takes place in educational settings such as K–12 classrooms or colleges. Emerging technologies need to be evaluated for their ability to support workplace learning, and not based on the assumptions of classroom-based learning.

We believe that much learning takes place in groups through cooperation, collaboration, and communication among members of teams and organizations. There is usually a social aspect to all individual learning, in that we learn little without the support and example of other people. Certain technologies are more supportive than others of collective learning, and any new technology should be evaluated for the support it gives to group processes.

Finally, the latest learning technologies offer a wide range of assessment techniques that need to be evaluated. The latest assessment techniques involve data collection and several types of analytics. Any emerging technology should be evaluated for its ability to provide data for analytics, especially if it uses artificial intelligence and learning algorithms.

Using the BUILDS framework, these are the kinds of questions you should ask about the support any new technology offers to learning in organizations:

1. Does this technology support both intuitive (experiential) and rational (instructional) ways of learning?
2. Is this technology flexible enough to support many different kinds of learning activities?

3. Has this technology been specifically designed for workplace learning?

4. Does this technology support individual and group learning? Does it embrace collaborative and collective learning?

5. Does this technology allow for a wide range of assessment tools, including support for organizational analytics and learning analytics?

Looking Ahead

The use of technologies for workplace learning has a long history and will continue to evolve as new technologies emerge. These need to be evaluated in terms of their usefulness for training employees on a case-by-case basis, depending on the types of learning that each technology supports. The very definition of learning is shifting and changing with the advent and use of these new technologies. It's likely that this change and the pace will widen the gap between true academic venues, such as K–12 and higher education, and workplace learning environments.

With more advanced tracking and assessment opportunities available in the emerging technology space, we should be able to more accurately record and report on our learners' activities. We hope this improvement and the iterative changes in curriculum and content it will enable will lead to more engaged and therefore better performing employees.

At the same time, the increase in data gathering and analytics adds layers of complexity to the new technologies that use these new capabilities. They also increase the number of dependencies that programmers and administrators need to deal with, increasing both the fragility of the software and the risk of failure. How to deal with dependencies is the subject of our next chapter.

CHAPTER 6

$\bullet$ ·· $\bullet$

Dependencies of Emerging Learning Technologies

The word dependency can have a lot of meanings attached to it—not just in everyday settings, where it can be a negative force or perhaps an impediment, but also in the technology world, where the effects of dependency may be seen as detrimental to achieving goals. After all, who hasn't been crushed when they discovered that their device was too old to run a newly released game or app? How about when your router, your phone, or your PC got the FINAL update from the manufacturer before being deemed obsolete? These are all the results of technical dependencies not being up to the task. Your device reached the end of the line because it simply couldn't run the latest software release.

In project management and the corporate world, dependencies can raise their heads in other ways. Your LMS project can't be completed until the company's IT group has updated the user provisioning and single sign-on process for the organization. You can't deploy apps for learning until your Mobile Center of Excellence has released its bring your own device (BYOD) policy and signed off on a mobile device management (MDM) software platform. You can't finish the rollout of your new social platform until the design group gets a chance to fully white-label the learning experience layer and run it by the corporate branding department.

In this chapter we'll explore that aspect of dependency: "You have to have this, if you are going to need or have that." We'll also explore the other more insidious side of dependency: "If I don't have this, I won't be able to do that." Both are challenging, but both have mitigation strategies you can employ to master the dependency traps you face. A third dependency is larger and more social: when humans are dependent on technology to function properly in daily life.

We'll address four kinds of dependencies in this chapter:

- Technical dependencies. Something must be in place for the new or next thing to happen—the minimum requirements for a new technology to function (you must have a computer at least this fast and this new to experience something that improves your current capabilities).

- Innovation dependencies. The deliberate and positive act of creating new dependencies through a process of recombinant innovation (combining affordances of technologies will produce new capabilities).

- Organizational dependencies. The knowledge, support, resources, and leadership needed to ensure an organization can implement, maintain, and operate a technology platform consistently for business success (budgets and guidance will be needed to ensure successful functioning).

- Infrastructure dependencies. The state of relying on basic reliable infrastructure to operate at a system level (given that most businesses now depend on computer networking to function, having the network shut down for an extended period of time could be devastating for the economy).

There are important reasons for considering these four aspects of dependencies and their implications for learning. After all, we commonly hear clichés such as "students today need to learn cursive, because if they don't they won't be able to function in modern society." In fact, the real reason for learning cursive writing can be more nuanced. We need well-rounded individuals who are flexible and can adapt and learn as new technologies emerge, methods of knowledge production and delivery change, and processes are improved. Reading and writing are not disappearing in the new digital culture, although their relative importance may be changing. A rigid approach is often detrimental.

We hope that by now you agree with us that that a black and white approach to technology simply doesn't work in today's marketplace. For more on this, you can read about the constantly evolving world laid out by futurists like Kevin Kelly (2016), in *The Inevitable: Understanding the 12 Technological Forces that Will Shape Our Future,* or Amy Webb (2016), in *The Signals Are Talking: Why Today's Fringe Is Tomorrow's Mainstream.* Not only are technologies changing, they are also changing us, as well as how we learn, what we need to learn, and what we are currently learning but don't actually *need* to learn anymore. We may even have to learn how to forget things so we can focus on what is new and important.

Dependency Path 1: How Technologies Are Interrelated, Build on Each Other, and Progress in a Sequential Manner

It's self-evident that technologies build on each other. You couldn't have an automobile without an engine, wheels, or (from our point of view) a way to hook up your favorite tunes while you drive. We are all "standing on the shoulders of giants," to borrow a phrase from Isaac Newton. Not only do you need to have some technologies in place if you are to advance existing ones or make new ones available, but technologies also often amplify one another.

For example, without broadband technology and ubiquitous access to fast web technology, the growth of e-commerce and the advanced use of the web for entertainment was slow. Once the tipping point was reached and a majority of U.S. households connected to broadband in 2007, Amazon's sales increased exponentially. YouTube, streaming, and other types of online video consumption also didn't take off until the broadband tipping point was reached. These new business models were considered, planned, and tested before the technologies were in widespread use, but the pervasive availability of the underlying technology—high-speed ubiquitous access—made the follow-on advancements possible.

This type of dependency can be a boon or, equally, an impediment to growth. If you can't adequately deliver content through the existing infrastructure, you can't deliver the content at all. If the technology you want to use is still months away from release or too expensive to afford because it is too new, it will be impossible to deliver a pilot, prototype, or production service on time.

These types of bottlenecks occur regularly with new technology and are to be expected. It's up to us, as innovators, designers, and project leads, to determine where these bottlenecks will happen and to plan risk mitigation strategies to deal with them. What can you do if your team is unable to purchase the latest smartphones with facial recognition? What other paths for content delivery might exist for your new augmented reality experience if the smart glasses your company wants to purchase are not compatible with your mobile device security protocols? Having a backup plan for technology is always a good idea, but when using technologies that are brand new, somewhat untested, and hard to come by, it's necessary to plan for what might go wrong!

One thing we have learned in working in the learning industry over the last decade is that designing for mobile devices requires different design techniques than the ones we previously used for creating desktop applications. The desktop computer revolution was driven by the needs of businesses, governments, and the military. The mobile technology revolution has largely taken place in the consumer space. Because users usually pay for apps themselves, their expectations for the usability, fit, and finish of the applications they buy are high. Users simply won't put up with buggy, poorly designed apps on their mobile devices and will alert fellow consumers about defects in apps through social media and word of mouth. Users also take for granted that newly purchased applications are progressively smarter than older versions. They expect any new applications to take advantage of the full range of capabilities afforded by their mobile device.

Consider this simple example. It's not enough to provide a map in an application to give users directions. The map in your application should leverage the GPS sensors of the user's device to triangulate their current location. The desired destination could even be inferred through the link that the user clicked in the message that triggered the map to load. The map should make all of this easy by understanding past usage patterns of the device's user, and the map could be invoked by scheduling meetings by the user in the device's calendar, or by any number of other contextual triggers.

Why do enterprises persist in designing old-school approaches to work-place problems? If innovative app design rules the day in your personal life, why do we keep building apps for mobile workers that are merely shrunken down versions of their desktop counterparts?

The need for new design processes for improved performance and productivity is clear. User requirements and functional or business case rules for the application design process are fluid and iterative. It's unlikely that an app will launch with all the features that it may eventually have. Only through constant testing and updates will an app be tuned to meet the needs of the mobile professional.

Dependency Path 2:
How Recombinant Innovation Can Create Dependency

Dependencies don't have to be an impediment to a properly functioning program. Recombinant innovation happens when one technology is added to or combined with another in new or unexpected ways, sometimes as "happy accidents" (Carayannis, Clark, and Valvi 2013). With recombinant innovation you can combine and leverage a number of different technologies for success based on the fact that many different technologies build on one another.

Technological affordances can be combined to create innovative, useful tools to solve common business problems. These solutions may not be readily apparent when viewing the disparate technologies that comprise them, but when they are taken up by someone who innovates and develops apps, new possibilities arise.

In music, you might call it a remix or a mashup. In cooking, you could call this fusion—combining American cuisine with Asian food styles, for example. "I'll take a Pad Thai wrap to go, please." We encounter this type of recombinant innovation in the digital space all the time, for example:

- dating + social networking = eHarmony, Tinder, and other web romance technologies

- taxis + mobile apps = Uber, Lyft, and other emerging transportation platforms
- videos + a recommendation engine = Netflix, YouTube, and other video platforms
- restaurant reviews + GPS = Yelp and other localized social eating apps.

That's just the start. When you take a service like Yelp and then layer over it things like communication capabilities and an application programming interface, you can use it to make reservations at a restaurant chosen from the app, a la OpenTable. This effect is not geometric or additive—it's exponential!

What Does This Mean for Innovation?

The problem is that with about 30 identified affordances of mobile technologies, the number of potential combinations is impossible for a single person to evaluate, even if you only combine three or four different features. With 30 choices, when you combine two affordances there are 870 possibilities, which is manageable. But when you combine three sets of features, it jumps to 24,360 possibilities. Combining four sets out of 30 affordances yields 657,720 different combinations, and combining five affordances produces more than 17 million different combinations. You get the picture.

As Erik Brynjolfsson and Andrew McAfee (2014) point out in their excellent book, *The Second Machine Age: Work, Progress, and Prosperity in a Time of Brilliant Technologies,* even when combining a small number of affordances it's clear you would need lots of eyeballs to produce and evaluate all the possibilities that can be formed by an innovation economy. The point here is that the creation of new features for a technology always runs the risk of producing new and unexpected dependencies, but this is the way innovation works.

With new and emerging technologies, combinations are truly limitless. Unlocking their recombinant potential is an impossible task if you try to take it on yourself or you do it in a vacuum. So, to help move things forward, be sure to listen to your users. Observe their work, understand their issues, and ideate on how the tools in front of you and on the horizon can solve their problems in new or unique ways. Don't analyze each piece of technology by itself but rather in the context of how it can be enhanced and bolstered by the other supporting technologies present on the devices, in the workplace, and in the cloud.

As part of a technology design process, we recommend recombining two or three affordances of digital technologies to design innovative solutions to problems that users bring to the table, or that present interesting market opportunities. If this all seems a little abstract to you now, let's dive down and look at a couple examples of how recombinant innovation could create a unique solution to some age-old workplace problems.

Example 1: A Three-Layer Recombinant Innovation

- collaboration + clock = automatic meeting requests and responses, group scheduling
- notification + geolocation = geofences and reminders including to-do lists or checklists
- context detection + cloud = files and info always available, tailored to your needs.

If you layer all of these together, you might end up with something like this:

> Collaborative clock + notification geolocation + contextual cloud = A universally accessible team scheduler and task delegation system that uses geofences.

So, what could you do with such a beast? How about creating a team to-do list that automatically adds maintenance calls for customer locations when you drive by a location (including relevant documentation or maintenance records), while simultaneously removing the call from another co-worker's to-do list to maximize productivity, minimize wasted drive time, and so forth?

Example 2: A Five-Layer Recombinant Innovation

All right, that was fun. Let's try another one—this time with additional components, including AR, a new, emerging technology.

- intelligent camera = a camera that understands what it is taking a picture or video of (semantic computer vision)
- wearable + geolocation = a wearable device that knows where you are or where you are going
- search + cloud = a large-scale repository of data and media, easily tagged for later retrieval
- AR + product information and repair manuals = instant product information and repair manuals displayed as interactive overlay in situ.

Now, let's layer them:

> Intelligent camera + wearable geolocation + search cloud + AR + product information and repair manuals = A work blogging platform that records and tags videos, marking the contents of the video with objects that it recognizes for later retrieval and search.

This would bring valuable information to people who need it as they travel, contextualizing and making real-world objects and images searchable and meaningful. All results would be overlaid directly in the technician's view, making accessing and interacting with the objects and information seamless.

So, what could you do with that? How about equipping your workers with wearable cameras to record service calls, and then allowing other service technicians to search for solutions to problems using keywords tagged to photos or videos of the job sites. A search for "rain," for example, could provide a list of images on how techs handled their duties when Mother Nature wasn't cooperating. A search for "power outage" might provide a video or image to help explain how to restart a specific machine when a blackout occurs or when a generator kicks in. When you combine these types of performance support use cases with head-worn technology, you create a cyborg of sorts—a meta-human ready to perform at the highest level and get things done quickly.

We need to explore the affordances of a variety of technical possibilities in order to be truly innovative, and then we need to find the combination that really works. Innovation doesn't just belong in the home or in our personal lives. The next burst of productivity growth is going to come from building on the platforms we've created and combining the building blocks of technology to design and develop powerful next-generation business tools. How do these types of technology dependencies apply to next-generation technologies? Let's dive in some more.

Using advanced technologies requires that we understand dependencies and are ready to use them creatively. The products and services we regularly depend on today all have dependencies that would have made them exotic or impossible even just a short time ago. For example, ride-sharing services like Lyft and Uber require all of the following to be usable:

- cars for hire (taxicabs)
- GPS
- mobile phones
- mobile apps
- mobile payment systems.

Four of the five items on this list didn't exist in a format suitable for this use until 2007. Now the service is everywhere and is used by millions daily. The dotcom boom of the late 1990s and early 2000s was largely driven by the early promise of the Internet. Many companies folded because the services they tried to supply to their customers didn't have all the necessary dependencies in place. For example, they needed widespread broadband, streaming services, and channel partners to fulfill their missions; some of them even needed products with more advanced features, like better cameras, faster processors, more memory, and cloud-based storage. As web 2.0 unfolded between 2005 and 2010, it was able to fulfill what those earlier offerings could only promise. Dependencies finally fell into place. It could be considered marketing made good, but services once promoted were finally better, easier, and more affordable. This allowed services like Amazon Prime, Netflix, and more to finally take root.

Many of these dependencies are just now falling into place for currently emerging technologies. Take, for example, virtual reality, which has been on the cusp of "happening" since the development of head-mounted displays in the late 1960s (Sutherland 1968). The Oculus Rift headset has been around since 2012. Before that, tools like Quicktime VR got their start in the 1990s. It's not really anything new per se. However, many of the key dependencies needed for VR to work are finally becoming a reality. VR needs high processing power, good graphics rendering, content creation tools, affordable hardware, and many other small but vital technologies before it can be viable as a storytelling platform.

Dependency Path 3: How Organizations Set the Stage for Success or Failure

Besides the obvious reliance on certain technologies being in place, there are other types of dependencies that can hold up widespread adoption of new technologies in the workplace. These may include having a specific kind of knowledge residing within a firm before an emerging technology can be exploited for its best advantage. Such knowledge dependencies "emphasize the role of inter-functional and inter-organizational knowledge linkages in determining the performance of a firm" (Al-Natour and Cavusoglu 2009).

New technologies require a person to set the stage and establish the vision for a new direction. This requires change management and messaging that clearly articulates the business value and illustrates the "what's in it for me?" questions that will certainly be raised. This also requires a show of high-level executive support, which could be achieved through demo days, videocasts, all-hands meetings, or any number of other mechanisms. It's less of a challenge to get the whole team on board if the strength and belief in the system comes from the top. This high-level support should be more than a hollow gesture delivered in a newsletter. It has to come in the form of ample time for design and deployment, proper resourcing for the rollout, marketing materials, and ongoing, publicly expressed interest. Launching a program and expecting it to work without this high-level care and nurturing is a recipe for failure.

Every plan for maintenance and upkeep has its own set of dependency traps. If you plan to roll out an emerging technology such as IoT, blockchain, or AR/VR, you'll need to make sure you have the following infrastructure in place:

- Wi-Fi and high-bandwidth connections with plenty of throughput and allowed connections
- power in the right locations for IoT or beacons
- solar or green power for energy-hungry use cases or remote users
- hardware that is purchased with enough lead time to harden and secure the infrastructure
- a process to upskill your IT team with software and implementation knowledge to make things smoother at launch and support time.

Before committing to a full rollout or even a prototype or pilot, you'll need to test that new infrastructure as well. Sales teams can be very persuasive, but a sales sheet with a lot of checked boxes doesn't mean the new technology will work for you. This is because context is very important; most of these new technologies are highly context dependent. They need to be tested in the environment in which they will be used. This type of contextual, environmental testing will enable you to see where things may or may not work for your workforce. You'll also need to ensure that any device or service provisioning policy and your company's technology governance support the new delivery methods and media. What does your company's safety policy say, for example, about the use of optical or eyewear equipment or personal protective equipment at the worksite? Do your new smart glasses conform or do adjustments need to be made to the chosen equipment or to company policy?

Once the dependencies for putting the technology in people's hands have been met, it's time to consider onboarding and ramp-up time. You're going to need to provide time for employees to learn the tech, provide feedback, and improve on or iterate the system, the content, and the task flow. Both the specifics of, and the time needed for, this adjustment period can be highly variable depending on company culture and whether the organization has a history of successfully delivering technology. After all, no one learns this stuff right away. It could be as easy as getting used to having a microwave in your breakroom like in the 1980s, or as slow as switching your business over to a cloud-based, web-data entry system as happened when we transitioned away from green screens and mainframes. Every technology is going to have its own timetable and hang-ups.

A related dependency is that expecting spectacular performance results to happen immediately is not realistic and may be harmful to the growth and adoption of new technologies. Some things take time.

As if it weren't tough enough to consider all the technologies that need to be in place right now for the rollout of your latest plan, you also have to be aware of the near-term advancements that are likely to take place. These are gaps in the punctuated equilibrium, as we discussed in the introduction to the book. In layman's terms, you need to be able to foresee, to some extent, whether the technology you are going to employ today will also work in the future. Chapter 7, on signals for the future, will guide you through this decision-making path, but a quick rule of thumb is that content is often tied to the delivery mechanism or media, whether it be LaserDisc, 8Track, VHS/Beta, Flash (SWF), or some other format. There will be winners and losers out there. Do you really want to bet it all on the minidisc equivalent of VR?

Dependency Path 4:
How People, Businesses, and Society Have Become Dependent on Technology

Shifting gears, it's clear that as a society, we are totally and completely dependent on (and addicted to) technology. This dependence or addiction can be as simple as alarm clocks and electric coffee makers, or as life-giving as CPAP machines and automatic insulin pumps. We need our beeping, blinking bots and appliances to keep us well, rested, on time, and happily caffeinated.

As if the need to hit the snooze bar, caffeinate, and use our electric toothbrushes every day before beginning the morning commute wasn't bad enough, there are plenty other insidious ways technologies are injected into our lives, making us dependent on them. Some sneaky (read: very effective) designers, developers, and organizations have taken advantage of our need for affirmation, validation, and "likability" in ways that have dramatically changed how we live. This is dependency through design, also known as the attention economy. Built on "like" buttons, hearts, favorites, and Snapchat Streaks, the attention economy has reshaped the way we interact with one another on a personal level, and it has also remade what it means to have an acceptable work-life balance. When your phone's home screen is ripe with red notification dots—including your work's Slack chat app—it can be hard to put the screen down, detach, and engage with the people around you. That's true dependency. When you add things like Amazon Dash Buttons, augmented reality games like Pokémon Go, and the sure-to-come AR games centered around Harry Potter, Marvel, or Star Wars universes, maybe it's time to admit we have a serious dependency on this dopamine drip.

Compulsive and addictive behaviors can be produced by these design patterns (Alter 2017). Mobile device dependency is an area of intense study right now. Researchers are studying the effects of a device's radio waves on the human body; the impact of a device's ergonomics on people's necks, hands, and postures; the rise of distracted driving; the effects of technology use on parenting; the effects of mobile social networks on the stress levels of the people using them; and, of course, the use of social media related to bullying, the digital divide, and other topics. It is likely that other emerging technologies will have similar ramifications because many of them are personal, easily transportable, and highly immersive. Will you use this power for good or something else?

As experience designers, it our responsibility to not only empower and augment our users via the new capabilities we provide in our emerging technology solutions, but also leverage design patterns that reinforce positive technology interactions. Some key areas of focus and respect we can offer our users in helping alleviate some technology dependencies (Hussang 2015):

- Do not encourage users to partake in unsafe activities like using mobile devices while driving, walking, or otherwise actively mobile.
- Do not create a cyclical or notification-driven experience that induces the fear of missing out (FOMO), or the fear of not being able to use one's phone or device (nomophobia).
- Do not encourage users to check or otherwise engage with your services and tools after normal working hours under normal circumstances.

- Whenever possible, enable or allow users to "see behind the wizard's curtain" to aid in understanding the decisions being made in presenting the information (for example, why was this recommendation made to me?).
- Whenever possible, provide an alternate means of interacting with a service in a way that may be less technology driven or offers a more work-life balance friendly way of completing a task (for example, offer a personal agent or contact number instead of requiring texting or an app to complete a transaction).

It's clear that Westerners are quickly becoming dependent on a variety of emerging technologies, such as voice control of home lighting and heating, chatbots in insurance and banking call centers, and automobiles with AI to help navigate a faster, safer commute. What effects are these new dependencies having on us? Am I just plain lazy because I tell Alexa to turn on my lights? Does it make me asocial if I don't want to talk to a human to resolve my insurance issues? Does lane assist and adaptive cruise control make me a worse driver? When things work smoothly it can seem like life is made easier by these new technologies and the enhancements they bring. But if you can't change your home thermostat's temperature because the Wi-Fi is on the blink, that might be a problem.

Businesses are even more dependent on technology than we are at home. Just try to purchase something at a retail store or a meal at a restaurant with a credit card when their Internet connection is not working. Other businesses are already dependent on emerging technology in myriad ways, including AI-driven logistics bots at shipping companies and Internet retailers, and farmers who use AI to help them know what and where to plant their crops for maximum effectiveness. These dependencies can often have cascading effects when there are technical difficulties. For example, a 2015 domino-style computer outage took out United Airlines, the New York Stock Exchange, and the *Wall Street Journal* (Associated Press 2015).

Western societies are already highly dependent on technologies considered fringe only a few years ago—the electric smart grid, electronic AI-driven stock and commodity trading, and computer vision–driven bots doing routine tasks like scrubbing floors in our homes and weeding our gardens are a few examples.

Other emerging technologies have the potential to become just as ingrained in our world of learning and development. It's not that difficult to envision the following use cases becoming commonplace:

- Blockchain records indicate who has been given access, experienced, and passed any relevant course, content, and assessments. This removes the need for extensive staff auditing, lengthy verification processes, or complex analytics review cycles to verify training has taken place, that employees are compliant with regulations, and that the organization is cleared of liability because of lack of access to content.

- Technicians using AR headsets to receive their next work orders, see step-by-step instructions on what to do next in a repair, or even have live-in-view video conversations with a senior-level tech or a computer vision–enabled bot that they can talk with to help them out.

- A near complete replacement of expensive learning labs that replicate everything from medical training centers to insurance claims training facilities by leveraging immersive VR.

- Eliminating training for call center workers, drivers and forklift operators, accountants and tax preparers, law clerks, and others because their jobs have been completely automated and replaced with machines, bots, or AI.

- Smart devices like IoT sensors and cameras providing real-time shop floor performance support and monitoring to managers, technicians, and other employees so that everyone is in sync, all workstations are humming along, and no one is in danger of missing their quota.

An interesting thing to consider in these performance-enhancing technology scenarios is that while the technology may have been introduced as an adjunct to an original learning initiative (for example, backing up a training program with a reference material sheet), some of these learning paths eventually become part of the operational flow of getting work done. The original need to train someone on the "old way" of doing things is no longer valid. Slide rules are pretty hard to find today, aren't they? Not only that, if you manage to get your hands on one, you'll probably need a YouTube video to learn how to use it. A similar effect can be seen with things like memorization tasks, such as remembering street addresses, phone numbers, and document and file locations and contents. Quite simply, if you can get a machine, a process, or a program to do it for you cheaper, easier, and faster, why wouldn't you?

These types of dependencies can make it seem like we've become slaves to the technologies we have produced. There certainly are some ways that it could play out like this if we were to believe the dystopian blockbusters in the movie theaters and the doomsday preppers we see on reality TV. However, there are things that will become important for us to understand to avoid having this dark vision take hold. We need to ensure that we are employing adaptive thinking and learning, and with them, proper contingency planning.

What happens when the sales training AI is offline, for example? Will your team just take a break, or will they have paths to get to the information or data in other ways? This sort of process redundancy is essentially the equivalent of having a backup generator. Fall over and switching have long been a core part of the information services function in your business, but are they tuned in to provide this sort of service-level agreement for your cloud-based computer vision–driven inventory application? Who watches the watchers? (That's a great *Star Trek TNG* episode, by the way.) A dependency you may want to put in place yourself to keep things humming would be active monitoring and preventative maintenance for these emerging systems. Numerous cloud infrastructure vendors have been building tremendously resilient systems in this arena, so do not think that you are in this alone with these concerns.

A wonderful side effect may also happen when we no longer need to devote so much training time to the mundane, rote memorization of tasks and processes. We may be able to become more human after all. By removing the need to focus on all the menial training we now fill our time with, we can finally start to improve our business practices in other ways. Training for soft skills such as customer service, conflict resolution, and mentoring and coaching may finally get the time it needs, even with new or less-senior workers in our workplaces. There are still lots of things that humans can do better than AI or robots.

Putting Dependencies to Work for You

It may seem a bit overwhelming when you read about these dependencies and how they interact with one another. You can start putting things in place with emerging technologies using a few planning tools that might be a little different from what you are used to. For example, traditional scheduling tools and techniques like the program evaluation and review technique (PERT) or critical path method (CPM) might not be the right fit here. Those tools are great for maintaining a schedule and keeping projects on time. But when you have many complicating factors like unreleased technologies or unproven business contextual applicability, it can be difficult to make a hard and fast deadline work. It's a good idea to explore alternate project management techniques when trying out new and innovative technologies. Some things to try as you introduce emerging learning technologies to your workforce could include:

- Lean methodologies akin to the Lean startup method pioneered by Eric Ries (2011). This method is focused on incremental improvements and measurements by releasing minimally viable products and testing value hypotheses against reality.
- Agile project management or extreme project management (XPM). These two methods allow for the unknown and unpredictable, and acknowledge that things will change as projects progress.
- Benefit realization management (BRM). A project management method focused around organizing and planning a project to maximize its end business benefits. Schedules and deliverables are more malleable in BRM-driven projects to protect the business investment and create positive change.
- Backcasting. A mindset that is focused on painting a vision of a successful outcome and then using time slices or intervals

working backward for that successful outcome to help chart a path that will lead the effort to the end state. These time slices can be incremental and introduce real and measurable change, but should be working toward a larger goal that by itself would be unobtainable or difficult to plan for.

It's a matter of adhering to a timetable, of course, but when dealing with these types of new and uncertain products, it's more important that you segment the timetable by working in quarters. You can use backcasting to help you start out far in the future and work backward, making each quarter attainable. This allows you to see incremental shifts and changes, and prove value to your business every step of the way by taking advantage of the punctuated equilibrium concept. When mapping your dependencies in backcasting, make sure you lead with business benefits, before linking them to process or tool changes and specific technologies at the end.

Evaluating Emerging Technologies for Dependencies

Evaluating emerging technologies for their dependencies is not a topic that is often discussed in learning and talent development gatherings. But it is of critical importance in evaluating whether to adopt and implement an emerging learning technology. There are at least four types of dependencies that need to be assessed: technical dependencies, innovation dependencies, organizational dependencies, and infrastructure dependencies. The point is not to get rid of dependencies (you can't eliminate all of them anyway), but to become aware of what they are, and how you and your organization are going to manage them.

Enterprise technologies are implemented within the context of an enterprise that is usually up and running, often with a set of enterprise-level technologies already in place. How will the new learning technology you want to adopt tie into and work with all the technologies already in use in your company? And, are the right technologies in place to support the new systems you want to deploy? The answers to these questions must fit within an organization's overall technology plan.

At the same time, there are also opportunities to be innovative by introducing new technologies. Sometimes new processes are called for, or you can discover new efficiencies when you start combining new technologies with those already in use. Because new technologies have affordances that you may not have seen before, be open to new possibilities any time you implement new software or hardware.

Of course, this means change—perhaps change that really shakes up the way you and your fellow employees are used to doing things. Be prepared for some level of discomfort when change happens, and try to mitigate any disruption with a clear change management plan and open communications. It is also very critical to have executive support because the road ahead may be bumpy.

In the excitement of implementing new technologies, it's easy to forget about security, but security issues are a critical set of dependencies that need to be evaluated as part of your implementation plan, and can never be ignored. Security breaches are often preventable, and can be dangerous, harmful, or just plain embarrassing to the company and customer relations. Yet, simple procedures like changing your default password for new equipment or software are often not followed, with unpleasant consequences. Data backup procedures must be impeccable.

Finally, you need a set of emergency procedures in place in case your organization experiences a real disaster that knocks out your infrastructure. What are your company's plans if a major fire, hurricane, or flood takes out power for days or destroys critical records? Disaster planning is essential for enterprises of any size.

Here are key questions that we suggest you ask as you undertake any evaluation of technology dependencies:

1.   What supporting technology needs to be in place to successfully deploy and use this emerging technology?
2.   What dependencies (both new and interesting or potentially disastrous) are introduced when this emerging technology is combined with existing technologies in your organization?
3.   What sorts of change management, communication plans, and executive support need to be put into place to successfully launch this new technology?

4. How secure is this technology? Do you have a strategy for handling user's private information? Do you have solid backup technologies and processes in place?

5. How will your users deal with being highly dependent on this new technology if there are service outages or other infrastructure problems?

Looking Ahead

Dependencies can seem like showstoppers at times, and it's easy to be dragged down into the details when you are fighting against them. With a bit of understanding about how to leverage dependencies as strengths, you can take advantage of how technologies interact with one another to create new and interesting possibilities for innovation. Putting steps in place that always keep the business value in focus is a great way to remember just why you are embarking on this path in the first place.

Dependencies will need regular monitoring; they will change as new technologies arrive or current technologies are updated with new versions. In order to anticipate what is coming and be prepared, we need to evaluate the signals that indicate the next technology or trend that is around the corner. How to gather and evaluate these signals is the topic of the next chapter.

CHAPTER 7

Signals of the Future

For learning and talent development professionals interested in the many technological developments that are happening right now, it is imperative to keep up with technological changes without being paralyzed by fear of information overload or getting too far ahead of others in your organization because of your euphoria over the latest gadget. Watching for signals and tracking technological changes can alert an organization well in advance of potential innovative disruptions. This early warning information can be used to evaluate the current business model and allow a company to consider options for change, such as developing a plan for business model innovation to complement the new technology (Osterwalder and Pigneur 2010). Being prepared can help insulate the company from disruption; it may also allow the company to outcompete less well-prepared rivals.

After evaluating an emerging learning technology for how it fits with business objectives, discovering whether it has outstanding user experiences, understanding its impact on the world beyond learning, ensuring it supports the forms of learning and talent development that you want to develop and foster, and determining that it doesn't have dependencies that cannot be managed, you need to evaluate its future. Is the technology just a fad or will it have a lasting impact on your organization's mission? Does it support your organization's need for training and lifelong learning? What does the technology's future look like—will it last, or will it all but disappear in a few years? To answer these questions, you need to assess both short-term and long-term signals in order to predict the future of any emerging technology.

Abraham Lincoln once said, "The best way to predict your future is to create it." By way of explaining why rapid change can be so disorienting, futurists Alvin and Heidi Toffler (1970), authors of *Future Shock*, contended that sanity depends on the ability to predict one's immediate future on the basis of information from the environment. And, as William Gibson (1999) famously noted, "The future is already here—it's just not very evenly distributed." Many of the technologies and events that we will encounter as "new" in the future have already been started, and may be available now if you know where to look.

Part of the skill in anticipating the future, then, is to understand that it is a complex outcome of the (often) unpredictable actions of many people. But, you can get a head start on anticipating possible futures by looking for clues in the present and recent past. As Tom Standage (2017) argues in *The Economist* blog, "Technologies have surprisingly long gestation periods; they may seem to appear overnight, but they don't. As a result, if you look in the right places, you can see tomorrow's technologies today. . . . It involves seeking out 'edge cases,' examples of technologies and behaviors that are adopted by particular groups, or in particular countries, before going on to become widespread."

As part of our work as new technology developers in the mobile devices area, we have at various points created maps and comprehensive "environmental scans" that look at the present deployment and near future possibilities of combining several emerging learning technologies in such diverse verticals as health, pharmaceuticals, and agriculture. We are mostly interested in the period between now and 10 years out because that's the period for making business decisions that fall within the usual timeframe considered reasonable by shareholders and executives.

The further one moves beyond 10 years, the more speculative predictions become. If we look back 30 years, for example, we would find that mobile devices suitable for use in learning were under development, but they were not ready for commercialization and widespread use. The Apple

Newton of the 1990s, for example, was "bleeding edge," but not visible enough to have a lasting impact on corporate learning. This all changed when the iPhone was released in 2007, and the iPad in 2010. These devices and their copycats, competitors, and partners ushered in the era of widespread mobile learning.

We track and predict the future of emerging learning technologies for our customers based on the simple fact that every new technology follows a set of developmental curves. But the early stages of an emerging technology are often hidden unless you really dig for them. In developing environmental scans on a specific emerging technology, we are looking for the signals that will help us answer these questions:

- What is the history of development of this technology?
- What other technologies need to be in place before this one becomes a commercial success?
- Is the technology real or is it "vaporware" (that is, being sold by vendors but not really viable)?
- How many competitors are creating and promoting this technology?
- Should we be collaborating with others and getting on board with this trend?
- How will this technology change specific industries, including learning and talent development?
- What signals can we detect to predict where this technology will end up in five or 10 years?
- What are the long-term implications of this technology?

Where to Gather Signals

Signals are everywhere. But some appear earlier than others and are indications of very early efforts at developing a new technology (Table 7-1). Science fiction writers and artists are often able to depict a plausible world in 100 to several hundred years in the future, based on their imaginations and their knowledge of the direction of current technologies. Practically speaking, however, this is not a great way for learning professionals to predict what will happen with a new technology over the next 10 years. Both literature and film are littered with artifacts of time gone by and devices, products, androids, and other fantastical creations that never came to fruition. The original *Blade Runner* film from 1982 showed us a world overrun by replicant humans (androids) in the year 2019. And, don't even get us started on how we were promised flying cars back in the 1950s.

Table 7-1. Signals About Emerging Learning Technologies Within Various Timeframes
Here is a rough breakdown of the timeframe of various kinds of signals that will help you determine the future of emerging learning technologies.

Timeframe	Types of Signals
Early signals	• Science fiction • Depictions of technology in art • Interviews with future oriented or fringe thinkers (e.g., Bush 1945)
Medium-term signals	• Science and maker fairs • Academic conferences, especially poster presentations by graduate students • Doctoral dissertations and master's theses • Industry announcements (e.g., from startups or incubators, awards, and grants) • Funding for companies and research, especially early funding from military or government sources • Industry magazines, especially lists of young innovators and up-and-coming companies • Patent applications
Late signals	• Alerts and notifications (Google and conference alerts) • Search engines, including academic databases • Visualization engines, to see what is increasing or decreasing • Industry conferences, which can be a source of business intelligence, and allow you to scan for what is new • Technology websites • Subscriptions to aggregators • Industry leaders on social media (e.g., blogs, Twitter, and Facebook) • Table of contents from relevant academic journals (refereed journals will have later signals than non-refereed journals) • Consulting reports (e.g., Ambient Insight, Gartner Hype Cycle, McKinsey, Accenture, PwC, Deloitte, and others prepare reports for their clients on emerging and future technologies) • Newly published books if they contain lots of relevant information that is unfamiliar • Vendor whitepapers and sales collateral

Early Signals

In addition to science fiction, nonfictional channels for long-term fore-casting also exist. These frequently take the shape of books and interviews with futurists and thought leaders, but also as essays and editorials, such as Bill Joy's pieces for *Wired* magazine (for example, the 2000 article "Why the Future Doesn't Need Us"). Vannevar Bush's famous essay, "As We May Think," published in the *Atlantic* in July 1945, forecast the Internet, hypertext, personal computers, the World Wide Web, speech recognition, and online encyclopedias such as Wikipedia.

Medium-Term Signals

As a new technology develops, medium-term signals tell you about its prog-ress. At this stage, prototypes are often available for a new technology, or demonstration materials may be hacked together to show a new concept. Examples of where you would find such demonstrations include research departments, science fairs, "maker" gatherings, and do-it-yourself labs. Similarly, academic technology conferences often have poster sessions by graduate students revealing their latest projects. A few years later the same graduate students often summarize the state of development of a new tech-nology in their doctoral dissertation or master's thesis.

At the end of the medium-term timeframe are often industry announce-ments about startups and incubators to develop the technology, or press releases about awards and grants that reveal a specific kind of technology being worked on. At this point, technology magazines often publish lists of young innovators (for example, "Top 40 under 40") who have launched a company and are wanting to publicize their new and growing technologies. Patent applications are often pending for these technologies, too.

Websites devoted to fostering innovations and sourcing companies able to undertake research and development on these medium-term tech-nologies host postings and solicitations for things that do not yet exist and seek solutions to problems that may be solved by new inventions. Some example sites we refer to regularly on these types of efforts include FBO.gov, GovWin, various SBIR/STTR trackers, and Innocentive. Even if you aren't actively seeking to win work in these types of ways, these sites are a good way to see what types of innovation are being sought and who is willing to invest in them.

Late Signals

Late signals include newly launched conferences on a specific developing technology, as well as academic articles in peer-reviewed journals, writing in industry trade magazines and those for the general public, books, and consulting reports, which are all based on knowledge that has often been available for many years. Because they fall later in the sequence of publicity, the first one or two books on an emerging learning technology often contain examples of its implementation, which can lead you to press releases, newsletters, or whitepapers that give more details. For example, Brandon Hall's (1997) *Web-Based Training Cookbook* contained descriptions of some of the earliest efforts in enterprise e-learning, giving managers who were contemplating adoption of this new technology some comfort in making the decision to put their training online.

Startup competitions, hackathons, and publications like Crunchbase or TechCrunch also offer some signposts on what we can expect around the corner. Subscribe to alerts and notifications (such as Google Alert) and you will receive a regular stream of signals based on how you craft your search string. If you have the budget and the desire to be even more tapped into these late signals, you can sign up for consulting packages with firms like Gartner or Forrester. These companies publish regular updates on what to expect from vendors and technology providers.

Once a body of literature has been built up about a specific technology it is possible to track that technology's growth trajectory by tracing the numbers of publications about it over time. This is a technique that will let you determine if interest in the technology is still growing or if it has peaked (Figure 7-1).

Figure 7-1. Growth of Academic Articles on Microlearning as an Example of a Signal About the Growth of a New Technology

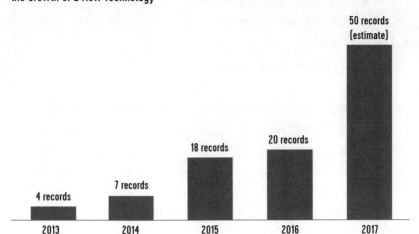

Every Technology has a Developmental Curve

Placing signals within a timeframe allows you to determine what stage of development a technology has reached. Of course, this is not a simple exercise because signals can be contradictory, missing, unfounded, or a product of hype (Webb 2016). To sort out all the signals around a new technology, it is helpful to produce a mind map of all the major signals, from the strongest to the weakest, laid out from the earliest to the latest. Only by laying out all the major signals about a technology in a visualization will you be able to see the big picture. This is because every technology has a time-based developmental curve that it follows. The overlapping stages of the growth of a technology are anticipation, development, adoption, publicity, trends, and scenarios. Taken together they make up what we call the ADAPTS curve.

- Anticipation
  - Has this technology shown up in early signals?
  - Are there converging trends that would support multiple reasons why this technology may take off?
  - Are there hackers who would have already tried this technology and written about it?
  - Who is excited about this?

- Who else is watching or investing in this technology?
- What human needs will be met through the development of this technology?

- Development
  - Are there prototypes of this technology that can be demonstrated?
  - Has any company taken out a patent on this technology?
  - Are there multiple companies operating in this space to create competition?
  - What is the product road map and the current velocity like?
  - What sorts of winding paths is the development taking?
  - Who is driving the development of this technology?

- Adoption
  - What are the drivers for adoption?
  - How widespread will it be?
  - What might hold it back?
  - Who is already buying this technology and how or where are they buying it? Look at the fringes of your industry to find early adopters or unconventional uses of this technology.
  - Are there other related industries where this technology might spill over?

- Publicity
  - Is this technology making headlines? Will it?
  - Has the publicity for this technology been received in a good way or a bad way?
  - Can you plot a curve of increased presence in the market for this technology?
  - Can you separate out marketing hype from reality?
  - Are the buzzwords warranted and are they understandable once you read up on them?
  - How many competitors are there already trying to develop this technology?
  - Has this technology already been adopted by one or more major companies?

- Trends
  - Is this technology following trends or setting them?
  - What are these trends?
  - Is interest growing at a pace at or above the technology's actual sales and development?
  - Can interest in this trend be quantified and plotted to visually show its direction and strength?
  - When will this trend start to taper off?
- Scenarios
  - What are possible, plausible, and probable scenarios for this technology?
  - How will the scenarios play out?
  - What happens if this technology succeeds?
  - What if it fails?

Futurist Amy Webb has developed an outstanding six-step methodology for tracking where any emerging technology is likely to be heading. In her 2016 book, *The Signals Are Talking: Why Today's Fringe Is Tomorrow's Mainstream,* she equips the reader with many tools to sort out which trends are real and which are likely to fade quickly. Here are her six steps:

1. Find the fringe and map it.
2. Search for contradictions, inflections, practices, hacks, extremes, and rarities (CIPHER) to uncover hidden patterns.
3. Ask the right questions and create counterarguments.
4. Calculate the estimated time of arrival for a trend to be fully developed.
5. Create scenarios and strategies.
6. Pressure-test your action.

These two approaches to detecting and reading signals of the future overlap and need to be adapted to your circumstances. Only a thorough analysis of signals will equip you to see where the future of an emerging technology lies, and how you should react to it. Let's briefly look at what can happen to companies that don't pay attention to what the signals are saying.

Is It a Fad or a Long-Term Shift?

Sometimes we become enamored with the latest "shiny object" and lose sight of a bigger and more general trend. For example, consider the impact of digital sound files on the music industry. The accessibility of high-quality, inexpensive (sometimes free) music files played on mobile devices such as iPods and MP3 players have largely displaced the formerly highly profitable compact disks, which in turn had displaced vinyl records. These rapid platform changes not only disrupted the business model of music publishers but also artists, music distributors, CD manufacturers, and graphic album designers, to name a few. And in a few short years the business model based on iPods and MP3 players has already been replaced by a new way of accessing music—streaming audio and video files. With the advent of cloud computing, which started at least a decade ago, we can see that the bigger trend is toward not owning any material goods at all, but using them under license at will for a relatively low subscription price.

As a second example, consider the impact of digital photography. Traditional film giants like Kodak and Polaroid were late in responding to digital files for imaging, and many film development companies went out of business. In addition, camera manufacturers went into the digital market with strength, but it now seems that they are being forced to compete with smartphones in the camera market! Not reading the signals correctly can mean disaster for large and seemingly successful companies.

A delay in understanding the ramifications of innovative technology can result in not only the loss of competitive opportunities but also the destruction an entire business model through innovative disruption (Christensen 1997). An innovative disruption is a product or service that effectively replaces both the previous product or service and the value chain that supports it. This is what happened to the music industry with the arrival of digital sound files and to both film developers and camera manufacturers when digital cameras burst on the scene. And, to bring things back to focus, it's what mobile and other digital learning technologies are now doing to the 20-year-old e-learning industry.

Mobile learning shares many affordances of e-learning and, to that extent, developers have simply ported over instructional models to hand-held devices that seemed to be successful for desktop learning. But mobile learning has many unique affordances not available to desktop learners. Here are some examples of what we, working for a mobile learning company, have developed using these unique affordances:

- Learn while on the move or from any location—we have gathered information while driving, flying, and crossing bodies of water.
- Use location and surrounding environment as contextual variables in instructional design—we have built geofences into learning games, which only yield information in a specific location.
- Learn at the time of need because our mobile device is always with us—we constantly look up information as we need it while working with clients.
- Collect and send out data while using your mobile device as a research tool—we have built mobile apps that collect data and produce visualizations for later analysis.
- Augment what a mobile camera is viewing with overlays of text or virtual objects—we have built augmented reality for Google Glass and a variety of virtual reality goggles.
- Use haptic technologies to recognize gestures and touch—we have built computer vision technology for people with visual impairments that reads the shape of the environment using Google Tango technology.

These are only a few of the disruptive possibilities of mobile learning that will change the way traditional learning and development is carried out. Disruption does not mean that opportunity has been extinguished. New companies are starting up that capitalize on the new technologies by using novel value chains that work with the disruptive technology, not against it. Apple's success with iTunes and the iPod is one example. Digital photo-sharing companies like Instagram are another. Recognizing a real shift is understanding how the technology meets basic human needs and desires to improve the experience of living.

Drivers for Change in Learning and Development

What are the forces for change in the world of learning and development? We think that there are significant changes coming for those who work in this industry. The demand for corporate profits and shareholder value will continue, often by cost-cutting when a particular department such as training is not seen as essential. But there are bigger forces at work.

The development of mobile learning, which started slowly in the 1950s, has accelerated dramatically in the past 10 years since the introduction of the iPhone and iPad along with the very popular Android operating system. The fact that most people have a highly sophisticated small computer in their pocket that is capable of delivering information on demand means that the need for organizing classes and training programs has diminished. The earliest examples of digital learning technologies—learning management systems and online courses—are being supplanted by newer technologies such as the Internet of Things, augmented reality, and virtual reality.

Because we can, we are collecting more data on learners than ever, which has led to the field of learning analytics, and a move to personalize content. At the same time, there has been a shift from instruction to self-directed learning as employees find and share useful resources. Many of these changes are being driven by new demographics, as Millennials and even newer generations enter the workforce.

We are constantly scanning the signals in our industry. Here are some examples of recent headlines and text we've gathered about learning and talent development. Each of these items caused one of us to take a closer look to see if there was something new to which we needed to pay attention:
- "Video and Mobile Have Taken Over Learning" (Bersin 2017a)
- "Learning in the Gig Economy" (EduMe.com 2017)
- "The Case for Employment Branding" (Recruiting.com 2018)
- "Digital Learning Anywhere With 'Direct to Device' Technology" (Talentedge 2015)
- "Explosive Growth in Micro-Learning" (The Eventful Group 2018)
- "Virtual and Augmented Reality Seem to Finally Come of Age" (Nordrum 2016)

- "Artificial Intelligence Was This Year's Fad." (ALTC 2018; by the way, we don't agree!)
- "Online Mentorship Programs" (Sharma 2018)
- "More people would not recommend their training department than would recommend it..." (The Eventful Group 2018)
- "Millennials are addicted to learning because it cures workplace boredom" (Juo 2017)

Each of these intriguing headlines or text fragments should trigger a deeper search for what they mean, and how they may signal a trend that you might want to monitor.

Evaluating Signals for an Emerging Technology

Signals indicating both near-term and long-term futures of a new technology that interests you are all around. But, if no one in your company is looking for these signals and evaluating them, the information they contain will never reach the decision makers and visionaries in your company. You need to give at least one person in your organization the responsibility of looking for signals by monitoring developments in your industry; we hope you choose someone who is widely read on the future of technologies. That person should prepare a monthly report or at least conduct a quarterly meeting to convey what they have learned and lead a discussion about what it all means. There are many other ways to disseminate the information gleaned from all the signals gathered, including blogs, whitepapers, lunch seminars, and professional development sessions.

Once you have focused on a specific emerging technology, and gathered data on where it is headed, you need to plot its location on a developmental curve. In our consulting, we've both met company executives who've claimed that their company has a unique product, one which the executives excitedly tell us is patentable. Yet a comprehensive search often turns up several competitive products already in development or on the market. Done early, a competitive analysis gives executives important data about whether to invest in developing their own technology or opt for buying it off the shelf.

Is it a fad or is there a deeper trend that will override this particular technology? There are ways to arrive at an answer to this question, including pulling back to get an even bigger picture of what is happening in the world, and by combining several related trends that may converge at a later date.

Because we can never predict the future for certain, it is necessary to develop several scenarios based on the possible, plausible, and probable futures for the technology under consideration (Cederquist and Golüke 2016). For each of the scenarios you develop, you need to map out a strategy if that one materializes.

Within the BUILDS framework, here are five questions we'd ask in evaluating the signals of an emerging technology:

1. Do you have at least one person in your company who is assigned to gathering signals about the future of emerging technologies?

2. Are signals about emerging technologies regularly distributed and discussed throughout your company?

3. Have you assessed where this emerging technology is on its developmental curve?

4. Has someone analyzed the trends for this technology to see whether it is a fad or a long-term shift?

5. Do you regularly develop scenarios and strategies to anticipate change over the next five years?

Looking Ahead

Based on the signals we are tracking in learning and talent development, we think that the most impactful emerging learning technology in L&D will be the use of artificial intelligence in the form of machine learning and algorithms that automate the task of delivering the right content to employees as needed. Several vendors, including Microsoft and IBM, are offering cognitive services, which have the potential to automate much of the work of learning and talent development departments. Artificial intelligence, robotics, and cognitive computing are changing business faster than many have realized. In the next chapter, we look at strategies to prepare for the new normal that is coming, until even more change comes along.

CHAPTER 8

Crafting Strategies for Emerging Learning Technologies

As we've discussed throughout this book, change has come quickly and is accelerating. Rapid changes in technologies are making many people uncomfortable, even shocked. This has less to do with the technologies themselves than with our inability to grasp just how profoundly things are shifting and our desire to return to familiar cycles and timeframes.

Are You Ready for the New Normal?

Accepting that nothing will be stable, stationary, or static is a vital first step in taking advantage of these amazing new technologies. In the past, it was possible to wait years before adopting new technologies because there was a lot of risk involved. It was prudent to wait and see if a technology made a difference. Many technologies stuck around for quite a while (the rotary phone rose to prominence in the 1920s and wasn't replaced en masse until the 1980s, for example). Technologies were often undependable. Even as late as the 1970s most automakers had one or two models in their lineups notorious for breakdowns and problems, and many of the automakers' innovations centered around emphasizing quality improvements. Now, with new products and services coming out every time you turn around, and with them becoming vital business tools nearly as quickly, we can no longer afford to "wait and see." We must take these tools and leverage them if we are to stay competitive.

Accelerating change, better quality and faster products with better results and increased reliability, more connected workforces and communities, and everything else we are seeing play out shouldn't come as a surprise. More than half a century ago, Marshall McLuhan (1964) wrote, "In the age of electricity and automation, the globe becomes a community of continuous learning, a single campus in which everybody irrespective of age, is involved in learning a living." His global village concept is now starting to happen—not just in our schools and workplaces, but now in our social spaces, our mobile devices, and with the advent of bots and the Internet of Things—in an automated fashion 24/7. Whether we are active participants or just watching time go by, everything is, or will soon be, connected.

The widespread acceptance of technological realities is bound to give a bit of an identity crisis to those who have been able to chart their own paths and create protected spaces inside their businesses. Futurists Alvin and Heidi Toffler (1970) projected this in their ground-breaking book, *Future Shock*. Just as the role of parenting shifts from providing basics like clean clothes, food, and shelter to providing support, counseling, and lots of money, the role of the workplace learning professional is shifting too. The role of provider of the curriculum, courses, assessments, content, and delivery mechanisms is giving way to that of support, counseling, and, you guessed it, money. The Tofflers' advice to those caught up in change was to shift emphasis and focus on "unlearning." Without the ability to change, adapt, learn, and unlearn, they said, we'll stay in a constant state of "future shock."

A question often posed to us at conferences is something along these lines: "What skills are required to support these new technologies? How can L&D help?" The good news is that there are many ways the learning and development department can have a positive impact by adopting these new technologies and using them to increase performance, improve employee job satisfaction, and drive real growth.

Don't Be Afraid to Throw Some Things Out

Self-examination and inquiry are good places to start. Ask yourself, your workmates, and your department members the following questions, especially when resistance to or fear of new technologies creeps in:

- Why do we exist in this department?
- What are our true goals?
- What's our role or function in this organization going to look like in five or 10 years?
- What will we do when a current training tool (workshops, LMS, courses, seminars, or other mode of delivery) no longer exists, isn't sustainable, or no longer provides the answers our employees seek?

You must get rid of the blockages first. It may be the only way new things get put into your ecosystem (Harder 2017).

Following that, you'll need to take your self-enquiry and newly cleaned slate to the rest of the organization if you want to truly succeed. This won't be a one-person show. No amount of planning on the part of a single person can overcome a workplace filled with old ideas and a steadfast grip on dying technologies. So, whether Peter Drucker ever really said that "Culture eats strategy for breakfast," the meaning of that phrase is crystal clear, and we see the signs of it in our workplaces today (Cave 2017).

In her 2015 *Training Journal* article "Piecing Together Digital," Ali Merifield lays out a good ground plan for taking this sort of transformation to the workplace. Her plan suggests a six-phase process for transforming digital technology and processes that includes discovery and analysis, developing a program plan, setting the stage for change by preparing the audience, delivering the new program, measuring, and evaluating. It's not that different from the ADDIE model (Molenda 2003), but a meaningful distinction worth mentioning is that she puts some stock in the Drucker adage and recommends including a feedback loop in every phase, where the strategists must come down from their mountaintop to see how things are going. This may mean slowing things down, speeding things up, (re-)training your staff, adding new hires, and getting detailed feedback from the learners.

Figure Out What You Are Good at and Run With It!

L&D isn't the only type of profession in the educational and information resource arena facing seismic shifts. Librarians are also seeing lots of change occur with the ever-growing use of Internet searches, e-books, and digital publications. A fascinating 2010 article in the *Library Journal*, "Coping with Continual Motion," by Betha Gutsche, likens the change occurring to that of an earthquake, where solid soil can seem like an ocean wave. Shrinking budgets, dwindling usership, and audiences moving to other online gathering places are all contributing to the library community's concern about how to deal with what's coming next. Gutsche's recommendation is introspective, but also action oriented. Figure out what you are good at and run with it! Librarians may be good information gatherers, researchers, connectors, and community empathizers or have myriad other skills. In Gutsche's view, that's OK—just go with it and amplify it. Use that as your superpower and fight back.

Learning and development professionals can also use this strategy to find their place in the technology landscape being created by 3-D printing and other new technologies. Maybe your role isn't that of technology soothsayer. Maybe your workgroup is not a hotbed of coders, UX designers, or IT implementation specialists. That's absolutely OK. Review what your group does really well and determine how their strengths integrate with this new technology.

When you identify the key strengths of your learning and talent development group, you may find that it is great at highlighting core performance gaps and then figuring out how to close them; maybe your group is better suited to research and curate information repositories; or, perhaps your designers are best at simulation and scenario modeling and creation. Any of these or myriad other strengths in instruction and learning bring something to technology rollouts that are valuable or vital skills. It is up to you and your fellow instructional designers, technologists, and managers to review your team makeup and figure out how best to leverage skills to better serve the interests of the organization. Once this is determined, approach the other groups in your business—operations, sales, IT, executives, or others—with news of this recast and provide a briefing on how it benefits them.

Focus on Action and Progress, Even If Incremental

Given that 45 percent of nearly 1,000 businesses surveyed by the Global Center for Digital Business Transformation have *not* made digital disruption a board- or executive-level priority, it's clear that planning for change is not on everyone's radar. Yet the same study found that respondents believe half of all top 10 market leaders in their verticals will be pushed out by digital disruption (Vey et al. 2017). But for many CEOs, digital transformation of their companies has risen to the top of their agendas (Siebel 2017). KPMG reports that in a 2017 survey, "six out of 10 CEOs now view technology as an opportunity, not a threat."

For those CEOs who are not moving forward on change, why aren't they focusing on digital disruption and putting plans in place to get change moving? In working with dozens of clients over the years, we can chalk it up primarily to three things:

- Business is, by definition, is a pretty cutthroat endeavor. There will be winners, there will be losers. Businesses obviously don't want to lose, and in the past a wait and see approach was beneficial. There was always plenty of time to observe a competitor's gambles, and, if they were successful enough, to copy their moves. Today, the rate of businesses taking gambles is increasing. But overall, the gambles taken are less risky, the changes brought about are much smaller, and it is possible to assess the outcomes quickly. Adopting change quickly reduces (not increases) overall risk.

- Businesses may not believe change has happened. But it is real, and it has the potential to threaten their existence. Moreover, change will not stop. One only needs to look at what is unfolding in the news where all sorts of people regularly deny any number of things are true or real to understand that applying that same level of skepticism to digital transformation is not only natural, but expected. A large number of businesses that were once juggernauts have been reduced to a shell of their former selves or have gone bankrupt and shuttered. Yet many businesses still think that this downturn is just something that affects other people, not themselves. And since many businesses live for the current quarter or perhaps the next one or two out, it's not surprising that planning for five years or more down the road is simply not possible for them.

- Business leaders are often cautious and pragmatic by nature (Moore 2014). This isn't meant as an insult. If you work on things like engines, airframes, retail, or food service, it can be an affront to be informed that your business's digital DNA is just as important as your factory floor and workers, storefronts, and real estate. The complicated pivot required to focus on investing in something that you cannot see, touch, or walk into is just too much for many people with backgrounds in finance, sales, or human resources. The CEOs of most companies in the Fortune 1000 are often not from liberal arts backgrounds where creativity is the currency. In addition to this limiting factor, more than three-quarters of all CEOs climbed the ladder inside their organization to reach the top spot. This type of internal promotion approach is less risky, less likely to topple internal processes and organization charts, and less likely to upend business models. These steadfast leaders deal with the harsh realities of numbers, and dollars and cents. They aren't necessarily motivated by the act of creation, invention, or anything of the sort. This can be overcome by putting trusted advisors in place to support top executives, but it's an uphill battle for sure. It is even tougher to get learning and talent development folks at the executive table. High-performing companies have shown themselves to be the exception to this rule, with 44 percent of CEOs surveyed by PriceWaterhouseCooper expressing some level of concern about the speed of technological change being a risk to their company's success.

But, there are ways to help overcome these obstacles. Let's take a look at how to get things moving, and join the rest of the technology community.

Adopting a process and a mindset that accepts learning from mistakes and improving on things iteratively is a big first step in being able to adapt to change and take more, but smaller gambles. This is counter to the mindset that learning and development has had for a long time, where the concept that you only "get one shot at reaching those employees" has held sway. Now, in the age of instant search and connectivity, it's almost expected that a technology product's user base is going to duck in and out of using it many times a day.

Don't believe it? Keep a piece of scratch paper at your desk and make a tally mark each time you use search to find something you are looking for. If you have just a little more time and presence of mind, write down the terms you searched for. Over a week or two, take a look; did you have any duplicates? Notice any patterns? You are using search—an emerging technology from the early 2000s—to get your work done dozens of times a week. Augmented reality, blockchain, and other emerging technologies will soon be like that, and just as seamless. You will have many chances to deploy and tune your product, so waiting and seeing is counterproductive.

Planning for the long term is a difficult skill to build when you are obsessed with quarterly results and annual goals. It's necessary to get out of a month-to-month mentality and take the long view every once in a while. Do you have a longer-term plan for your life? Maybe where you'd like to live, trips you want to take, people you want to spend time with, or maybe some personal goals or milestones? If you do, great! Why can't you do the same for your workplace? It doesn't have to be an exhaustive list or even tremendously detailed, but outlining some key thoughts and principles and maybe even a couple of measurable performance goals could suffice.

A big problem we are facing as a society is an epidemic of short-termism, where we think little about the effects we will have on future generations or even ourselves later in life. Ari Wallach (2016), director of LongPath, a consulting company focused on solving "wicked problems," advocates using "Telos thinking," in which you consider the "ultimate purpose" of an effort, and what will come after it is completed. If you put a line in the sand and start to work back from it, you'll find incremental success along the way that will allow you to continue to get the support you need to execute against that long path.

It is always your job as the thought leader, the vanguard, and the trail-blazer to bring new solutions to old problems. You can be imaginative instead of leaving it to the C-suite or other groups in your business that seemingly "don't get it." Learning professionals are usually people who like to learn, by letting new ideas roll around in their heads. In your next evolutionary step as a leader in your organization, take advantage of that characteristic and introduce activities and discussions that help bring a culture of innovation to your work group and beyond. This can take a lot of different forms, both big and official (funded research, proof of concept projects, and things like fellowships or grand challenges like those given to IBM's Watson) or small "skunkworks" type activities (such as lunch and learns, private projects, self-development, and self-directed learning time) (Vey et al. 2017).

Be Pro-Active About Decision Making and Investing in the Future

To put emerging technology in place, the final major obstacle for L&D lies in finding a path for successful governance and moving to a more proactive decision-making stance. Learning and development departments at most businesses we have consulted with are often not at the leading edge of technology in their organizations. This isn't really all their fault. Learning and talent development have a lot of organizational dependencies that have to be in place before they can reasonably be expected to try out new things. For example, by the time L&D got around to being able to use PowerPoint for workshops, the meeting rooms had to be switched over to support it, the business had to buy the software, the sales teams had to get familiarized with it, and then all the content had to be created.

A similar sequence played out with LMS platforms. Companies making that purchase also needed a web presence, an IT staff capable of running servers, administrators to run the servers, courseware creators, and, of course, the content. Mobile learning software followed the same pattern— the technology had to be in place, tools had to be procured, and content had to be created.

Learning and development can move to a more proactive state with the newer tools now available. The equilibrium period is getting shorter between bursts of innovation, so you better buckle up. These periods of calm are becoming less and less a time of no new products coming out, but rather periods where people get familiar with what's available and adapt and figure out how to use it.

These periods of relative calm can not only be used to try things that were just released from the labs and into your hands, but they can also serve as a time to see what is on the horizon and begin a plan for what will happen when the next equilibrium occurs. As this planning takes place, a bit of anticipatory governance should be exercised (Guston 2010, 2014).

For instance, you may not be in the middle of delivering a pilot on AI and adaptive learning paths right now. More likely you are transitioning all your learning content to mobile-friendly formats. But, almost certainly, in the next three to five years you will have to face some sort of test on how your workforce will leverage AI to make them more informed and more productive. What is your department's view on AI and human interaction? Will AI be allowed? Will it be encouraged? What types of use cases do you think would be most effective for some early tests? Who owns the AI? How will it be supported? Now is the time to start these discussions.

Most of those decisions can be made without even touching the technology. It's common sense for anyone who, as a student, liked to work ahead in their study halls.

Putting It All Together

Here we are, at the end of a book full of forward-looking statements and a good number of pointers on how to put this amazing new world to work for you and your organization.

No doubt it's going to be a fun next few years in learning and development. This new normal offers lots of opportunity to enable real change and improve performance in ways we'd only dreamed about just a couple years ago. Get ready and enjoy the shock of the new.

ACKNOWLEDGMENTS

An African proverb tells us that it takes a village to raise a child. Writing a book can be a bit like raising a child and it took many villages to help bring this one to completion. Both of us live in small communities—Chad in Metamora, Illinois, and Gary in Belleville, Ontario—where immediate family and surrounding friends form the basis of the support groups that give meaning, care, and encouragement for our projects.

Beyond our immediate personal communities, we are both part of a much larger international network of technology professionals who make the world of learning and talent development an exciting place to work and who contribute so much to our understanding of the many new developments currently taking place. The global nature of emerging technologies is evident in the hundreds of references and resources we used in writing this book—research and writing that comes from all over the world.

We couldn't have written *Shock of the New* without countless conversations—at conferences with attendees, online with members of our personal learning networks, and, of course, at Float with our co-workers and colleagues. We'd especially like to thank John Feser and Tom Marchal, leaders at Float, for their ongoing encouragement and support, and for giving us the freedom to pursue projects we both enjoy.

This book wouldn't have happened without the initiative and advocacy of Justin Brusino, associate director, communities of practice, at the Association for Talent Development, or without the fabulous editing of our developmental editor, Kathryn Stafford, and our copy editor, Melissa

Jones. Thank you to this team, and to the many others who worked on this project behind the scenes at ATD Press.

Chad would personally like to thank his mentors and the friends he has made over the years in the industry—the crew from Rollingstone.com, Toons.com, The Iona Group, the eLearning Guild, and ATD. He's thankful for having a great family with his wife, Renee, and three kids, Sophia, Liam, and Carter. They gave him all the support he needed to begin this project, and the strength and reason to keep going and get it done.

Both authors are grateful to Brandon Hall for writing the foreword to the book, and Gary thanks Brandon for giving him five years of experience working as a consultant and researcher. Gary would also like to thank his research assistant on this project, Emma Clare, for her careful Internet research and bibliographic searches. Most of all, he is grateful for the loving support of his wife, Karen Anderson, who acted as the first-tier editor for the entire manuscript, suggesting improvements and turning our first drafts into much better prose.

It really does take a global village to produce a big view of learning and technology today.

●————————————————●

BUILDS Evaluation Rubric

The 30-question evaluation rubric that follows is the sum of the six five-question sets appearing at the end of those chapters in which the BUILDS framework is presented.

Business Value

1. Have you conducted a value proposition analysis for adopting this new technology? Does the new technology fit your business needs?
2. Have you identified any problems in adopting this new technology?
3. Does adopting this emerging technology open up new opportunities for your organization? Have you assessed these opportunities?
4. Will you have a risk management plan in place when these technologies are adopted?
5. Have you gathered case studies of other companies in your industry that have adopted this technology that you can present to your executive team?

User Experience

6. Do you have a thorough analysis of the affordances of this technology? What new capabilities does it offer your users?

7. Has your company carried out an observational (ethnographic) study of how users would employ this technology?

8. Has your team carried out a use case analysis for your company for this technology? Who are the primary, secondary, and tertiary users, and how would each category of users employ this technology?

9. Does this technology collect enough data to allow it to be personalized for each user? Have you gathered feedback from users on how this technology can be iterated and improved?

10. Is the technology supplying a high-polish end user experience comparable to consumer technologies that they may be familiar with and use at home?

Impact

11. Is the emerging learning technology accessible for persons with a disability? Does it have any obvious biases or barriers for specific groups (for example, groups based on gender, race, or culture)?

12. Would the adoption of this technology introduce new work experiences into your company? Does it allow for mobile learning?

13. How would the adoption of this technology change your company's organizational structure?

14. Does this technology introduce ethical issues or problems (such as at-risk populations, privacy, or control)?

15. Is this emerging technology environmentally friendly and sustainable?

Learning

16. Does this technology support both intuitive (experiential) and rational (instructional) ways of learning?

17. Is this technology flexible enough to support many different kinds of learning activities?

18. Has this technology been specifically designed for workplace learning?

19. Does this technology support individual and group learning? Does it embrace collaborative and collective learning?

20. Does this technology allow for a wide range of assessment tools, including support for organizational analytics and learning analytics?

Dependencies

21. What supporting technology needs to be in place to successfully deploy and use this emerging technology?

22. What dependencies (both new and interesting or potentially disastrous) are introduced when this emerging technology is combined with existing technologies in your organization?

23. What sorts of change management, communication plans, and executive support need to be put into place to successfully launch this new technology?

24. How secure is this technology? Do you have a strategy for handling the user's private information? Do you have solid backup technologies and processes in place?

25. How will your users deal with being highly dependent on this new technology if there are service outages or other infrastructure problems?

Signals

26. Do you have at least one person in your company who is assigned to gathering signals about the future of emerging technologies?

27. Are signals about emerging technologies regularly distributed and discussed throughout your company?

28. Have you assessed where this emerging technology is on its developmental curve?

29. Has someone analyzed the trends for this technology to see whether it is a fad or a long-term shift?

30. Do you regularly develop scenarios and strategies to anticipate change over the next five years?

APPENDIX B

Applying the BUILDS Framework

To show you how to use the BUILDS evaluation framework described in chapters 2 through 7 and listed in appendix A, here we've applied its six perspectives—business, user experience, impact, learning, dependencies, and signals—to six specific technologies:

- blockchain
- adaptive learning and personalization
- 3-D printing
- the Internet of Things/Internet of Everything (IoT/IoE)
- artificial intelligence and machine learning
- augmented reality and virtual reality.

Blockchain

What It Is

Blockchains are trustworthy, distributed digital ledgers (databases)—records of transactions replicated across many computers and cryptographically guaranteed to be immutable. A blockchain creates trust without any intermediary institution supervising the trusted relationship. Applications of blockchain technology include cryptocurrencies (such as Bitcoin), smart contracts, records of identity, registries of credentials, electronic medical records, and intellectual property records.

How It Works

A blockchain is a ledger distributed across a network; but, unlike a Distributed Database Management System (DDBMS) with multiple logically related databases, every computer node in the network holds a complete and identical copy of the ledger. This means there can be no single point of failure, and any changes to the ledger are replicated across every computer in the network. New blocks of information are added at regular intervals to the chain after being mathematically encrypted using public key infrastructure (PKI) technology and validated using a consensus protocol. Once added, a block can never be changed.

BUILDS Evaluation
Business Value

Blockchain technology has the potential to move us from the Internet of Information to the Internet of Value. The father-son team of Don and Alex Tapscott (2016) have written a book on blockchain and explain it this way: "The blockchain can be programmed to record virtually everything of value and importance to humankind, starting with birth certificates and moving on to educational transcripts, social security cards, student loans, and anything else that can be expressed in code." Ledra Capital (2014) keeps a master list of applications for blockchain, which includes 84 categories of records. The broad classifications, with a few examples, are:

- financial instruments, records, and models: digital currencies, bonds, mortgage records
- public records: land titles, passports, birth certificates
- private records: contracts, wills, escrows
- semi-public records: degrees, HR records, business transaction records
- physical asset keys: car keys, betting records, safety deposit box keys
- intangibles: patents, trademarks, online identities
- other records: documentary records, gun unlock codes, nuclear launch codes.

Blockchain clearly has the potential to disrupt financial institutions and other organizations that manage assets of high value by displacing them as the institutions who manage trust.

User Experience

The user experience of blockchain technology will vary greatly depending on the clarity and ease-of-use of any interface design for this technology. In many cases, blockchain functions operate in the background and while users aren't even aware of them, they will see their effects.

Impact

According to Tapscott and Tapscott (2017), "blockchain represents nothing less than the second generation of the Internet, and it holds the potential to disrupt money, business, government, and yes, higher education." In addition, the consulting firm McKinsey cites a World Economic Forum survey that suggested that 10 percent of global GDP will be stored on blockchain by 2027 (Carson et al. 2018).

In terms of the learning industry, blockchain storage means that anyone's credentials can easily be verified and made available to anyone else with consent. In effect, a record of all credentials will be owned by each learner, allowing an aggregation of badges, certificates, diplomas, awards, and degrees to be managed by the person who earned them.

However, there is a major downside to blockchain technology—its high use of electricity by "miners" who play the essential role in creating and validating new blocks in the chain. "By some estimates, to ensure that a decentralized ledger can't be monopolized by any one group, blockchain miners already burn as much energy as the nation of Cyprus on an ongoing basis," writes David McArthur (2018). In the same article, he also notes that "simply establishing trust does not ensure a record's enforceability, quality, value, or accuracy." That is, while the blockchain is immutable, the information it contains may or may not be of value.

Learning

There are several applications of blockchain of interest to the learning and talent development industry. The technology can be used to store standards and issue credentials. It can be used to manage massive open online courses (MOOCs) by verifying that a person who signed up for the course finished it. It can be used to track payments and allow learners to set up "smart contracts" as part of their lifelong learning plans. It can also be a repository of badges and other forms of recognition that would credit the learner with a variety of acquired competencies. Badges issued by different learning providers could be assembled into an "open badge passport" that learners can share with whomever they wish (Skiba 2017).

Dependencies

The value of blockchain records are dependent on the quality of the off-chain assets recorded in the immutable chain. The recorded transactions may still be subject to government regulations or require licensing that could nullify any transaction even if it was recorded in a blockchain. McArthur (2018) warns that "[a]n even more basic problem is that statements that are now true but could later prove false can be immutably placed on the public blockchain."

Signals

Blockchain is still "three to five years away from feasibility at scale, primarily because of the difficulty of resolving the 'coopetition' paradox to establish common standards" (Carson et al. 2018). The market in learning and talent development looks strong, as the demand for a secure method of recording digital credentials is growing by employers "as they move away from degrees being the only method to demonstrate one's abilities" (Skiba 2017). We are starting to see movement on this front, with the development of the Smart City University in the United Arab Emirates. The university is a decentralized learning platform for digital skills development that uses blockchain technology to enable learners to chart their careers (UAE 2018). At the same time, we have taken note of a magazine article titled "Is This the End of Blockchain?" which claims "a recent study into 43 initiatives reported that despite a great number of promises and convincing arguments, none of the projects have been able to show that they have been able to use blockchain technology to achieve their objectives" (Marr 2018b).

The Bottom Line

We recommend a wait and see strategy for blockchain technology. We think that most learning and talent development departments don't need blockchain technology in the next five years because learning is a noncore industry for this technology. Blockchain is still immature, and a clear strategy for success has not emerged to justify experimentation unless you are in the financial services, government, or healthcare sectors. We think that learning and talent development should be a follower rather than a leader in the use of blockchain technology. We therefore recommend the advice of Brant Carson and colleagues (2018):

> Most companies do not have the capability to influence all necessary parties, especially when applications of blockchain require high standardization or regulatory approval. Such companies . . . should keep a watching brief on blockchain developments and be prepared to move fast to adopt emerging standards. Just as businesses have developed risk and legal frameworks for adopting cloud-based services, they should focus on developing a strategy for how they will implement and deploy blockchain technology.

Further Reading:

Casey, M., and P. Vigna. 2018. *The Truth Machine: The Blockchain and the Future of Everything.* New York: St. Martin's Press.

Mougayar, W. 2016. *The Business Blockchain: Promise, Practice, and Application of the Next Internet Technology.* Hoboken, NJ: John Wiley & Sons.

Tapscott, D., and A. Tapscott. 2016. *Blockchain Revolution: How the Technology Behind Bitcoin Is Changing Money, Business, and the World.* New York: Portfolio/Penguin.

Adaptive Learning and Personalization

What It Is

Adaptive learning and the personalization of digital learning experiences are rooted in common digital marketing practices. Nonetheless, this technology offers an opportunity to learning and development departments to provide tailored, curated learning experiences and content to individual learners through a variety of design techniques and data analysis tools. Personalized learning can mean different things in the context of workplace learning:

- instructional methods can be tailored to meet each learner's needs
- each person can learn at his or her own speed
- different content can be made available for different learners, depending on their interests or needs (Willingham 2017).

How It Works

Over time a learning platform can collect a lot of data and provide short assessments to evaluate if the relevant learning material is being mastered. An algorithm can be used, along with the data and the assessment results, to determine the learning approach an individual prefers and the speed at which they work. Mistakes can trigger more instruction, review, and support. Learners can also indicate their interests or issues, which, in turn, cause the learning platform to offer content specific to their interests. Personalization software can also offer recommendations for new materials, based on congruence with the choices made by other learners with similar interests or abilities.

BUILDS Evaluation

Business Value

Training is expensive to produce, takes workers out of their day-to-day routines, and can be a drain on productivity. It's certainly not a magic bullet for increasing performance and producing results. But offering learners materials personalized to their interests and needs can be more motivating in the long run than if the same learning materials are offered to everyone regardless of need or interest. If only there were ways to better understand your learners' needs, deliver only the most useful content, and be sure to follow up with the user after they've taken the training to see that they get the next steps right and are able to go through a focused, orderly progression in the curriculum. Oh, wait! That's adaptive learning and personalization in a nutshell.

User Experience

It's no secret that learners are often not fans of e-learning content and believe that it's a waste of time. Harsh judgment for sure, but some of that is due to the one-size-fits-all approach to content delivery. The same basic tenets that drive web marketing—stickiness, engagement, dwell time, revisiting, retargeting, and conversion paths—can be successfully applied to learning and development to provide learners with a more pleasant and useful learning experience. Providing a tailored learning experience layer is a good start, but going one step further and curating the content or controlling content access or sequencing based on predictive analytics, user preferences, and organizational performance needs is where you need to be heading.

Impact

Cutting down on unneeded training is a common reason for using personalized and adaptive learning. But don't discount the significance of learners' overall satisfaction with training. To maximize the benefits of an investment in training you need to ensure the content that is produced is actually used and possibly even enjoyed.

Organizations with the funds, data, and workforce size will see the impact of these technologies most quickly, because they often have a strong set of dependencies, requiring an increase in the amount of content needed and making the production of content more complex.

Learning

Adaptive learning and personalization are directly applicable to digital learning programs because they serve a vital role by improving the signal-to-noise ratio and providing a focused curriculum that is more directly applicable to the learner. This approach can potentially increase the value of the content to the user, reduce overhead in reviewing and wading through extraneous content, and provide relevant content to learners when they need it, sometimes even before they know they need it.

Adaptive learning systems naturally focus on flexibility. Personalized adaptive assessments, in which tasks are automatically matched to the real-time performance of individual learners, are possible. A focus on understanding and applicability rather than some sort of a memorization exercise where simple facts are tested using static multiple-choice tests can also be managed by adaptive algorithms.

Advances in data-driven learning content management systems allow for on-the-fly adaptation of what is presented to each learner, and can provide high-quality feedback to the learner and the instructor. Data collected can produce expert knowledge on common learner errors and misunderstandings. Adaptive tutoring can also provide more meaningful engagements with the learner and move away from the assembly line–like approach of older web-based training systems. Adaptive learning and personalization are consistent with an adult learning approach to training in that users only learn what they don't know or material that is directly relevant to the task at hand.

Dependencies

Adaptive and personalized digital learning experiences share a dependency with several other emerging technologies discussed in this book. The single biggest thing that may be holding up widespread deployment and adoption of adaptive and personalized digital learning is not having enough data. Creation of lots of data is necessary to feed an adaptive algorithm, to parse the data to provide insights, and to supply data for a recommendation system.

xAPI (the new data standard for interoperability) can help close this gap, but it isn't the only tool you are going to need. You'll also need a team of data analysts and designers able to make sense of all the digital bread crumbs left by learners.

Signals

Government adaptive learning programs like GIFT (Generalized Intelligent Framework for Tutoring) and PERLS (PERvasive Learning Systems) are two systems undergoing extensive research and development at this time. Both seem to have an interesting future, and, due to the development path they are on, these open-source projects are likely to influence commercial products in the years to come. Commercial personalization products like ALEKS from McGraw Hill and Alta from Knewton are also gaining traction, but mostly among educational users in K–12 and higher education.

The Bottom Line

Adaptive data engines are common in tools like marketing automation, customer relationship management, and other areas of web-based software, but the technology is still trickling into the learning ecosystems of today. Keep an eye on this technology, and make sure your next learning content delivery system at minimum supports content personalization features such as favorites, bookmarks, powerful analytics, and customized portal pages.

Adaptive learning is an emerging learning technology with a promising future; but, there's also a lot of murkiness around the immediate path for its development and deployment. Small experiments focused on specific roles, workgroups, or use in a contained business unit might be a good way to try things out. Start small and grow from there.

Further Reading:

Chaplot, D., E. Rhim, and J. Kim. 2016. "Personalized Adaptive Learning using Neural Networks." Proceedings of the Third ACM Conference on Learning @ Scale, Edinburgh, Scotland, UK, April 25–26.

Crossley, S., and D. McNamara. 2016. Adaptive Educational Technologies for Literacy Instruction. New York: Routledge.

Feldstein, M., and P. Hill. 2016. "Personalized Learning: What It Really Is and Why It Really Matters." EDUCAUSE Review, March 7.

3-D Printing

What It Is

3-D printing is a process where various materials can be joined together or solidified under computer-control to create a three-dimensional object, usually with a device called a 3-D printer.

How It Works

A 3-D printer operates like an inkjet printer and is controlled by 3-D computer-assisted design (CAD) software. It builds a 3-D model from the bottom up one layer at a time by repeatedly printing over the same area until the desired object is formed. A 3-D printer deposits layers of molten plastic or powder and fuses them together with adhesive or ultraviolet light. Many other materials can be used with 3-D printers, including metals, sand, wood composites, biological cells, and food.

BUILDS Evaluation

Business Value

3-D printers come in different sizes and with many options and capabilities. Very simple 3-D printers can be obtained for a few hundred dollars, but printers for enterprise training may cost thousands of dollars. There is also the ongoing supply cost—instead of ink or toner, 3-D printers require continuous refilling of specialized plastics or metals. Creating all the objects needed for a specific training workshop may require purchasing several different kinds of 3-D printers, along with 3-D scanners. However, the value of using realistic objects may easily outweigh the costs of printers and materials, especially for critical missions in the military or medicine.

User Experience

Using a 3-D printer and the objects it creates is engaging and interactive for many learners. Before they can be printed, 3-D models must be created with a computer-aided design package, often using a 3-D scanner or digital camera. This process can be complicated. 3-D printing can be a slow process, because layer after layer needs to be built up to create each object. In addition, each 3-D printer has a maximum size object it can print. If a trainer needs an object that is larger than any given printer's maximum, it may be necessary to print several different pieces and then assemble them into the final object to be used in training.

Impact

Except for hobbyists, 3-D printing is mostly used in collaborative work where the printer can be used by many different people. It is currently being used for rapid prototyping in manufacturing, and in the medical industry. Emerging uses of 3-D printing include the development of food products made from layers of extruded edible materials, and personalized clothing and eyewear for the fashion industry. It is also used in the transportation industry for the manufacture of customized cars and airplanes.

3-D printing may result in a drastic reduction in manufacturing costs as computer designs can be shipped anywhere in the globe and then printed locally, reducing employment in the manufacturing sector and reducing transportation costs for goods. A controversial example of this use of 3-D printing is the sale of designs for print-your-own firearms.

Learning

The use of 3-D printing and 3-D printed objects for learning supports an active learning strategy based on manipulating tactile objects. This strategy uses real objects for teaching and allows for experimentation and failure as learners try using these objects for the tasks they are learning. At the same time, hands-on objects and pieces of equipment increase learner motivation because of their novelty.

3-D printers are used for creating objects for training workshops and simulations where realistic learning materials are important. This is especially appropriate for objects that are expensive, difficult or impossible to obtain, dangerous to use, or hard to visualize. The technology is often used for building prototypes, models, and visualizations for training purposes.

Examples include medical workshops with a 3-D printed heart, land mine removal training with 3-D printed mines with basic electronics, and creation of 3-D welding joints for supervisor review based on a student's use of an online welding simulator.

Dependencies

There are several significant dependencies for 3-D printing. First, employees with skills in computer-aided design are needed to build models. Second, 3-D printers and scanners are relatively expensive, and must be of industrial quality if they are used regularly by a group of people. Supplies such as plastics and metal need to be purchased and stocked. Finally, you need a physical location for a lab of 3-D printers and scanners, with adequate security for such high-value items.

The maximum size of the 3-D object depends on the size of the printer. Pricing of 3-D printers can range from less than $1,000 to millions.

Signals

Indications are that the field of 3-D printing is going to continue to grow and be used in many more diverse ways. A database search for "3-D printing" in academic literature found nearly 10,000 articles on the topic between 2008 and 2017, with 2018 on track to be a record year. However, only 90 of those publications were in the field of education, and only 14 had "learning" in the subject line. This would indicate that there has been little uptake of 3-D printing in education and training.

What is coming in the longer term is on-demand printing of human organs, and the hyper-local manufacturing of objects ranging from jewelry to cars. There will also be local (or regional) manufacturing of larger objects (such as houses) as communities invest in maker spaces, and schools and universities introduce 3-D printing into science, technology, engineering, and math (STEM) programs.

The Bottom Line

3-D printing has its uses in the learning and development environment, but unless there is a need to teach about real objects, or for students to handle them, buying all the equipment and supplies that are necessary for 3-D printing is probably not a wise investment for most learning and talent development departments at this time.

Further Reading

Bothmann, O. 2015. *3D Printers: A Beginner's Guide*. East Petersburg, PA: Fox Chapel Publishing.

Kloski, L., and N. Kloski. 2018. *Getting Started With 3D Printing: A Hands-on Guide to the Hardware, Software, and Services That Make the 3D Printing Ecosystem*, 2nd Ed. Sebastopol, CA: Maker Media.

The Internet of Things (IoT) and the Internet of Everything (IoE)

What It Is

The Internet of Things (IoT) is a developing network of uniquely address-able objects connected through standard Internet communication proto-cols. As defined by Cho and Kim (2016), IoT is "an instance of the more general class of cyber-physical systems, which encompasses technologies such as smart grids, smart homes, smart cities and smart educational insti-tutes." Add people, processes, and data collection, and the IoT becomes the IoE—the Internet of Everything (McEwan and Cassimally 2013). By giving each networked object a unique identifier, the IoT seems to turn things into "enchanted objects" with hidden capabilities that appear magical to most users (Rose 2014). Technologies involved with IoT and IoE include AI, network connectivity, sensors, wearables, smartphones, barcodes, GPS, drones, voice activation and recognition software, digital cameras, and microphones.

How It Works

The basic architecture of the IoT and IoE is described as "physical object + controller, sensor and actuators + internet" (McEwan and Cassimally 2013). The objects connected to the IoT may have additional capabilities, such as memory, data processing, or communication with other objects (Adorni, Coccoli, and Torre 2012).

BUILDS Evaluation

Business Value

A 2015 study by the Gartner consulting firm estimated that the size of the market for IoT will grow to $1.9 trillion by 2020, and connect 30 to 50 billion discrete objects by 2025 (Grebow 2015). This may be a gross underestimate of business value, as the website Statista projects that the IoT market will grow from "$2.99T in 2014 to $8.9T in 2020, attaining a

19.92% compound annual growth rate (CAGR)" (quoted in The Pitcher 2015). Clearly this is a big deal for firms that use this technology.

The main impact of IoT and IoE on learning and talent development will be in the area of performance support. Information, especially job aids, will be embedded directly into tools that employees use, which will be able to sense when a user needs help or updated information. Connected digital information using IoT—referred to as "digital materiality" (Pink, Lingard, and Harley 2016)—is already part of a workflow for many people.

User Experience

The user experience of IoT and IoE varies depending on the clarity and ease of use of any interface designed for this technology. In many cases, IoT functions operate in the background, and while users are not aware of them, they will experience their effects.

One approach that may accompany any IoT design is that of tangible user interfaces (TUIs), a new form of electronically embedded physical artifacts that combines digital information to produce a wide range of user interactions (such as gesturing or grasping) and system behaviors (Shaer and Hornecker 2009; Domingo and Forner 2010). Other experiences of using IoT could include work-related equipment that teaches the user, in their native language, what they need to know to operate it correctly; offers textual, audio, or video help embedded in the object; or automatically helps the user contact someone in an emergency (Grebow 2017).

Impact

With billions of devices connected to the Internet, the IoT will be everywhere that can be connected to the network. The most impactful result of this will be a sharp increase in surveillance (and loss of privacy), for good or bad. Sensors in buildings will monitor intrusions by strangers and may even trigger an automatic lockdown if a significant enough threat, such as the sound of gunfire, is ascertained. Police would be notified immediately, and drones launched to provide aerial views of the scene.

Given the rise in use of electricity for computing in general, IoT technologies will collect data on energy consumption in buildings and advise on ways to reduce use of electricity or heat (Hu et al. 2013). By monitoring farming practices and teaching farmers to improve their productivity in a sustainable way, IoT technologies will "help feed the world" (Fries 2018).

IoT-enabled remote laboratories will allow for training to take place in realistic (virtual) STEM environments while students remain located in the classroom with an instructor (Gibbs 2016; Kalashnikov et al. 2017). In fact, IoT and IoE are already being used on an experimental basis to educate and train. For example, students in one school conducted virtual investigations of possible microbial outbreak scenarios and attempted to solve an epidemiological mystery (Bennani, Novak, and Vaidya 2015). Heart or brain monitors will be used to provide instant data on how a trainee is performing during a high-intensity task, such as the kind often found in police work or the military.

Learning

IoT will support many types of learning (Domingo and Forner 2010), including:

- lifelong learning
- pervasive learning
- personalized learning
- collaborative learning
- learning by doing
- microlearning
- open learning
- game-based learning
- geo-located scenario learning
- tangible learning.

IoT may also reduce the need to rely on memory by sending out reminders, or by making information available as needed through a mobile device. For example, some pill containers have "smart" lids, which are capable of checking whether medications have been removed from the bottle (Rose 2014). This technology could easily be extended to the workplace.

Dependencies

The emergence of IoT and IoE is an exponential rise in the complexity of the Internet, with sharp increases in the problem of dependencies. For example, researchers in Chicago are building an "Array of Things" (AoT), which is a network of interactive, modular sensor boxes that installed around the city to collect real-time data on the environment, infrastructure, and activities for research and public use (Thornton 2018). If bracelets that monitor health and fitness activities were linked to the array, then the amount of data that could be collected would explode. If drones connected to the AoT could monitor the pulse of the city, then terabytes of video would be available every day for processing. This example alone shows how complex dependencies and data collection can grow at a very fast pace.

A major problem for connecting many different kinds of digital objects is interoperability. Hu and colleagues (2013) advocate for "serendipitous interoperability," "where devices which were not necessarily designed to work together (e.g., built for different purposes by different manufacturers at different times) should be able to discover each other's functionality and data, and be able to make use of it." New Internet protocols, such as the Smart Objects for Intelligent Applications (SOFIA) Interoperability Platform (IOP), have been developed to improve the interoperability, efficiency, security, and speed of the IoT.

Signals

There are a few examples of the application of IoT and IoE in schools, but almost none for enterprise learning. The 2017 Horizon Report predicts that the "time to adoption horizon" for the IoT in schools and higher education is two to three years, but we believe this is too optimistic for enterprise learning and talent development (NMC 2017). We expect that this technology will arrive in a big way in corporate learning in the next five to 10 years.

Some signals we have seen include the growth of Internet-connected wearable devices for personal monitoring of actions and emotions. For example, researchers at the University of Texas Arlington's LINK Lab are using wearables to monitor biological factors that correspond to emotional states to monitor learning. At the University of the Pacific, Kinect sensors in classrooms are used to track students' skeletal positions to find correlations between posture and learner engagement (NMC 2017). In the medium-term future, autonomic assessments based on monitoring a learner's body's autonomic nervous system to detect emotional engagement with and interest in learning activities will be available as data points (Beissner et al. 2013; Mendes 2016).

In smart city developments, the IoT is being used to monitor utilities, provide geo-located information to citizens about their city, and set up a "smart city university" (Domingo and Forner 2010; Thornton 2018; UAE 2018).

The Bottom Line

While billions of devices are interconnected through the Internet, most of the action has been in the field of "domotics" (home automation systems), monitoring of large buildings, and in the tentative buildout of smart cities. Aside from embedded sensors and screens in equipment for performance support, we see little impact of IoT in the field of learning and talent development, and don't think this will change much in the next five years.

Further Reading

Greengard, S. 2015. *The Internet of Things*. Cambridge, MA: MIT Press.

McEwan, A., and H. Cassimally. 2014. *Designing the Internet of Things*. New York: Wiley.

Rose, D. 2014. *Enchanted Objects: Design, Human Desire, and the Internet of Things*. New York: Scribner.

Artificial Intelligence and Machine Learning

What It Is

Artificial intelligence (AI) and machine learning are disciplines within computer science that seek to enable computers to "think," or, more accurately, use statistical probability and predicative analytics via algorithmic processing. This is done to increase decision-making capabilities and enhance a computer program's overall capability by making them "smarter."

How It Works

A model of how people are expected to behave based on two or more variables is programmed into the computer by a person. A prediction is then made, performance data are collected, and then results are compared with the data predicted by the model. The parameters of the model are then adjusted and the program is run again. This is repeated many times until the program's predictions come as close as possible to the actual outcomes. This information is then stored as machine learning and used for further predicting what other people will do in the same situation. In deep learning, a variation of machine learning, a computer program creates its own model of how something works without being programmed first by humans.

BUILDS Evaluation

Business Value

AI and machine learning costs are rapidly dropping, and the availability of existing software development kits (SDK) and application programming interfaces (API) is making the initial investment a minor cost in the overall development of training programs that use AI. The upside for these technologies from a business perspective can be profound as businesses are able provide expert-level guidance to all employees regardless of location, context, or time of service. This type of approach enables all employees to essentially become as skillful as the company's best employee.

The trend is moving away from companies setting up their own AI on in-house servers; instead they're using cloud-based, software as a service (SaaS) approaches by renting cognitive services from providers like Amazon, Microsoft, and IBM.

User Experience

AI and machine learning's main enhancement to the overall user experience is often centered around providing predictive or adaptive advice, feedback, and output based on a user's activities—either implicit or explicit. The user interface and user experience are less centered around pixels and buttons, but more focused on task flows, empathetic approaches to user-centered design, and providing adequate user cues, coaching, and alternate input methods like cameras, voice, and gestures.

Impact

Learning and development departments often spend thousands of hours creating training that may or may not be used, needed, or even engaged with more than once by a user, essentially showing no real return on investment through increased performance or knowledge building. It's clear that placing a system in an organization that dramatically reduces the need for retention in the first place could have profound impacts on what gets turned into training. Using AI agents to serve as coaches, mentors, and mediators could reduce the impact of these issues.

At the same time, new learning systems based on AI and machine learning may eventually replace human instructors as the automation of teaching takes hold.

Learning

AI is useful for assisting employees where decision-making processes are complicated or tedious, or if the work contains steps that are easily missed or mixed up. It is especially appropriate for work where things like lack of motivation, fatigue, or distraction can impede proper performance. AI can also be used to impart or share institutional knowledge that may have been gained by fitting users performing tasks efficiently with sensors and then modeling the best practices after them. Examples include adaptive paths in learning and curriculum delivery, assistive checklists based on other user activities in a system, and chatbots with an answer and response user experience to provide conversational assistance and just-in-time answers. Integration with operational business systems—such as supply chain management, customer relationship management, and others—may reduce overall training needs.

The use of AI and machine learning in training supports an active learning strategy based on reducing overall cognitive load and offloading intelligence to a more dependable process than human thought. This refocusing of what makes something worth teaching versus something that can be, in the words of Kevin Kelly (2016), "cognified," will shake some foundational concepts of what constitutes a learning experience. Once learning and development professionals move past this initial awkward phase, though, learners will find themselves with free time to pursue other learning paths, including more time to be spent on mentoring, coaching, soft skills, leadership, and any number of professional development tasks of their own choosing.

Dependencies

There are several significant dependencies for AI in the workplace. First, employees with skills in algorithmic design will be needed to build neural networks and models. Second, AI toolkits are becoming more accessible, but are still not simple enough to easily set up, integrate, and deploy widely. A big area of uncertainty for many organizations is obtaining the high volumes of data needed for fueling these AI processes. Servers and services to train and house the AI must also be bought, subscribed to, or leased. There are a number of cloud-based vendors and SaaS providers popping up in this space now. The end users' devices must be web connected and provide adequate processing power to leverage these AI.

Signals

With two major boom and bust cycles of AI behind us—the AI winter of the 1970s and the second one in the 1990s, well chronicled in *Human+Machine* by Paul Daugherty and H. James Wilson (2018)—it seems that the stage is set for another boom cycle of AI. With the advent of millions of mobile devices all capable of running AI processes and tool-kits, it's also clear that the audience is primed for it. Consumer products like thermostats, home brewing kits, smartwatches, and more come with AI embedded, and now big-ticket items like automobiles have AI in them too. The future looks bright for this next burst of activity in the AI space.

The Bottom Line

AI has a big upside, as long as you can obtain the necessary data and implement it with expert advice. The costs are dropping to the point where experimentation and prototypes are certainly within the reach of most organizations. With the pace that things are changing and growing here, and with the expectations that many of your employees have because of their exposure to Alexa, Siri, Cortana, and other agents, it's time to give AI a try.

Further Reading

Daugherty, P., and H.J. Wilson. 2018. *Human + Machine: Reimagining Work in the Age of AI*. Boston: Harvard Business Review Press.

Lamson, M., and A. von Redwitz. 2018. "The Impact of AI on Learning and Development." *Training Industry,* May 8.

Meister, J. 2017. "The Future of Work: The Intersection of Artificial Intelligence and Human Resources." *Forbes,* March 1.

Augmented Reality and Virtual Reality

What It Is

Augmented reality (AR) and virtual reality (VR) are two related technologies that enable users to engage with digital content and environments in highly immersive, interactive ways. Augmented reality is typically understood as the mixing of digital assets such as 3-D models and objects, or other digital content added to images or video of the real world. Virtual reality is a more immersive experience, with the user's entire field of view and sometimes even other senses, such as hearing and touch, being stimulated and engaged by a virtual environment.

How It Works

AR places objects or text into images and video of the real world by adding an information overlay to a display screen or by projecting a computer-generated image into a space. Gijevski (2017) distinguishes among three kinds of AR experiences:

- 3-D viewers allow users to place life-size 3-D models in their surroundings with or without the use of trackers
- browsers enrich the user's camera display with contextual data
- gaming allows users to display virtual creatures that are hidden throughout a map of the real environment.

VR uses a headset to show you an image. As soon as you move your head, the image changes in sync with your head's motion to make it seem that you are in a real environment. 3-D audio or haptic feedback can enhance the VR experience. The latest VR apps let you see a world around you in a 360-degree field of vision.

BUILDS Evaluation

Business Value

Both AR and VR are considered emerging technologies because they are still gaining acceptance and have a long way to go in terms of widespread adoption. However, companies that are employing these technologies in place are seeing benefits. For example, assembly technicians at Boeing who are using AR have seen a reduction in time on task by more than 30 percent. VR can similarly reduce costs in training by fully virtualizing worksites, reducing the need for travel or costly learning lab setups, and a wide variety of other cost-saving measures.

User Experience

AR and VR are both highly personal technologies, with each of them either replacing or significantly changing the way that the user perceives the reality around them. It is of paramount importance that the AR and VR experiences themselves be designed with a high level of usability, with a focus on user acceptance and making things frictionless. Both AR and VR have the potential to be disorienting or introduce facets of the "uncanny valley" problem, so designers should take ample time to design and test the deliverables in the actual contextual settings and on the actual required computer or mobile hardware (Mashable 2014).

Impact

AR is in some ways the fullest embodiment of the original electronic performance support system (EPSS) concepts from the 1990s—an always available, in-situ assistant that knows and understands an employee's true issues in real time and provides quick answers in a seamless fashion. This is a big deal in the workplace and will undoubtedly change the way that things like checklists, competency assessments, and many other aspects of how a field or factory floor worker's day-to-day tasks are accomplished.

VR looks to be a great equalizer. Companies that lack the seemingly unlimited training and travel budgets of their bigger and better funded competitors will no longer be constrained by their physical locations. Workers who may benefit from being thrust into high-pressure or risky situations will be able to do so with impunity once the immersive headsets are put on and the new VR learning environments are made available.

Learning

AR and VR have different applications for learning. AR is often used for just-in-time information delivery or performance support. VR is best used for creating ahead-of-time training content for situations when immersive learning experiences are important. VR is especially appropriate for simulations that are expensive, difficult or impossible to obtain, dangerous to use, or hard to visualize. It also works well when used for gaming or scenario testing and more advanced visualizations for training purposes. AR is a great tool for helping people visualize step-based processes like repairs, assemblies, and other checklist-based things where steps may be difficult to remember or users could benefit from help.

These immersive learning tools offer powerful spatial and locative learning tools. VR and AR also offer immense opportunities for creating experiential learning content and virtualized, but still hands-on training. Recent developments in the AR and VR space also hint at powerful potential for shared experiences with two or more learners, possibly with coaches or teachers by their side, setting the stage for virtualized or augmented collaborative learning experiences. It has been suggested that VR, especially the kind that uses 360-degree videos, may be a powerful tool for teaching empathy, because it immerses learners in the environment of others. However, this claim needs to be researched and proven before it can be fully accepted.

It seems at first glance that AR and VR offer most of the affordances and models that the traditional classroom and e-learning offer, while adding a layer of additional sensory interaction that provides a wealth of new learning opportunities previously only imagined.

Dependencies

There are several significant dependencies for AR and VR. These mediums are immersive and rich in design, so you will need content creators capable of working in 3-D environments. VR content creation is also demanding in terms of scenario design, akin to game design or even film direction (in some cases).

AR content is often best when connected to enterprise data systems and operational software, with a heavy need to be tied to the SCM, ERP, or CRM software to provide true value.

Both AR and VR can have steep hardware and software requirements, including the need for multiple new systems and programs.

Signals

Investments and new product introductions in the AR and VR space are currently on a steep upward trajectory (Carter 2016). It seems with every new mobile OS launch or CES event there are multiple developments happening in this space. When you consider that today's biggest players in technology (including Google, Apple, Microsoft, and Facebook) are just getting started with this technology and the penetration rate of AR and VR compatible devices hasn't yet reached anything close to saturation, it's clear there is still a lot of room for growth here.

The Bottom Line

The largest study to date in the United Kingdom on the use of VR e-learning shows that 95 percent of learning and development professionals intend to integrate the technology into their organizational learning, with a third planning to roll out VR over the next three years (Carter 2016). AR and VR technologies are widely available and appear to be here to stay. If you aren't already trying them out in your organizations, you are behind schedule.

Further Reading

Bailenson, J. 2018. *Experience on Demand: What Virtual Reality Is, How It Works, and What It Can Do.* New York: Norton.

Morey, S., and J. Tinnell, eds. 2016. *Augmented Reality: Innovative Perspectives Across Art, Industry, and Academia.* Anderson, SC: Parlor Press.

Sanjiv, K.R. 2016. "How VR and AR Will Be Training Tomorrow's Workforce." *Venture Beat,* February 21.

GLOSSARY

360-degree virtual worlds. Computer-generated scenes or videos that cover a full field of vision accessed through goggles. The viewer can turn completely around and see the scene in all directions.

3-D printing. A variety of processes to print a three-dimensional object, which may range from very small to the size of a house, depending on the size of the 3-D printer being used. Various materials, including plastic, metal, concrete, and biomaterials, can be used to build objects.

A/B testing. A technique to compare two versions of a single variable, such as a choice between two designs of a web page, to determine which version is preferred by a majority of users.

Active beta testing. A software quality improvement program where unfinished programs are released for trial use to a community of people who agree to give feedback to the developers.

Adaptive tutoring system. A software program designed to teach or train that uses artificial intelligence algorithms to change what information or problems are presented to a learner based on their current and past performance.

Affective computing. A computer program that senses and interprets the emotional state of humans and responds with an appropriate simulated emotional reaction.

Affordances. The technologies, features, and conveniences that make a particular product, service, or device usable and more capable than alternatives of accomplishing a specific outcome.

Agile project management. An approach to software development based on collaboration among self-organizing and cross-functional teams and end users. Agile methods include early delivery, rapid feedback, and iterative improvement.

Algorithm. A specification or formula for solving a problem.

Amazon Web Services (AWS). A cloud computing platform offered by Amazon for use by third parties for storage, processing, and hosting of applications.

Ambient intelligence. Aspects of a computing platform that are aware of human presence and respond appropriately without any specific user input or even awareness that the computer program has acted.

Analytics. The detection and interpretation of patterns in data that have meaning for the context in which the data are collected. Organizational analytics refers to data collected in a group setting while learning analytics refers to patterns about individual learners.

Application programming interface (API). Commands, methods, properties, and variables in a computing platform that enable developers to create apps using a common set of features or to extend existing ones. Used to connect two or more programs so they can work together.

Artificial intelligence (AI). A discipline in computer science where traditional programming practices are augmented by creating programming enhancements through "smart" algorithms generated by statistics from large data sets.

Attribution modelling. The rule or process in which something can be attributed or credited to something else for making the final conversion or action possible. Used in marketing to analyze purchasing decisions.

Augmented reality (AR). The integration of digital artifacts—media, text, 3-D models, and more—with the physical world. Often interactive, these systems enhance or augment the user's reality and provide new layers of information to increase performance.

Autonomic assessment. Monitoring a person's autonomic nervous system to detect the amount of emotional engagement, stress, or interest in learning activities.

Backcasting. A planning method where a state of success—usually in the somewhat distant future—is used as a goal, and then the ideation process works backward from that spot to create intermediary goals and steps of progress to meet the desired end state.

Badge. A visual element in game design or in the gamification of learning that indicates a specified level of achievement.

Beacon. A small Bluetooth radio transmitter that can send or collect information wirelessly with mobile devices, including smartphones and tablets. Often used to track the movements of customers in a retail environment.

Benefit realization management (BRM). A project management approach where business change managers work to ensure that a change produces the expected benefits for the right people, on time and within budget.

Big data. Large data sets that are used to reveal patterns, trends, or relationships. Big data is used in statistical analysis, but also in things like machine learning and AI.

Binary code. Any two-symbol system used to represent data—including text, computer code, and communications—to any device that can read the code. The binary code in most frequent use is the system of zeros and ones used in most computers today.

Bioelectronics. Use of biological materials and biological architectures for information processing systems and electronic devices. It also refers to the interface between biological and electronic systems.

Biometrics. Computer processing of biological data for the purposes of recognition and identity confirmation.

Blockchain. An encrypted, immutable list of records (also known as a ledger) dependent on having multiple computers sharing the same record to create shared trust to verify the veracity and immutability of the information stored in the encrypted records.

Bots. Short for "robots" or sometimes "chatbots." Computer programs that perform tasks or automate work through preprogrammed steps or even simple AI. *See also* chatbots.

Bring your own device (BYOD). A policy companies use to allow employees to use their own personal digital devices (such as smartphones or tablets) to connect to company systems, apps, or other digital communications tools.

CD-ROM (compact disc read-only memory). A pre-pressed optical compact disc that contains data read by a small laser. The read-only memory part of the name refers to the fact that the laser can only read, and cannot write to the disc.

Central processing unit (CPU). The "brains" of a computer system. This is the processor that executes programming code.

Chatbot. A computer program that can carry on a conversation through text or a synthetic voice. Often used for customer service, training, or information acquisition and transmission.

Cloud computing. A model of computer server usage where shared resources not typically owned by the user are leased or managed remotely with no requirement to own or maintain the hardware.

Cognitive services. Cloud-based computer vision, speech, language, translation, and knowledge capabilities offered by subscription from large companies like Microsoft, IBM, and Amazon.

Complex adaptive system. A system in which the individual parts do not give an understanding of the system operating as a whole, but which shows dynamic emergent behavior, often after unpredictable phase transitions.

Computer vision. Robotic vision in which one or more video cameras capture a scene that can be used for navigation or object recognition by robots or people with a visual impairment. It is also an interdisciplinary field studying how computers gain high-level understanding from digital images or videos.

Critical path method (CPM). A project management approach that uses a mathematical algorithm to determine the timeline in which a project should take place, the required resources, and the order of activities that need to be undertaken.

Dashboard. A control panel and display element in software that shows a summary of the state of a system and a summary of data on features of software that are being tracked.

Deep learning. A subset of machine learning where algorithms determine if a prediction is accurate or not. With deep learning it is not necessary to teach a computer if its responses are correct, because it figures this out on its own.

Dependency. A condition or state that requires something else to be in place prior to being able to use it. Also, a state of need where a person requires a thing in order to continue working or producing.

Design thinking. An iterative process based on developing a deep understanding of those for whom products or services are being designed by observing and developing empathy with the target user. It involves ongoing experimentation and trying out different concepts and ideas.

Digital bread crumbs. Indications of activity in an online environment or website through records left behind from user interactions, such as recorded clicks or keystrokes. This term also refers to web navigation, by showing a trail of where users have been in an online environment.

Digital divide. Inequality of access to information and communication technologies or bandwidth usually due to differing socioeconomic levels or other demographic variables.

Digitization. The process of making information available and accessible in a digital format.

Distributed denial of service (DDoS). A coordinated method of attacking a computer system where the network or server is overwhelmed by a wave of requests from many devices or computers.

Domotics. Home automation systems based on digital platforms, networking, and artificial intelligence algorithms to produce "smart homes." These systems, part of the growing Internet of Things (IoT), will control lighting, temperature, humidity, entertainment systems, access to the home, alarm systems, and appliances.

Drill and practice programs. Programs that encourage the acquisition of knowledge or skill through repetitive practice.

Dual coding. A theory of cognition wherein an idea can be stored or remembered in multiple ways (such as the word representing the item and an image of the same item).

Dual process theory. A belief that there are two kinds of thinking, recently popularized by Nobel laureate Daniel Kahneman in his book *Thinking, Fast and Slow*, where he distinguishes between intuition and reasoning.

DVD (digital video disc). A digital optical disc developed in 1995 that can be read or written to by a small laser. Also known as a "digital versatile disc" because it can be used for more than just video.

Edge case. A problem or situation that occurs at the extreme of a phenomenon, away from the average or middle. Often the place where innovation begins.

Embodied digital devices. An approach to integrating digital devices with bodies and vice versa. Could include embedding sensors in our bodies to assist in knowing more about them, or integrating our senses and brain functions with IoT devices or other digital processes.

Emerging technologies. New, potentially disruptive technologies still being developed and capable of changing how a specific process or task is completed.

End user development. Methods, techniques, and tools that allow users of software, acting as non-professional software developers, to create, modify, or extend some aspect of the software. Enables users to customize the user interface and functionality of the software.

Ethnography. The study of people and cultures, usually through observation that captures the point of view of the subject being observed.

Extreme project management (XPM). A short, flexible approach to project management that allows you to alter your project plan, budget, and final outcome to fit changing needs.

Facial recognition software. Software that is capable of identifying or verifying a person from a digital image or video frame.

Fall over. Fall over is a plan for system control and recovery in the event of a disaster, such as a fire, earthquake, flood, or infrastructure failure. Automatic fall over is designed to maintain data integrity and application usability using a backup system that can quickly be brought online to minimize or eliminate downtime of a computer system.

Filter bubble. Intellectual isolation caused by algorithms that make assumptions about what a user wants to see and only gives that information to the user. Filter bubbles can cause users to get significantly less contact with contradictory points of view.

Fourth Industrial Revolution. A fusion of technologies that blurs the lines between the physical, digital, and biological spheres. Characterized by rapid breakthroughs of new technologies that in turn become connected to one another through computer networking.

Gamification. The application of game design elements and principles to non-game contexts. Often used for motivation in e-learning. GDPR (General Data Protection Regulation). A regulation in European Union law on data protection and privacy. It applies to all individuals living in the European Union and the European Economic Area, as well as the export of personal data outside these areas.

GovWin IQ. A service offered by the company Delteck to help companies identify and win government contracts.

GPS (Geographical Positioning System). A U.S. government–owned global satellite-based navigation system operated by the U.S. Air Force. Provides geolocation and time information to a GPS receiver anywhere on earth.

Graphical user interface (GUI). A computer program that lets a person communicate with the computer through the use of symbols, visual metaphors, or pointing devices.

Graphics processing unit (GPU). A highly optimized computer chip originally intended to perform specialized calculations for graphics-intensive applications like games or engineering applications. GPUs are now commonly used for systems with AI components due to their parallel processing capabilities, which allow many calculations to be performed simultaneously.

Heuristics. A trial-and-error approach to problem solving that uses any method that gets you close to your goal, such as a mental shortcut or "rule of thumb" that helps in decision making.

Human–computer interaction (HCI). A field of computer science and design that focuses on the interfaces between people and computers.

Human–machine symbiosis. The integration of humans and machines so that they act together.

IMS Global Learner Information Package (LIP). A digital container of information and identity about a specific learner. A template for the collection of learner information offered by IMS Global.

Information and communications technology (ICT). A term used for technologies based on the convergence and integration of audiovisual devices, telephone networks, computer networks, and middleware.

Information explosion. The rapid exponential increase in the amount of recorded information or data in the world.

Information spillover. The exchange of ideas and information among individuals, organizations, or countries, especially those in close physical proximity or those linked to each other through computer networks.

Infrastructure as a service (IaaS). A form of cloud computing that provides virtualized computing resources over the Internet that act as physical infrastructure.

Innocentive. An open innovation and crowdsourcing platform that allows corporations, government, and nonprofit organizations to use crowdsourcing to solve problems.

Innovative disruption. A form of innovation where a new market, system, or segment is created by disrupting or making an old model obsolete.

Interface. A system of commands or methods, properties, and variables in a computing platform that enables developers to create apps that use a common set of features or extend the existing ones.

Internet. The global system of interconnected computer networks that use the Internet protocol (IP) to link devices worldwide.

Internet of Everything (IoE). A network that connects people to the Internet of Things (IoT).

Internet of Things (IoT). A network of physical devices, vehicles, appliances, and other objects with embedded electronics and sensors that can be connected to the Internet. It is a network of uniquely addressable objects connected via the standard Internet protocol (IP).

Intertwingled. The condition of virtually everything being connected and mixed together in some way or another. People, places, communications, software, tools, processes, contexts, and more are now all dependent on one another. *Intertwingularity* is a term coined by Ted Nelson in his self-published books *Computer Lib and Dream Machines* (1974), to express the complexity of interrelations in human knowledge. Nelson is also the inventor of hypertext.

Lambda server instance. A flexible computing service from Amazon. Lambda executes code only on demand, operating in a SaaS business model.

Laserdisc. The first commercial optical disc storage medium. Each disk was 12 inches in diameter and made of two single-sided aluminum discs layered in plastic. It was used to store analog audio and video.

Lean methodologies. The aim of the Lean approach is to create an enterprise that minimizes cost overruns and waste.

Learning. The process of acquiring knowledge, skills, or behaviors by interaction between a person and their environment. Can be the result of habituation, play, traumatic events, imitation, or direct instruction.

Learning content management system (LCMS). A server application used to create, manage, host, and track digital learning content.

Learning management system (LMS). A server application used to track learner data such as course enrollment, assessment data, and e-learning completion information.

Learning record store (LRS). A server application that stores and reports on learning data produced by xAPI activity providers, such as xAPI-enabled apps, courses, and LMS interactions.

Liquid enterprise. A flexible and responsive organization that is able to change rapidly to meet new operating and market conditions.

Livecasting. The process of broadcasting real-time live video footage or a video feed to an audience.

Machine learning. A subset of artificial intelligence where statistics and probability are used to tune an algorithm that a computer program can use in its decision-making processes.

Mainframe computer. A large computer usually enclosed in a set of giant cabinets called "main frames" and housed in a climate-controlled room. Also known as "big iron" within the computer industry.

Mashup. A web page or application that integrates elements from two or more online sources. A content mashup brings together material from two or more websites and presents it in a single webpage or other user experience, such as an app.

Massive open online course (MOOC). An open-access online web-based course with no limits on the number of participants. Many MOOCs have community participation features.

Meta-design. Literally, designing design. Meta-design is the creation and establishment of frameworks for designing a host of things, from processes and tools to conceptual models used to create, sustain, and advance existing systems.

Microlearning. A way of teaching and delivering content to learners in small chunks through online devices based on an immediate need for learning.

Mimetic learning. Learning by imitation or memorization of what is mandated to learn.

Mirai botnet. Malware that was used to mount a massive distributed denial of service (DDoS) attack on many websites on October 12, 2016.

Mixed reality. The merging of elements of both real and virtual worlds to produce new environments. A form of augmented reality.

Mobile device management (MDM). A software service that enables provisioning and governance of a mobile device to place it under organizational control. Typically used to maintain and secure company-provided mobile devices.

Mobile learning. A person learning while on the move or being able to move while learning. It is asking for and receiving information just-in-time, from any place, at the moment a person needs or wants it.

Multivariate A/B testing. A/B testing analyzed using multivariate statistics.

Nanotechnology. Manufacture and use of technology at an extremely small scale.

Natural language processing (NLP). A branch of artificial intelligence that helps computers understand, interpret, and manipulate human language.

Neuro-electronics. A field of science that works on connecting brains and computers. Projects range from producing robotic limbs controlled directly by brain activity to altering memory and mood with implanted electrodes.

Nomophobia. Also known as no-mobile-phone-phobia, this is the fear or anxiety of not having one's mobile phone or the fear of not being connected to information and to other people if one's mobile phone is switched off.

Nudging. Setting up a choice architecture or arranging an environment to influence people's behavior in a predictable and desirable way.

Open learning resources. Freely accessible, openly licensed text, media, and other online assets that are useful for learning.

Optical character recognition (OCR). A function of computer vision where printed text is converted to digital text to be processed or understood by other computer programs.

Peer network. A network of people with equal status without central management or control by experts.

Performance support. The delivery of appropriate information meant to help employees with on-the-job support at the precise moment it is needed.

Personalization of learning. Instruction in which the pace and specific instructional materials used are optimized for the needs of each learner.

Platform as a service (PaaS). A category of cloud computing services that allows customers to develop, run, and manage applications without maintaining their own infrastructure.

PLATO Learning System. The first computer-assisted instruction or e-learning system in the world. It was developed on a mainframe computer at the University of Illinois in 1960 and eventually supported several thousand terminals around the world.

Podcasts. Audio programs delivered online, and playable on mobile and desktop computers.

Program evaluation and review technique (PERT). A statistical tool used in project management, designed to analyze the tasks involved in completing a project.

Prototype. An incomplete and often rudimentary version of a software program that is being developed, which may simulate only a few features of the proposed final product. It is used to elicit feedback from clients and potential users as a program is being developed and to see if the software is being developed according to specifications agreed upon between the developers and the client.

Punctuated equilibrium. A concept from evolutionary biology where bursts of change and abrupt speciation are interjected between relatively stable periods of stasis.

Quantified self. The results of self-tracking using digital wearable devices.

Quantum computing. A form of computing that uses quantum mechanical characteristics such as superposition and entanglement in its calculations. Development of quantum computers is just starting out, but the potential to disrupt how computing works and the potential increase in computing speed and power is huge.

Rating inflation. An increase in the value of a rating over time so that anything less than the top value is seen as a rebuke or negative rating.

Recombinant innovation. The combination of existing ideas or affordances to produce new innovations.

Remixing. The act of altering a piece of media from its original state by adding, removing, or changing elements.

RFID (radio frequency identification device). A technology that uses embedded sensors or small chips to aid in identifying or tracking items.

Robotics. A branch of engineering concerned with creating automated machines and software agents.

SBIR and STTR trackers. Software that tracks two U.S. government business seed funding programs: the Small Business Innovation Research (SBIR) program, and the Small Business Technology Transfer (STTR) program.

Scaffolding. Clues, wayfinding, or other stepped instructions that allow learners to work within their zone of proximal development (ZPD) to achieve things that they otherwise might not be able to learn by themselves.

Sensor. A device, module, or subsystem to detect events or changes in the environment and send the information to another computer system for processing.

Situated learning. A theory that there is a connection between learning and the social situation in which it occurs. In situated learning, new learners go through a cognitive apprenticeship via legitimate peripheral participation in a social group as they move toward becoming part of a community of practice.

Six Sigma. A quality-control program developed in 1986 by Motorola. Since that time, Six Sigma has evolved into a more general business management methodology of eliminating variation in a product.

Skeuomorphism. The use of design cues to increase the perceived realism of a digital item by making it appear or behave like its physical counterpart.

Skunkworks. A secret or hidden research and development team focused on innovation and new product or service design and development. Often found in a separate location from the main enterprise.

Smart dust. A network of small sensors, chips, robots, or other IoT devices used to create a localized cloud of information to be processed by other larger systems.

Socio-technical system (STS). The intersection of social structures and technology that creates the modern world we live in.

Software as a service (SaaS). A software licensing and subscription model where software is centrally hosted and delivered as a service. The software is then updated and maintained by the hosting company.

Sousveillance. Use of a mobile device to monitor and record the actions of authorities in power—the reverse action to surveillance.

Speech to text. A subset of artificial intelligence and computer algorithms concerned with processing speech and transforming it into written text.

Switching costs. Amount of time and money that may need to be spent changing from one service to another.

Tango. An augmented reality computing platform that was developed and authored by the Advanced Technology and Projects (ATAP) group, a division of Google.

Text to speech. A subset of artificial intelligence and computer algorithms concerned with processing written text and transforming it into speech.

Tensor processing unit (TPU). A specialized GPU product from Google, which was made to process and deliver machine learning models and artificial intelligence–based algorithms rapidly and at a low cost using a cloud computing approach.

Uncanny Valley. The uneasy feeling that occurs as humans interact with a system, robot, or other technology that exhibits human-like characteristics. The valley is actually the dip in affinity felt for the system due to the fact that it is unable to successfully replicate human qualities.

Use case analysis. A technique used to identify the requirements of a software system by identifying the actors and processes that will be considered in designing the system. The results are often placed in a use case diagram.

User-centered design. A creative approach to problem solving that starts with finding the needs of the people for whom you are designing. User experience (UX). The attributes and emotional response of a person's interactions with a computer system. Essentially the "feel" in the "look and feel" of the system.

User interface (UI). The space where interactions between a person and a computer occur, in order to control the computer and provide feedback to the person operating the computer.

Vaporware. Software that doesn't yet exist but may be hyped and sold as if it does. Often has a negative connotation, as if the software will never be released or will fall short of expectations.

Virtual reality (VR). A computer program that simulates a real or imaginary physical environment with audio, video, and, perhaps, haptic features, often in 3-D, using a set of goggles or wearable items such as VR gloves or suits.

Wearables. Smart electronic devices incorporated into clothing, jewelry, watches, activity trackers, rings, or other accessories, as well as body implants.

White-label. A version of an application or service that can be easily customized or configured to reflect an organization's branding and specific communication needs.

xAPI. Also known as the Experience API or Tin Can API, xAPI is a new specification for recording events and achievements related to a person's learning experiences, both online and offline. xAPI collects data about a person's activities from many sources, including self-reporting.

ADDITIONAL RESOURCES

Chapter 1. Digital Transformation

Bounfour, A. 2016. *Digital Futures, Digital Transformation*. Cham, Switzerland: Springer.

Bughin, J., T. Catlin, M. Hirt, and P. Willmott. 2018. "Why Digital Strategies Fail." Whitepaper. McKinsey& Company, January. www.mckinsey.com /business-functions/digital-mckinsey/our-insights/why-digital-strategies-fail.

Dearborn, J. 2017. "The Role of Corporate Learning & Development in the Digital Transformation of the Fourth Industrial Revolution." Video Recording. www.hci.org/lib/role-corporate-learning-development -digital-transformation-fourth-industrial-revolution.

Herbert, L. 2017. *Digital Transformation: Build Your Organization's Future for the Innovation Age*. London, UK: Bloomsbury.

Lowenthal, S. 2018. "How Is Digital Transformation Affecting L&D?" eLearning Industry blog, January 16. https://elearningindustry.com /digital-transformation-affecting-l-and-d.

Main, A., B. Lamm, and D. McCormack. 2017. "Winning With Digital: What Boards Need to Know About Digital Transformation." Whitepaper, October. www2.deloitte.com/content/dam/Deloitte/us /Documents/center-for-board-effectiveness/us-oct-2017-winning-with -digital-on-the-boards-agenda.pdf.

Westerman, G., D. Bonnet, and A. McAfee. 2014. *Leading Digital: Turning Technology Into Business Transformation*. Boston, MA: Harvard Business Review Press.

Wilen, T. 2018. *Digital Disruption: The Future of Work, Skills, Leadership, Education, and Careers in a Digital World*. New York: Peter Lang.

Chapter 2. Business Needs

Benson-Armer, R., A. Gast, and N. van Dam. 2016. "Learning at the Speed of Business." *McKinsey Quarterly*, May. www.mckinsey.com/business -functions/organization/our-insights/learning-at-the-speed-of-business.

Bersin, J. 2017. "AI, Robotics, and Cognitive Computing Are Changing Business Faster Than You Thought." Josh Bersin blog, March 8. https://joshbersin.com/2017/03/ai-robotics-and-cognitive-computing -are-changing-business-faster-than-you-thought

Blank, S. 2013. *The Four Steps to the Epiphany: Successful Strategies for Products that Win*, 2nd ed. Louisville, KY: Cafe Press.

Cerra, A., K. Easterwood, and J. Power. 2012. *Transforming Business: Big Data, Mobility, and Globalization*. Indianapolis: John Wiley & Sons.

Gordon, E.E. 2014. "Talent Creation and the Bottom Line." *Training*, November 13. https://trainingmag.com/trgmag-article/talent-creation -and-bottom-line.

IBM Training. 2014. "The Value of Training." IBM whitepaper. www-03 .ibm.com/services/learning/pdfs/IBMTraining-TheValueofTraining.pdf

Jain, P., and P. Sharma. 2014. *Behind Every Good Decision: How Anyone Can Use Business Analytics to Turn Data Into Profitable Insight*. New York: AMACOM.

Osterwalder, A., and Y. Pigneur. 2010. *Business Model Generation: A Handbook for Visionaries, Game Changers, and Challengers*. Hoboken, NJ: John Wiley & Sons.

Ries, E. 2011. *The Lean Startup: How Today's Entrepreneurs Use Continuous Innovation to Create Radically Successful Businesses*. New York: Crown Business.

Williams van Rooij, S. 2017. *The Business Side of Learning Design and Technologies*. New York: Routledge.

Chapter 3. User Experience

Draper, C. 2015. "Ships Passing in the Night? E-learning Designers' Experiences With User Experience." Doctoral dissertation. Brigham Young University, Provo, UT. https://scholarsarchive.byu.edu/cgi /viewcontent.cgi?referer=&httpsredir=1&article=6486&context=etd.

Fischer, G. 2013. "Meta-Design: Empowering All Stakeholders as Co-Designers." Chap. 12 in *Handbook on Design in Educational Computing*, edited by N. Winters et al. London, UK: Routledge. http://l3d.cs.colorado.edu/~gerhard/papers/2012/paper-handbook.pdf

Fischer, G. 2014. "Supporting Self-Directed Learning With Cultures of Participation in Collaborative Learning Environments." Chap. 1 in *In Problem-Based Learning for the 21st Century: New Practices and Learning Environments*, edited by E. Christiansen et al. Aalborg, Denmark: Aalborg University Press. http://l3d.cs.colorado.edu/~gerhard /papers/2014/Scandinavia-PBL.pdf

Krishna, G. 2015. *The Best Interface Is No Interface: The Simple Path to Brilliant Technology*. San Francisco: New Riders.

Krug, S. 2014. *Don't Make Me Think, Revisited: A Common Sense Approach to Web Usability*. San Francisco: New Riders.

Morville, P. 2014. *Intertwingled: Information Changes Everything*. Ann Arbor, MI: Semantic Studios.

Rosenfeld, L., P. Morville, and J. Arango. 2015. *Information Architecture: For the Web and Beyond*, 4th ed. Sebastopol, CA: O'Reilly.

Szabo, P. 2017. *User Experience Mapping: Enhance UX With User Story Map, Journey Map and Diagrams*. Birmingham, UK: Packt Publishing.

Chapter 4. Impact

Bolukbasi, T., K. Chang, J. Zou, V. Saligrama, and A. Kalai. 2016. "Man Is to Computer Programmer as Woman Is to Homemaker? Debiasing Word Embeddings." *Proceedings of the 30th International Conference on Neural Information Processing Systems*. https://dl.acm.org/citation .cfm?id=3157584.

Brynjolfsson, E., and A. McAfee. 2012. *Race Against the Machine: How the Digital Revolution is Accelerating Innovation, Driving*

Productivity, and Irreversibly Transforming Employment and the Economy. Digital Frontier Press.

Cameron, N. 2017. *Will Robots Take Your Job? A Plea for Consensus.* Cambridge, UK: Polity Press.

Daugherty, P., and H.J. Wilson. 2018. *Human + Machine: Reimagining Work in the Age of AI.* Boston: Harvard Business Review Press.

De Gagne, J. 2010. "Ethical and Legal Issues in Online Education." *Journal of eLearning and Online Teaching* 1(7): 2–13.

Design Work Group and West Michigan Sustainable Business Forum. 1999. "Designing Products and Services With Sustainable Attributes." http://nbis.org/nbisresources/product_design/designing_products%20_sustainable_attributes.pdf.

Gazzaley, A., and L. Rosen. 2016. *The Distracted Mind: Ancient Brains in a High-Tech World.* Cambridge, MA: MIT Press.

Gunn, C. 2010. "Sustainability Factors for E-Learning Initiatives." *ALT-J, Research in Learning Technology* 18(2): 89–103.

Horrigan, J. 2016. Lifelong Learning and Technology. Pew Research Center, March 22. www.pewinternet.org/2016/03/22/lifelong-learning-and-technology.

Lee, K.-F. 2018. *AI Superpowers: China, Silicon Valley and the New World Order.* Boston: Houghton Mifflin Harcourt.

McCann, L. 2015. "Experimental Modes of Civic Engagement in Civic Tech: Meeting People Where They Are." Chicago: Smart Chicago Collaborative. www.smartchicagocollaborative.org/wp-content/uploads/2015/10/experimental-modes.pdf.

World Economic Forum. 2018. "Mastering a New Reality." World Economic Forum, February 21. www.youtube.com/watch?time_continue=163&v=a9OQLNvgf2Y.

Chapter 5. Learning

Crawford, M.B. 2015. *The World Beyond Your Head: On Becoming an Individual in an Age of Distraction.* New York: Farrar, Straus and Giroux.

Dichev, C., and D. Dicheva. 2017. "Gamifying Education: What Is Known, What Is Believed and What Remains Uncertain: A Critical Review." *International Journal of Educational Technology in Higher Education* 14(1): 9. http://educationaltechnologyjournal.springeropen.com /articles/10.1186/s.

Dirksen, J. 2016. *Design for How People Learn,* 2nd ed. San Francisco: New Riders.

Fiorella, L., and R. Mayer. 2015. *Learning as a Generative Activity: Eight Learning Strategies That Promote Understanding.* Cambridge, UK: Cambridge University Press.

Hill, P., and M. Barber. 2014. *Preparing for a Renaissance in Assessment.* London: Pearson UK. www.pearson.com/content/dam/one-dot-com/ one-dot-com/uk/documents/educator/primary/preparing_for_a_ renaissance_in_assessment_and_summary_text_december_2014.pdf.

Hopwood, N. 2014. "Four Essential Dimensions of Workplace Learning." *Journal of Workplace Learning* 26(6/7): 349–363. https://doi.org/10.1108/JWL-09-2013-0069.

Leech, R. ed. 2015. "Learning Assessments: Designing the Future - Research Conference 2015." Melbourne, Australia: Australian Council for Educational Research. www.acer.org/files/Research-Conference -Proceedings-2015.pdf

Miglino, O., A. Di Ferdinando, R. Di Fuccio, A. Rega, and C. Ricci. 2014. "Bridging Digital and Physical Education Games Using RFID/ NFC Technologies." *Journal of E-Learning and Knowledge Society* 10(3): 89–106.

National Academies of Sciences, Engineering, and Medicine. 2018. *How People Learn II: Learners, Contexts, and Cultures,* 2nd ed. Washington, D.C.: National Academies Press. www.nap.edu/catalog /24783/how-people-learn-ii-learners-contexts-and-cultures

Tozman, R. 2012. *Learning on Demand: How the Evolution of the Web Is Shaping the Future of Learning.* Alexandria, VA: ASTD Press.

Chapter 6. Dependencies

Associated Press. 2015. "Growing Dependence on Technology Raises Risks of Malfunction." *Crain's New York Business,* July 9. www.crainsnewyork.com/article/20150709/TECHNOLOGY/150709895/growing-dependence-on-technology-raises-risks-of-malfunction.

De Bono, E. 2016. *Six Thinking Hats.* London: Penguin UK.

Ebeling, M. 2017. *Not Impossible: The Art and Joy of Doing What Couldn't Be Done.* New York: Atria.

Eno, B. 2001. "Oblique Strategies: Over One Hundred Worthwhile Dilemmas." Card deck. www.enoshop.co.uk/product/oblique-strategies.html.

Ferguson, K. 2012. "Embrace the Remix." TED Talk, June. www.ted.com/talks/kirby_ferguson_embrace_the_remix?.

Gilbert, E. 2009. "Your Elusive Creative Genius." TED Talk, February. www.ted.com/talks/elizabeth_gilbert_on_genius?.

Hussung, T. 2015. "Emerging Trends in Psychology: Technology Dependency." Concordia St. Paul Blog and News Updates, October 16. https://online.csp.edu/blog/psychology/technology-dependency.

Lee, A., V. Shirazi, P. Gangu, O. Wyman, M. Leonard, and L. McKay. 2017. "Mitigating Risks in the Innovation Economy." World Economic Forum Whitepaper, October 12. www.weforum.org/whitepapers/mitigating-risks-in-the-innovation-economy.

Middleton, R., and M. Cantor-Grable. 2015. "Emerging Risks: Opportunities and Threats of Disruptive Technology." Presentation slides. London. www.actuaries.org.uk/documents/e8-emerging-risks-opportunities-and-threats-disruptive-technology.

Rodrigues, I., and J. Gonzaga. 2015. "Empirical Studies on Fine-Grained Feature Dependencies." Doctoral dissertation. Universidade Federal de Alagoas, Maceio, Brazil. www.repositorio.ufal.br/bitstream/riufal/1724/1/Empirical%20studies%20on%20fine-grained%20feature%20dependencies.pdf.

Strategic Foresight Initiative. 2011. "Technological Development and Dependency Long-Term Trends and Drivers and Their Implications for Emergency Management." FEMA. www.fema.gov/pdf/about/programs/oppa/technology_dev_%20paper.pdf.

Strode, D.E. 2016. "A Dependency Taxonomy for Agile Software Development Projects." *Information Systems Frontiers* 18(1): 23–46.

Chapter 7. Signals

Al-Khalili, J. ed. 2018. *What the Future Looks Like: Scientists Predict the Next Great Discoveries—and Reveal How Today's Breakthroughs Are Already Shaping Our World.* New York: The Experiment.

Bauer, M.R. 2017. "Quantum Computing Is Coming for Your Data." *Wired,* July 19. www.wired.com/story/quantum-computing-is-coming -for-your-data.

Bersin, J. 2017. "AI, Robotics, and Cognitive Computing Are Changing Business Faster Than You Thought." Josh Bersin blog, March 8. https://joshbersin.com/2017/03/ai-robotics-and-cognitive-computing -are-changing-business-faster-than-you-thought.

Bostrom, N. 2014. *Superintelligence: Paths, Dangers, Strategies.* Oxford: Oxford University Press.

Captain, S. 2018. "Quantum Computing Comes Out of the Closet." *Fast Company,* October 4. www.fastcompany.com/90245982/quantum -computing-comes-out-of-the-closet-d-wave-leap.

Daugherty, P., and H.J. Wilson. 2018. *Human + Machine: Reimagining Work in the Age of AI.* Boston: Harvard Business Review Press.

Franklin, D. ed. 2017. *Mega Tech: Technology in 2050.* New York: Public Affairs.

Gorbis, M. 2013. *The Nature of the Future: Dispatches From the Socialstructed World.* New York: Free Press.

Harari, Y.N. 2017. *Homo Deus: A Brief History of Tomorrow.* New York: Harper.

Howard, P.N. 2015. "Pax Technica: How the Internet of Things May Set Us Free or Lock Us Up." New Haven, CT: Yale University Press.

Husain, A. 2017. *The Sentient Machine: The Coming Age of Artificial Intelligence.* New York: Scribner.

Lanier, J. 2013. *Who Owns the Future?* New York: Simon & Schuster.

Lee, E.A. 2017. *Plato and the Nerd: The Creative Partnership of Humans and Technology.* Cambridge, MA: MIT Press.

Manyika, J., M. Chui, J. Bughin, R. Dobbs, P. Bisson, and A. Marrs. 2013. *Disruptive Technologies: Advances That Will Transform Life, Business, and the Global Economy*. San Francisco: McKinsey Global Institute.

Milner, G. 2016. *Pinpoint: How GPS Is Changing Technology, Culture, and Our Minds*. New York: W.W.Norton.

Mosco, V. 2014. *To the Cloud: Big Data in a Turbulent World*. New York: Routledge.

O'Reilly, T. 2017. *WTF?: What's the Future and Why It's Up to Us*. New York: HarperBusiness.

Rees, M. 2018. *On the Future: Prospects for Humanity*. Princeton, NJ: Princeton University Press.

Ross, A. 2016. *The Industries of the Future*. New York: Simon & Schuster.

Chapter 8. Strategies for a New Normal

Carson, B. 2017. *Learning in the Age of Immediacy: 5 Factors for How We Connect, Communicate, and Get Work Done*. Alexandria, VA: ATD Press.

Fong, P.S.W. 2006. "Project Professionals and Workplace Learning." Paper presented at New Directions in Project Management, Montréal, Québec, Canada. www.pmi.org/learning/library/project-professional-workplace-learning-initiatives-8079.

Johnson, M., and R. Davis. 2014. "A Future-Back Approach to Creating Your Growth Strategy." Innosight whitepaper, February. www.innosight.com/insight/a-future-back-approach-to-creating-your-growth-strategy

Loon, M. 2014. "L&D: New Challenges, New Approaches." Whitepaper. London: Chartered Institute of Personnel and Development. www.cipd.co.uk/Images/l-and-d_2014-new-challenges-new-approaches_tcm18-9172.pdf

Taylor, D.H. 2017. *Learning Technologies in the Workplace: How to Successfully Implement Learning Technologies in Organizations*. London: Kogan Page.

Yao, M., A. Zhou, and M. Jia. 2018. *Applied Artificial Intelligence: A Handbook for Business Leaders*. San Francisco: Topbots.

REFERENCES

Abel, A. 2008. "The Development of a Conceptual Framework and Taxonomy for Defining and Classifying Corporate Universities." Doctoral Dissertation. New York University, New York.

Adams, T. 2011. "How the Internet Created an Age of Rage." *Guardian,* July 24. www.theguardian.com/technology/2011/jul/24/internet-anonymity-trolling-tim-adams.

Adorni, G., M. Coccoli, and I. Torre. 2012. "Semantic Web and Internet of Things: Supporting Enhanced Learning." *Journal of E-Learning and Knowledge Society* 8(2): 23–32. https://pdfs.semanticscholar.org/4d5d/2c1fa7c6e1999d20972c74e28383c22f9d43.pdf.

Ahmed, A. 2018. "How Blockchain Will Change HR Forever." *Forbes,* March 14. www.forbes.com/sites/ashikahmed/2018/03/14/how-blockchain-will-change-hr-forever/#2836181d727c

Al-Khalili, J. 2018. *What the Future Looks Like: Scientists Predict the Next Great Discoveries and Reveal How Today's Breakthroughs Are Already Shaping Our World.* New York: The Experiment.

Al-Natour, S., and H. Cavusoglu. 2009. "The Strategic Knowledge-Based Dependency Diagrams: A Tool for Analyzing Strategic Knowledge Dependencies for the Purposes of Understanding and Communicating." *Information Technology and Management* 10(2–3): 103–121. www.researchgate.net/publication/225359925_The_strategic_knowledge-based_dependency_diagrams_A_tool_for_analyzing_strategic_knowledge_dependencies_for_the_purposes_of_understanding_and_communicating/download.

ALTC. 2018. "Emerging Learning Technologies: Conference Reviews." #ALTC blog, February 13. https://altc.alt.ac.uk/blog/2018/02/emerging-learning-technologies.

Alter, A.L. 2017. *Irresistible: The Rise of Addictive Technology and the Business of Keeping Us Hooked.* New York: Penguin Press.

Anderson, L., and D. Krathwohl, eds. 2001. *A Taxonomy for Learning, Teaching, and Assessing: A Revision of Bloom's Taxonomy of Educational Objectives, Complete Edition.* New York: Pearson.

Andreessen, M. 2011. "Why Software Is Eating the World." *Wall Street Journal,* August 20. https://a16z.com/2016/08/20/why-software-is-eating-the-world.

Andres, H.P. 2013. "Team Cognition Using Collaborative Technology: A Behavioral Analysis." *Journal of Managerial Psychology* 28(1): 38–54. www.emeraldinsight.com/doi/abs/10.1108/02683941311298850.

Antonelli, P. 2017. "What Is Your Digital Learning Strategy?" *Chief Learning Officer,* February 1. www.clomedia.com/2017/02/01/digital-learning-strategy.

Ashman, H., T. Brailsford, A. Cristea, Q. Sheng, C. Stewart, E. Toms, and V. Wade. 2014. "The Ethical and Social Implications of Personalization Technologies for E-Learning." *Information and Management* 51(6): 819–832. www.sciencedirect.com/science/article/abs/pii/S0378720614000524.

Asif, M., C. Searcy, A. Zutshi, and O. Fisscher. 2013. "An Integrated Management Systems Approach to Corporate Social Responsibility." *Journal of Cleaner Production* 56:7–17. www.sciencedirect.com/science/article/pii/S0959652611004203.

Associated Press. 2015. "Growing Dependence on Technology Raises Risks of Malfunction." Crains New York, July 9. www.crainsnewyork.com/article /20150709/TECHNOLOGY/150709895/growing-dependence-on-technology -raises-risks-of-malfunction.

Bailenson, J. 2018. *Experience On Demand: What Virtual Reality Is, How It Works, and What It Can Do.* New York: Norton.

Bain, R. 1937. "Technology and State Government." *American Sociological Review* 2(6): 860–874. www.jstor.org/stable/2084365.

Bates, T. 2014. "Why Lectures Are Dead (or Soon Will Be)." Tony Bates, July 27. www.tonybates.ca/2014/07/27/why-lectures-are-dead-or-soon-will-be.

Batson, T. 2011. "Situated Learning: A Theoretical Frame to Guide Transformational Change Using Electronic Portfolio Technology." *International Journal of EPortfolio* 1(1): 107–114. www.theijep.com/pdf/ijep34.pdf.

Behrens, J.T., and K.E. DiCerbo. 2014. "Technological Implications for Assessment Ecosystems: Opportunities for Digital Technology to Advance Assessment." *Teachers College Record* 116(11): 1–22. www.gordoncommission.org/rsc/pdf /behrens_dicerbo_technological_implications_assessment.pdf.

Beissner, F., K. Meissner, K.-J. Bar, and V. Napadow. 2013. "The Autonomic Brain: An Activation Likelihood Estimation Meta-Analysis for Central Processing of Autonomic Function." *Journal of Neuroscience* 33(25): 10503–10511. www.ncbi.nlm.nih.gov/pmc/articles/PMC3685840.

Bennani, F., K. Novak, and A. Vaidya. 2015. "The Internet of Things and STEM: How to Use IoT to Take Biology Out of the Classroom and Into the World." Presented at the EdMedia 2015, Montreal, Quebec. www.learntechlib.org /primary/p/151527.

Benson-Armer, R., A. Gast, and N. van Dam. 2016. "Learning at the Speed of Business." *McKinsey Quarterly.* www.mckinsey.com/business-functions /organization/our-insights/learning-at-the-speed-of-business.

Berlinski, D. 2000. *The Advent of the Algorithm: The Idea That Rules the World.* New York: Harcourt.

Bersin, J. 2007. "Death of the Corporate University." Josh Bersin Blog, June 26. https://joshbersin.com/2007/06/26.

Bersin, J. 2017a. "Video and Mobile Have Taken Over Learning." Keynote at L&D Innovation & Tech Fest, October 29-30. Sydney, Australia. www.techfestconf.com/ld/aus/blog/blog/learning-development/3-trends-that -will-shape-your-ld-strategy-in-2018.

Bersin, J. 2017b. "AI, Robotics, and Cognitive Computing Are Changing Business Faster Than You Thought." Josh Bersin Blog, March 8. https://joshbersin.com /2017/03/ai-robotics-and-cognitive-computing-are-changing-business-faster -than-you-thought.

Bersin, J. 2017c. "Watch Out, Corporate Learning: Here Comes Disruption." *Forbes,* March 28. www.forbes.com/sites/joshbersin/2017/03/28/watch-out -corporate-learning-here-comes-disruption.

Biech, E. 2018. *ATD's Foundations of Talent Development: Launching, Leveraging, and Leading Your Organization's TD Effort.* Alexandria, VA: ATD Press.

Biggs, J., and C. Tang. 2011. *Teaching for Quality Learning at University,* 4th ed. Berkshire, UK: Open University Press.

Blank, S. 2013. *The Four Steps to the Epiphany: Successful Strategies for Products that Win,* 2nd ed. Louisville, KY: Cafe Press.

Bloom, B.S., M.D. Engelhart, E.J. Furst, W.H. Hill, and D.R. Krathwohl. 1956. *Taxonomy of Educational Objectives: The Classification of Educational Goals.* New York: David McKay.

Borne, K. 2014. "Association Rule Mining – Not Your Typical Data Science Algorithm." MAPR blog, April 28. https://mapr.com/blog/association-rule -mining-not-your-typical-data-science-algorithm.

Bostrom, N. 2014. *Superintelligence: Paths, Dangers, Strategies.* Oxford: Oxford University Press.

Bothmann, O. 2015. *3D Printers: A Beginner's Guide.* East Petersburg, PA: Fox Chapel Publishing.

Bounfour, A. 2016. *Digital Futures, Digital Transformation*. Cham, Switzerland: Springer.

Brandenburg, L. 2018." How to Write a Use Case." Bridging the Gap blog. www.bridging-the-gap.com/what-is-a-use-case.

Bridle, J. 2018. *New Dark Age: Technology and the End of the Future*. New York: Verso.

Broussard, M. 2018. *Artificial Unintelligence: How Computers Misunderstand the World*. Cambridge, MA: MIT Press.

Brynjolfsson, E., and A. McAfee. 2014. *The Second Machine Age: Work, Progress, and Prosperity in a Time of Brilliant Technologies*. New York: Norton.

Bughin, J., T. Catlin, M. Hirt, and P. Willmott. 2018. "Why Digital Strategies Fail." *McKinsey Quarterly*. www.mckinsey.com/business-functions/digital -mckinsey/our-insights/why-digital-strategies-fail.

Burrow, G. 2017. "Data Spotlight: Fierce Demand for UI/UX Designers." Emsi Blog, January 12. www.economicmodeling.com/2017/01/12/data-spotlight -fierce-demand-uiux-designers.

Bursztein, E. 2017. "Inside Mirai the infamous IoT Botnet: A Retrospective Analysis." Elie Blog, December. https://elie.net/blog/security/inside-mirai- the-infamous-iot-botnet-a-retrospective-analysis.

Bush, V. 1945. "As We May Think." *The Atlantic Monthly* 176(1): 101–108. www.theatlantic.com/magazine/archive/1945/07/as-we-may-think/303881.

Cacciattolo, K. 2013. "Organizational Politics and Their Effect on Workplace Learning." *European Scientific Journal* 4. www.researchgate.net/publication /265560952_Organisational_Politics_and_their_effect_on_Workplace_Learning.

Calinger, M., and B.C. Howard. 2008. "Evaluating Educational Technologies: a Historical Context. *International Journal of Information and Communication Technology Education* 4(4): 9.

Cameron, N. 2017. *Will Robots Take Your Job? A Plea for Consensus*. Cambridge, UK: Polity Press.

Campbell, C. 2015. "How We Respond to Learning." *Training & Development* 42(2).

Captain, S. 2018. "Quantum Computing Comes Out of the Closet." *Fast Company*, October 4. www.fastcompany.com/90245982/quantum-computing-comes-out -of-the-closet-d-wave-leap

Carayannis, E.G., S.C. Clark, and D.E. Valvi. 2013. "Smartphone Affordance: Achieving Better Business Through Innovation." *Journal of the Knowledge Economy* 4(4): 444–472. https://link.springer.com/article/10.1007/s13132 -012-0091-x.

Carson, B. 2017. *Learning in the Age of Immediacy: 5 Factors for How We Connect, Communicate, and Get Work Done*. Alexandria, VA: ATD Press.

Carson, B., G. Romanelli, P. Walsh, and A. Zhumaev. 2018. "Blockchain Beyond the Hype: What Is the Strategic Business Value?" McKinsey & Company, June. www.mckinsey.com/business-functions/digital-mckinsey/our-insights /blockchain-beyond-the-hype-what-is-the-strategic-business-value

Carter, D. 2016. "95 Per Cent of L&D Practitioners in a New Survey See Virtual Reality as the Way to Enhance Their Practice." *Training Journal,* July 27. www.trainingjournal.com/articles/news/95-cent-ld-practitioners-new-survey -see-virtual-reality-way-enhance-their-practice?.

Casey, M., and P. Vigna. 2018. *The Truth Machine: the Blockchain and the Future of Everything.* New York: St. Martin's Press.

Cave, A. 2017. "Culture Eats Strategy for Breakfast. So, What's for Lunch?" *Forbes,* November 9. www.forbes.com/sites/andrewcave/2017/11/09/culture -eats-strategy-for-breakfast-so-whats-for-lunch.

CBC Radio. 2018. "'It's Like Christmas for Repressive Regimes': China Is Selling Surveillance Technology all Over the World." Day 6, November 30. www.cbc. ca/radio/day6/episode-418-when-gm-leaves-town-loud-restaurants-the-hit-series -dogs-mummers-china-surveillance-and-more-1.4927175/it-s-like-christmas-for -repressive-regimes-china-is-selling-surveillance-technology-all-over-the-world -1.4927185.

Cederquist, A., and U. Golüke. 2016." Teaching With Scenarios: A Social Innovation to Foster Learning and Social Change in Times of Great Uncertainty." *European Journal of Futures Research* 4(1): 17. https://link.springer.com/article/10.1007/s40309-016-0105-1

Cela-Ranilla, J.M., F.M. Esteve-Mon, V. Esteve-González, and M. Gisbert-Cervera. 2014. "Developing Self-Management and Teamwork Using Digital Games in 3D Simulations." *Australasian Journal of Educational Technology* 30(6). https://ajet.org.au/index.php/AJET/article/view/754.

Cerra, A., K. Easterwood, and J. Power. 2013. *Transforming Business: Big Data, Mobility, and Globalization.* Indianapolis: John Wiley & Sons.

Chamorro-Premuzic, T., D. Winsborough, R. A. Sherman, and R. Hogan. 2016. "New Talent Signals: Shiny New Objects or a Brave New World?" *Industrial and Organizational Psychology* 9(3): 621–640. www.cambridge.org/core /journals/industrial-and-organizational-psychology/article/new-talent-signals-shiny -new-objects-or-a-brave-new-world.B301CCE93DDCFC658257E36B80B5E695.

Chandok, P., H. Chheda, and M. Rosendahl. 2018. "Detailing the New Landscape for Global Business Services." *McKinsey & Company,* February 23. www .mckinsey.com/business-functions/digital-mckinsey/our-insights/detailing-the -new-landscape-for-global-business-services.

Chaplot, D., E. Rhim, and J. Kim. 2016. "Personalized Adaptive Learning Using Neural Networks." *Proceedings of the Third ACM Conference on Learning @ Scale*. Edinburgh: ACM. www.cs.cmu.edu/~dchaplot/papers/las16_chaplot.pdf

Cheng, B., M. Wang, J. Moormann, B. Olaniran, and N. Chen. 2012. "The Effects of Organizational Learning Environment Factors on E-Learning Acceptance." *Computers & Education* 58:885–899. www.sciencedirect.com/science/article/pii/S0360131511002582.

Cho, S.P., and J.G. Kim. 2016. "E-Learning Based on Internet of Things." *Advanced Science Letters* 22(11): 3294–3298.

Choi, G. 2016. "[Data Mining] Association Rules in R (Diapers and Beer)." Data Science Central blog, August 22. www.datasciencecentral.com/profiles/blogs/data-mining-association-rules-in-r-diapers-and-beer.

Christensen, C. 1997. *The Innovator's Dilemma: When New Technologies Cause Great Firms to Fail*. Boston: Harvard Business School Press. www.hbs.edu/faculty/Pages/item.aspx?num=46.

Christensen, C., M. Raynor, and R. McDonald. 2015. "What Is Disruptive Innovation?" *Harvard Business Review*, December. https://hbr.org/2015/12/what-is-disruptive-innovation.

Cochrane, T. 2012. "Secrets of Mlearning Failures: Confronting Reality." *Research in Learning Technology* 20(sup1): 123–134. http://citeseerx.ist.psu.edu/viewdoc/download?doi=10.1.1.689.9129&rep=rep1&type=pdf.

Crossley, S., and D. McNamara. 2016. *Adaptive Educational Technologies for Literacy Instruction*. New York: Routledge.

Daugherty, P., and H.J. Wilson. 2018. *Human + Machine: Reimagining Work in the Age of AI*. Boston: Harvard Business Review Press.

De Bono. 2016. *Six Thinking Hats (International)*. London: Penguin UK.

de Sola Pool, I. 1983. *Technologies of Freedom*. Cambridge, MA: Belknap Press.

Dear, B. 2017. *The Friendly Orange Glow: The Untold Story of the PLATO System and the Dawn of Cyberculture*. New York: Pantheon.

DeGusta, M. 2012. "Are Smart Phones Spreading Faster Than Any Technology in Human History?" *MIT Technology Review*, May 9. www.technologyreview.com/s/427787/are-smart-phones-spreading-faster-than-any-technology-in-human-history

Deshpande, P. 2017. "Understand How Content Is Influencing Buyers: A Primer on Attribution Models." Content Marketing Institute, February 10. https://contentmarketinginstitute.com/2017/02/primer-attribution-models.

Design Work Group. 1999. *Designing Products and Services With Sustainable Attributes*. Grand Rapids, MI: West Michigan Sustainable Business Forum. http://nbis.org/nbisresources/product_design/designing_products%20_sustainable_attributes.pdf.

Dichev, C., and D. Dicheva. 2017. "Gamifying Education: What Is Known, What Is Believed and What Remains Uncertain: A Critical Review." *International Journal of Educational Technology in Higher Education* 14(9). https://link .springer.com/content/pdf/10.1186%2Fs41239-017-0042-5.pdf.

Dillenbourg, P. 2013. "Design for Classroom Orchestration." *Computers & Education* 69:485–492. https://edisciplinas.usp.br/pluginfile.php/2745230 /mod_resource/content/7/Dillenbourg-CE-A8Extra.pdf.

Dillon, J. 2017. "L&D Digital Transformation Begins With Rethinking the LMS." *Learning Solutions*, June 5. www.learningsolutionsmag.com/articles/2345/ld -digital-transformation-begins-with-rethinking-the-lms.

Dinsmore, T. 2016. *Disruptive Analytics: Charting Your Strategy for Next-Generation Business Analytics.* New York: Apress.

Dirksen, J. 2016. *Design for How People Learn,* 2nd ed. San Francisco: New Riders.

Dixon, H. 2018. "Regulate to Liberate: Can Europe Save the Internet?" *Foreign Affairs* 97(5): 28–32. www.foreignaffairs.com/articles/europe/2018-08-13 /regulate-liberate.

Domingo, M., and J. Forner. 2010. "Expanding the Learning Environment: Combining Physicality and Virtuality - The Internet of Things for eLearning." Presented at the 10th IEEE International Conference on Advanced Learning Technologies, Sousse, Tunisia. https://ieeexplore.ieee.org/document/5572673.

Doornbos, A.J., S. Bolhuis, and P.R.-J. Simons. 2004. "Modeling Work-Related Learning on the Basis of Intentionality and Developmental Relatedness: A Noneducational Perspective." *Human Resource Development Review* 3(3): 250–274. https://journals.sagepub.com/doi/abs/10.1177/1534484304268107.

Draper, C. 2015. "Ships Passing in the Night? E-learning Designers' Experiences With User Experience." Doctoral dissertation. Brigham Young University, Provo, UT. https://scholarsarchive.byu.edu/cgi/viewcontent.cgi?referer=&httpsredir=1& article=6486&context=etd.

Dreyfus, H., and S. Dreyfus. 1986. *Mind Over Machine.* New York: Free Press.

Drucker, P. 1974. *Management: Tasks, Responsibilities, Practices.* New York: Harper & Row.

Dyson, G. 2012. *Turing's Cathedral: The Origins of the Digital Universe.* New York: Pantheon.

Ebeling, M. 2017. *Not Impossible: The Art and Joy of Doing What Couldn't Be Done.* New York: Atria.

EduMe.com. 2017. "Learning in the Gig Economy." EduMe blog, December 18. www.edume.com/blog/2017/11/20/learning-in-the-gig-economy.

Eno, B. 2001. "Oblique strategies: Over One Hundred Worthwhile Dilemmas." www.enoshop.co.uk/product/oblique-strategies.html.

Eschner, K. 2017. "The Roots of Computer Code Lie in Telegraph Code." *Smithsonian,* September 11. www.smithsonianmag.com/smart-news/roots -computer-code-lie-telegraph-code-180964782.

Farrell, J. 2012. "Social Media Takes Workplace Harassment to New Levels." HR.BLR, November 7. https://hr.blr.com/HR-news/Discrimination/Sexual -Harassment/zns-Social-Media-Takes-Workplace-Harassment-New-Le.

Feldstein, M., and P. Hill. 2016. "Personalized Learning: What It Really Is and Why It Really Matters." EDUCAUSE Review, March 7. https://er.educause.edu /articles/2016/3/personalized-learning-what-it-really-is-and-why-it-really-matters.

Ferguson, K. 2012. "Embrace the Remix." TED Talk. www.ted.com/talks/kirby _ferguson_embrace_the_remix?language=en.

Fields, K. 2016. "When Ethics and Compliance Training Fails." *ELearning Industry,* October 14. https://elearningindustry.com/ethics-and-compliance-training-fails.

Fiorella, L., and R. Mayer. 2015. *Learning as a Generative Activity: Eight Learning Strategies That Promote Understanding.* Cambridge: Cambridge University Press.

Fischer, G. 2003a. "Meta-Design: A Framework for the Future of End User Development (EUD)." Presented at the EUD-Net Symposium, Fraunhofer, Birlinghoven, Germany. http://l3d.cs.colorado.edu/~gerhard/presentations /eud-meta-d-slides-final.pdf.

Fischer, G. 2003b. "Meta—Design: Beyond User-Centered and Participatory Design." In Proceedings of HCI International 2003, vol. 4. Crete, Greece. http://l3d.cs.colorado.edu/~gerhard/papers/hci2003-meta-design.pdf.

Fischer, G. 2013. "Meta-Design: Empowering All Stakeholders as Co-Designers."In *Handbook on Design in Educational Computing.* London, UK: Routledge. http://l3d.cs.colorado.edu/~gerhard/papers/2012/paper-handbook.pdf.

Fischer, G. 2014. "Supporting Self-Directed Learning With Cultures of Participation in Collaborative Learning Environments." In *Problem-Based Learning for the 21st Century: New Practices and Learning Environments.* Aalborg, Denmark: Aalborg University Press. http://l3d.cs.colorado.edu/~gerhard/papers/2014 /Scandinavia-PBL.pdf.

Fischer, G., D. Fogli, and A. Piccinno. 2017. "Revisiting and Broadening the Meta-Design Framework for End-User Development." In *New Perspectives in End-User Development.* Cham, Switzerland: Springer. www.springer.com/us/book /9783319602905.

Fischer, G., and E. Giaccardi. 2006. "Meta-Design: A Framework for the Future of End-User Development." In *End User Development - Empowering People to*

Flexibly Employ Advanced Information and Communication Technology. Dordrecht, The Netherlands: Kluwer. Third International Conference on Designing InteractiveSystems. www.researchgate.net/publication/226719061_ Meta-design_A_Framework_for_the_Future_of_End-User_Development/download.

Fischer, G., and T. Herrmann. 2015. "Meta-Design: Transforming and Enriching the Design and Use of Socio-Technical Systems." In *Designing Socially Embedded Technologies in the Real-World.* London: Springer.

Fischer, G., and E. Scharff. 2000. "Meta-Design—Design for Designers." Presented at the 3rd International Conference on Designing Interactive Systems. New York: ACM. http://l3d.cs.colorado.edu/~gerhard/papers/dis2000.pdf.

Foer, F. 2017. *World Without Mind: The Existential Threat of Big Tech.* New York: Penguin Press.

Fong, P.S.W. 2006. "Project Professionals and Workplace Learning." Presented at New Directions in Project Management Conference, Montréal, Québec: PMI. www .pmi.org/learning/library/project-professional-workplace-learning-initiatives-8079.

Frank, J. 2017. "Bound to the Mimetic or the Transformative? Considering Other Possibilities." *Education and Culture* 33(1): 23–40. https://philpapers.org/rec /FRABTT.

Freedom House. 2018. "Freedom on the Net: The Rise of Digital Authoritarianism (Annual)." https://freedomhouse.org/sites/default/files/FOTN_2018_Final%20 Booklet_11_1_2018.pdf.

Fries, L. 2018. "How The Internet of Things Could Help Feed the World." *Forbes*, August 19. www.forbes.com/sites/lorinfries/2018/08/19/how-the-internet-of -things-could-help-feed-the-world

Gagné, R. 1985. *The Conditions of Learning and Theory of Instruction*, 4th ed. Belmont, CA: Wadsworth.

Gagné, R., L.J. Briggs, and W.W. Wager. 1992. *Principles of Instructional Design,* 4th ed. Fort Worth, TX: Harcourt Brace Jovanovich.

Galloway, S. 2017. *The Four: The Hidden DNA of Amazon, Apple, Facebook, and Google.* New York: Portfolio/Penguin.

Gallup. 2013. "State of the American Workplace." Gallup. www.gallup.com/file /services/176708/State_of_the_American_Workplace.

Gartner. 2018. "Gartner Says Worldwide IoT Security Spending Will Reach $1.5 Billion in 2018." Press release. www.gartner.com/newsroom/id/3869181.

Gazzaley, A., and L. Rosen. 2016. *The Distracted Mind: Ancient Brains in a High-Tech World.* Cambridge, MA: MIT Press.

Geertz, C. 1973. *The Interpretation of Cultures: Selected Essays.* New York: Basic Books.

Geisler, E. 1999. "The Metrics of Technology Evaluation: Where We Stand and Where We Should Go From Here." Presented at the 24th Annual Technology Transfer Society Meeting. www.inderscienceonline.com/doi/abs/10.1504/IJTM .2002.003060.

Gibbons, M., and R. Voyer. 1974. "A Technology Assessment System." Background Study no. 30. Ottawa: Science Council of Canada, Information Canada.

Gibbs, D. 2016. "What's the Internet of Things and What Does It Have to Do With My Classroom?" STEM Learning, August 1. www.stem.org.uk/news-and-views /opinions/what%E2%80%99s-internet-things-and-what-does-it-have-do-my -classroom.

Gibson, D., and D. Ifenthaler. 2017. "Preparing the Next Generation of Education Researchers for Big Data in Higher Education." In *Big Data and Learning Analytics in Higher Education: Current Theory and Practice*. Switzerland: Springer.

Gibson, W. 1999. "The Science in Science Fiction." NPR, November 30. www.npr.org/templates/story/story.php?storyId=1067220

Gijevski, N. 2017. "How Does Augmented Reality Work?" Quora, November 5. www.quora.com/How-does-Augmented-Reality-Work.

Gilbert, E. 2009. "Your Elusive Creative Genius." TED Talk. www.ted.com/talks /elizabeth_gilbert_on_genius?.

Goldin, I., and C. Kutarna. 2016. *Age of Discovery: Navigating the Risks and Rewards of Our New Renaissance*. London: Bloomsbury.

Gordon, E.E. 2014. "Talent Creation and the Bottom Line." *Training Magazine*, November 13. https://trainingmag.com/trgmag-article/talent-creation-and -bottom-line.

Grand-Clement, S. 2017. "Digital Learning: Education and Skills in the Digital Age." RAND Europe. www.rand.org/content/dam/rand/pubs/conf_proceedings/CF300 /CF369/RAND_CF369.pdf.

Grebow, D. 2015. "Coming Soon to Your Workplace: The Internet of Smart Things." David Grebow Knowledge Star blog, June 25. https://knowledgestar. blog/2015/06/25/coming-soon-to-your-workplace-the-internet-of-smart-things.

Grebow, D. 2017. "The Internet of Smart Things – Humanizing the IOT." David Grebow Knowledge Star blog, October 2. https://knowledgestar.blog/2017/10 /02/the-internet-of-smart-things-humanizing-the-iot.

Greengard, S. 2015. *The Internet of Things*. Cambridge, MA: MIT Press.

Guston, D.H. 2010. "The Anticipatory Governance of Emerging Technologies." *Journal of the Korean Vacuum Society* 19(6): 432–441. http://cspo.org/legacy /library/101214F2RN_lib_GustonD2010Antic.pdf.

Guston, D.H. 2014. "Understanding 'Anticipatory Governance.'" *Social Studies of Science* 44(2): 218–242. https://journals.sagepub.com/doi/10.1177/0306 312713508669.

Gutsche, B. 2010. "Coping With Continual Motion." *Library Journal* 135(4): 28–31. https://eric.ed.gov/?id=EJ925259.

Hagel, J. 2017. "Ask the Expert: John Hagel on the Future of Work." In *Learning in the Age of Immediacy: 5 Factors for How We Connect, Communicate, and Get Work Done.* Alexandria, VA: ATD Press.

Hagel, J., J.S. Brown, M. Wooll, R. Mathew, and W. Tsu. 2015. *The Lifetime Learner: A Journey Through the Future of Postsecondary Education.* www2. deloitte.com/insights/us/en/industry/public-sector/future-of-online-learning.html.

Hall, B. 1997. *Web-Based Training Cookbook.* New York: John Wiley & Sons.

Hall, D. 2004. "The Protean Career: A Quarter-Century Journey." *Journal of Vocational Behavior* 65(1): 1–13. www.sciencedirect.com/science/article /abs/pii/S0001879103001647.

Hamzelou, J. 2017. "Brain Implant Boosts Human Memory by Mimicking How We Learn." *New Scientist,* November 18. www.newscientist.com/article/215 3034-brain-implant-boosts-human-memory-by-mimicking-how-we-learn.

Harari, Y. N. 2017. *Homo Deus: A Brief History of Tomorrow.* New York: Harper.

Harder, D. 2017. "Becoming Active 'Unlearners': Why We Must Unlearn Our Past." *Training and Development Excellence,* August: 1–3.

Harris, I., R.C. Jennings, D. Pullinger, S. Rogerson, and P. Duquenoy. 2011. "Ethical Assessment of New Technologies: A Meta-Methodology." *Journal of Information, Communication and Ethics in Society* 9(1): 49–64. www.emeraldinsight.com/doi/abs/10.1108/14779961111123223.

Harris, R. 1999. "Lifelong Learning in Work Contexts." *Research in Post-Compulsory Education* 4(2): 161–182. www.tandfonline.com/doi/pdf/10.1080/1359674990 0200055.

Harris, T. 2016. "How Technology is Hijacking Your Mind—From a Magician and Google Design Ethicist." *Medium,* May 18. https://medium.com/thrive-global /how-technology-hijacks-peoples-minds-from-a-magician-and-google-s-design -ethicist-56d62ef5edf3.

Heath, J. 2014. *Enlightenment 2.0: Restoring Sanity in Our Politics, Our Economy and Our Lives.* Toronto: HarperCollins.

Heaven, D. ed. 2017. *Machines That Think: Everything You Need to Know About the Coming Age of Artificial Intelligence.* London: Nicholas Brealey.

Heinecke, W., L. Blasi, N. Milman, and L. Washington. 1999. "New Directions in the Evaluation of the Effectiveness of Educational Technology." Washington, D.C. https://files.eric.ed.gov/fulltext/ED452825.pdf.

Helbing, D. 2015. "Societal, Economic, Ethical and Legal Challenges of the Digital Revolution: From Big Data to Deep Learning, Artificial Intelligence, and Manipulative Technologies." https://arxiv.org/ftp/arxiv/papers/1504/1504 .03751.pdf.

Hinchcliffe, D. 2017. "The Digital Transformation of Learning: Social, Informal, Self-Service, and Enjoyable." Enterprise Web 2.0, September 27. www.zdnet .com/article/digital-transformation-of-learning-social-informal-self-service -enjoyable-mooc-education.

Hinton, A. 2014. *Understanding Context: Environment, Language, and Information Architecture.* San Francisco: O'Reilly.

Holland, J. 2012. *Signals and Boundaries: Building Blocks for Complex Adaptive Systems.* Cambridge, MA: MIT Press.

Holland, P., and A. Bardoel. 2016. "The Impact of Technology on Work in the Twenty-First Century: Exploring the Smart and Dark Side." *The International Journal of Human Resource Management* 27(21): 2579–2581. https://doi.org /10.1080/09585192.2016.1238126.

Homer-Dixon, Thomas. (2000). The Ingenuity Gap. How Can We Can Solve the Problems of the Future? New York, NY: Knopf.

Hopwood, N. 2014. "Four Essential Dimensions of Workplace Learning." *Journal of Workplace Learning* 26(6/7): 349–363. www.emeraldinsight.com/doi/abs /10.1108/JWL-09-2013-0069.

Horrigan, J. 2016. *Lifelong Learning and Technology.* Pew Research Center. www.pewresearch.org/wp-content/uploads/sites/9/2016/03/PI_2016.03.22 _Educational-Ecosystems_FINAL.pdf.

Howard, P.N. 2015. *Pax Technica: How the Internet of Things May Set Us Free or Lock Us Up.* New Haven, CT: Yale University Press.

Hsu, T. 2018. "For Many Facebook Users, a 'Last Straw' That Led Them to Quit." *New York Times,* March 21. www.nytimes.com/2018/03/21/technology/users -abandon-facebook.html.

Hsu, Y.-C., and Y.-H. Ching. 2015. "A Review of Models and Frameworks for Designing Mobile Learning Experiences and Environments." *Canadian Journal of Learning and Technology* 41(3): 1–22. https://doi.org/10.21432/T2V616.

Hu, J., B. van der Vlist, G. Niezen, W. Willemsen, D. Willems, and L. Feijs. 2013. "Designing the Internet of Things for Learning Environmentally Responsible Behaviour." *Interactive Learning Environments* 21(2): 211–226.

IBM Training. 2014. "The Value of Training." IBM whitepaper. www-03.ibm.com /services/learning/pdfs/IBMTraining-TheValueofTraining.pdf.

IMS Global. 2018. "IMS Learner Information Package Specification." IMS Global Learning Consortium. www.imsglobal.org/profiles/index.html.

Ito, J., and J. Howe. 2016. *Whiplash: How to Survive Our Faster Future*. New York: Grand Central Publishing.

Johnson, M., and R. Davis. 2014. "A Future-Back Approach to Creating Your Growth Strategy." Innosight whitepaper. www.innosight.com/insight/a-future-back-approach-to-creating-your-growth-strategy.

Johnston, J., and L.T. Barker. 2002. "Assessing the Impact of Technology in Teaching and Learning: A Sourcebook for Evaluators." Institute for Social Research, University of Michigan.

Joy, B. 2000. "Why the Future Doesn't Need Us." *Wired,* April 1. www.wired.com/2000/04/joy-2/

Juo, J. 2017. "5 Learning Trends You Need to Know to Keep Your Workforce Ahead of Innovation." Udemy for Business, March 15. https://business.udemy.com/blog/5-learning-trends-need-know-keep-workforce-ahead-innovation.

Kahneman, D. 2011. *Thinking, Fast and Slow.* New York: Farrar, Straus and Giroux.

Kahuna.com. 2015. "How App Store Ratings Impact App Downloads." Infographic. www.kahuna.com/resources/how-app-store-ratings-impact-app-downloads.

Kalashnikov, A., H. Zhang, J. Jennings, and M. Abramriuk. 2017. "Remote Laboratory: Using Internet-of-Things (IoT) for E-Learning." Sheffield Hallam University Research Archive. http://shura.shu.ac.uk/15845/1/Section_3_Kalashnikov_IoT_E-learning.pdf.

Kaplan, R., and D. Norton. 1992. "The Balanced Scorecard—Measures That Drive Performance." *Harvard Business Review*, February. https://hbr.org/1992/01/the-balanced-scorecard-measures-that-drive-performance-2.

Kaplan, R., and D. Norton. 1996. *The Balanced Scorecard: Translating Strategy Into Action.* Boston: Harvard Business Review Press.

Kapp, K. 2013. "Once Again, Games Can and Do Teach!" *Learning Solutions Magazine*, March 4. www.learningsolutionsmag.com/articles/1113/once-again-games-can-and-do-teach.

Kapp, K. 2018. "Gamification in Learning – 10 Tips from Karl Kapp." E-Learning Art blog, January 31. https://elearningart.com/blog/gamification-tips-karl-kapp.

Kelly, K. 2016. *The Inevitable: Understanding the 12 Technological Forces That Will Shape Our Future.* New York: Viking.

Kloski, L., and N. Kloski. 2018. *Getting Started With 3D Printing: A Hands-on Guide to the Hardware, Software, and Services That Make the 3D Printing Ecosystem,* 2nd ed. Sebastopol, CA: Maker Media.

Kornbluh, K. 2018. "The Internet's Lost Promise and How America Can Restore It." *Foreign Affairs* 97(5). www.foreignaffairs.com/articles/world/2018-08-13/internets-lost-promise.

KPMG. 2017. "U.S. CEO Outlook 2017 (Survey)." KPMG. https://home.kpmg.com
/us/en/home/insights/2017/06/us-ceo-outlook-2017.html.

Krishna, G. 2015. *The Best Interface Is No Interface: The Simple Path to Brilliant Technology.* San Francisco: New Riders.

Krom, C. 2012. "Using FarmVille in an Introductory Managerial Accounting Course to Engage Students, Enhance Comprehension, and Develop Social Networking Skills." *Journal of Management Education* 36(6): 848–865. https://journals.sagepub.com/doi/pdf/10.1177/1052562912459029.

Krug, S. 2014. *Don't Make Me Think, Revisited: A Common Sense Approach to Web Usability.* San Francisco: New Riders.

Lachman, S. 1997. "Learning Is a Process: Toward an Improved Definition of Learning." *Journal of Psychology* 131(5): 477–480. www.tandfonline.com /doi/abs/10.1080/00223989709603535.

Ladner, S. 2014. *Practical Ethnography: A Guide to Doing Ethnography in the Private Sector.* New York: Routledge.

LaGrow, M. 2017. "From Accommodation to Accessibility: Creating a Culture of Inclusivity." Educause Review, March 13. https://er.educause.edu/articles/2017 /3/from-accommodation-to-accessibility-creating-a-culture-of-inclusivity.

Lamson, M., and A. von Rewitz. 2018. "The Impact of AI on Learning and Development." Training Industry blog, May 8. https://trainingindustry.com /articles/learning-technologies/the-impact-of-ai-on-learning-and-development.

Lanier, J. 2013. *Who Owns the Future?* New York: Simon & Schuster.

Lave, J., and E. Wenger. 1991. *Situated Learning: Legitimate Peripheral Participation.* Cambridge: Cambridge University Press.

Ledra Capital. 2014. "The Mega-Master Blockchain List." Ledra Capital, March 11. http://ledracapital.com/blog/2014/3/11/bitcoin-series-24-the-mega-master -blockchain-list.

Lee, C.-Y., and T. Cherner. 2015. "A Comprehensive Evaluation Rubric for Assessing Instructional Apps." *Journal of Information Technology Education: Research* 14:21–53. www.jite.org/documents/Vol14/JITEV14ResearchP021 -053Yuan0700.pdf.

Lee, E. 2017. *Plato and the Nerd: The Creative Partnership of Humans and Technology.* Cambridge, MA: MIT Press.

Lee, K.-F. 2018. *AI Superpowers: China, Silicon Valley, and the New World Order.* New York: Houghton Mifflin Harcourt.

Leech, R. 2015. "Learning Assessments: Designing the Future—Research Conference 2015." In *Learning Assessments: Designing the Future.* Melbourne: Australian Council for Educational Research. www.acer.org/files/Research-Conference -Proceedings-2015.pdf.

Leinonen, T., J. Purrna, K. Ngua, and A. Hayes. 2013. "Scenarios for Peer-to-Peer Learning in Construction With Emerging Forms of Collaborative Computing." In Technology and Society 2013 IEEE International Symposium. Toronto: IEEE.

Lejarraga, J. 2010. "Do the Sources of Learning Affect Entrepreneurial Risk-Taking?" *European Management Review* 7:73.

Levy, S. 2017. "Google Glass 2.0 Is a Startling Second Act." *Wired,* July 18. www.wired.com/story/google-glass-2-is-here.

Liang, T., C. Huang, Y. Yeh, and B. Lin. 2007. "Adoption of Mobile Technology in Business: A Fit-Viability Model." *Industrial Management & Data Systems* 107(8): 1154–1169. https://doi.org/10.1108/02635570710822796.

Lin, H., and J. Kolb. 2006. "Ethical Issues Experienced by Learning Technology Practitioners in Design and Training Situations." ERIC Document No. ED492813. https://files.eric.ed.gov/fulltext/ED492813.pdf.

Loon, M. 2014. *L&D: New Challenges, New Approaches.* London: Chartered Institute of Personnel and Development. www.cipd.co.uk/Images/l-and-d _2014-new-challenges-new-approaches_tcm18-9172.pdf.

Lowenthal, S. 2018. "How Is Digital Transformation Affecting L&D?" *E-Learning Industry,* January 16. https://elearningindustry.com/digital-transformation -affecting-l-and-d.

Lukic, D., A. Littlejohn, and A. Margaryan. 2012. "A Framework for Learning From Incidents in the Workplace." *Safety Science* 50(4): 950–957. www.sciencedirect.com/science/article/pii/S0925753511003511.

Lynskey, D. 2015. "How the Compact Disc Lost Its Shine." *Guardian,* May 28. www.theguardian.com/music/2015/may/28/how-the-compact-disc-lost-its-shine.

Main, A., B. Lamm, and D. McCormack. 2017. "Winning With Digital: What Boards Need to Know About Digital Transformation." Deloitte whitepaper. www2.deloitte.com/content/dam/Deloitte/us/Documents/center-for-board -effectiveness/us-oct-2017-winning-with-digital-on-the-boards-agenda.pdf.

Mann, S., J. Nolan, and B. Wellman. 2003. "Sousveillance: Inventing and Using Wearable Computing Devices for Data Collection in Surveillance Environments." *Surveillance and Society* 1(3): 331–355. https://ojs.library .queensu.ca/index.php/surveillance-and-society/article/view/3344.

Manyika, J., M. Chui, J. Bughin, R. Dobbs, P. Bisson, and A. Marrs. 2013. *Disruptive Technologies: Advances That Will Transform Life, Business, and the Global Economy.* McKinsey Global Institute. www.mckinsey.com /business-functions/digital-mckinsey/our-insights/disruptive-technologies.

Mark, C.L. 2014. *Growth and Decline of Second Life as an Educational Platform.* Doctoral Dissertation, University of Southern Mississippi. ERIC Document ED557541.

Marr, B. 2018a. "The 4th Industrial Revolution Is Here - Are You Ready?" Forbes, August 13. www.forbes.com/sites/bernardmarr/2018/08/13/the-4th-industrial -revolution-is-here-are-you-ready.

Marr, B. 2018b. "Is This the End of Blockchain?" Forbes, December 10. www .forbes.com/sites/bernardmarr/2018/12/10/is-this-the-end-of-blockchain.

Mashable. 2014. "What Is the Uncanny Valley? | Mashable Explains." Mashable video, June 19. www.youtube.com/watch?v=aYuBDkto2Vk.

Mason, R.O. 1986. "Four Ethical Issues of the Information Age." MIS Quarterly, 10, 5–12. www.researchgate.net/publication/242705009_Four_Ethical_Issues _of_the_Information_Age.

Masters, G. 2015. "Learning Assessments: Designing the Future." *2009 - 2018 ACER Research Conferences.* https://research.acer.edu.au/cgi/viewcontent. cgi?article=1251&context=research_conference.

Mayes, R., G. Natividad, and J.M. Spector. 2015. "Challenges for Educational Technologists in the 21st Century." *Education Sciences* 5:221–237. www.mdpi.com/2227-7102/5/3/221/pdf.

McAfee, A. 2009. *Enterprise 2.0: New Collaborative Tools for Your Organization's Toughest Challenges.* Boston: Harvard Business School Publishing.

McArthur, D. 2018. "Will Blockchains Revolutionize Education? *Educause Review,* May 21. https://er.educause.edu/articles/2018/5/will-blockchains-revolutionize-education.

McEwan, A., and H. Cassimally. 2013. *Designing the Internet of Things.* New York: Wiley.

McGrath, R. 2013. "The Pace of Technology Adoption Is Speeding Up." *Harvard Business Review,* November 25. https://hbr.org/2013/11/the-pace-of-technology -adoption-is-speeding-up.

McLuhan, M. 1964. *Understanding Media: The Extensions of Man.* New York: McGraw-Hill.

McLuhan, M. 1966. "Quote About Fish Not Discovering Water." *Technology and World Trade: Proceedings of a Symposium.* Gaithersburg, MD. https://quoteinvestigator.com/2013/12/23/water-fish.

McLuhan, M., and Q. Fiore. 1967. *The Medium Is the Massage: An Inventory of Effects.* New York: Bantam Books.

Meadows, D. 2008. *Thinking in Systems: A Primer.* White River Junction, VT: Chelsea Green Publishing.

Meister, J. 1998. *Corporate Universities: Lessons in Building a World-Class Work Force,* 2nd ed. New York: McGraw-Hill.

Meister, J. 2017. "The Future of Work: The Intersection of Artificial Intelligence and Human Resources." *Forbes,* March 1. www.forbes.com/sites/jeannemeister

/2017/03/01/the-future-of-work-the-intersection-of-artificial-intelligence-and
-human-resources/#2f7efe3a6ad2.

Mendes, W. 2016. "Emotion and the Autonomic Nervous System." Chap. 9 in
Handbook of Emotions, 4th ed, edited by L.F. Barrett, M. Lewis, and J.M.
Haviland-Jones. New York: Guilford Press. https://static1.squarespace.com
/static/59a5d96b8dd041d469d4304e/t/59b1ccf28dd04187fccd1ffb/150482
4563654/emotion_ANS_2016.pdf.

Merifield, A. 2015. "Piecing Together Digital." *Training Journal,* January 1.
www.trainingjournal.com/articles/feature/piecing-together-digital.

Middleton, R., and M. Cantor-Grable. 2015. "Emerging Risks: Opportunities and
Threats of Disruptive Technology." Powerpoint presented at the Institute and
Faculty of Actuaries, October 30. www.actuaries.org.uk/documents/e8
-emerging-risks-opportunities-and-threats-disruptive-technology.

Miglino, O., A. Di Ferdinando, R. Di Fuccio, A. Rega, and C. Ricci. 2014.
"Bridging Digital and Physical Educational Games Using RFID/NFC
Technologies." *Journal of E-Learning and Knowledge Society* 10(3): 89–106.
www.learntechlib.org/p/150734.

Molenda, M. 2003. "In Search of the Elusive ADDIE Model." *Performance
Improvement* 42(5): 34–36. www.researchgate.net/publication/251405713
_In_search_of_the_elusive_ADDIE_model.

Momeni, M., M. Jamporazmey, M. Mehrafrouz, and F. Bahadori. 2013.
"Comprehensive Framework for Evaluating E-Learning Systems: Using BSC
Framework." *International Journal on E-Learning* 12(1): 81–98.
www.learntechlib.org/p/36052.

Moore, G. 2014. *Crossing the Chasm: Marketing and Selling Disruptive Products
to Mainstream Customers,* 3rd ed. New York: HarperBusiness.

Morey, S., and J. Tinnell, eds. 2016. *Augmented Reality: Innovative Perspectives
Across Art, Industry, and Academia.* Anderson, SC: Parlor Press.

Morville, P. 2014. *Intertwingled: Information Changes Everything.* Ann Arbor,
MI: Semantic Studios.

Mougayar, W. 2016. *The Business Blockchain: Promise, Practice, and Application
of the Next Internet Technology.* Hoboken, NJ: John Wiley & Sons.

Mozur, P. 2018." Inside China's Dystopian Dreams: A.I., Shame and Lots of
Cameras." *New York Times,* July 8. www.nytimes.com/2018/07/08/business
/china-surveillance-technology.html.

Musk, E (@elonmusk). 2018. "We will add a feature to allow." Twitter, April 5.
https://twitter.com/elonmusk/status/981975289403076610.

National Academies of Sciences, Engineering, and Medicine. 2018. *How People
Learn II: Learners, Contexts, and Cultures,* 2nd ed. Washington, D.C.:

National Academies Press. www.nap.edu/catalog/24783/how-people-learn
-ii-learners-contexts-and-cultures.

Negroponte, N. 1995. *Being Digital.* New York: Knopf.

Nelson, T. 1974. *Computer Lib: You Can and Must Understand Computers Now.* South Bend, IN.

Nieva, R., and L. Hautala. 2018. "Facebook, Twitter Still Have Fake Account Problems. But They're Making Progress." Cnet, August 22. www.cnet.com/news/facebook-twitter-still-have-fake-account-problems-but-theyre-making-progress.

Nilekani, N. 2018. "Data to the People: India's Inclusive Internet." *Foreign Affairs* 97(5): 19–26. www.foreignaffairs.com/articles/asia/2018-08-13/data-people.

NMC. 2017. "Horizon Report: 2017 Higher Education Edition (Annual)." *New Media Consortium and EDUCAUSE.* www.nmc.org/publication/nmc-horizon-report-2017-higher-education-edition.

Noeth, R.J., and B.B. Volkov. 2004. *Evaluating the Effectiveness of Technology in Our Schools.* ACT Policy Report. American College Testing ACT. https://files.eric.ed.gov/fulltext/ED483855.pdf.

Nordrum, A. 2016. "The Fuzzy Future of Virtual Reality and Augmented Reality." IEEE Spectrum, November 15. https://spectrum.ieee.org/tech-talk/consumer-electronics/gadgets/can-you-see-it-the-future-of-virtual-and-augmented-reality.

Norman, D. 1988. *The Psychology of Everyday Things.* New York: Basic Books.

Oliver, M. 1998. "Innovation in the Evaluation of Learning Technology." Learning and Teaching Innovation and Development, University of North London.

Oliver, M. 2000. "An Introduction to the Evaluation of Learning Technology." *Educational Technology & Society* 3(4): 20–30. www.researchgate.net/publication/255672817_An_introduction_to_the_Evaluation_of_Learning_Technology.

O'Reilly, T. 2017. *WTF?: What's the Future and Why It's Up to Us.* New York: HarperBusiness.

Osterwalder, A., and Y. Pigneur. 2010. *Business Model Generation: A Handbook for Visionaries, Game Changers, and Challengers.* Hoboken, NJ: John Wiley & Sons.

Otterbacher, J. 2016. "New Evidence Shows Search Engines Reinforce Social Stereotypes." *Harvard Business Review,* October 20. https://hbr.org/2016/10/new-evidence-shows-search-engines-reinforce-social-stereotypes.

Ozkan, B.C., and B.K. McKenzie. 2006. "Evaluating Educational Technologies: Technology Connoisseurs in the Campus." Presented at the Annual Meeting of Eastern Educational Research Association, Hilton Head, SC. https://files.eric.ed.gov/fulltext/ED491403.pdf.

Pardo, A., and G. Siemens. 2014. "Ethical and Privacy Principles for Learning Analytics." *British Journal of Educational Technology* 45(3): 438–450. https://onlinelibrary.wiley.com/doi/abs/10.1111/bjet.12152.

Pariser, E. 2011. *Filter Bubble: What the Internet Is Hiding From You.* New York: Penguin Press.

Parlavantzas, E. 2015. "Learning Motivation for Employee Engagement." ELearning Industry, April 9. https://elearningindustry.com/learning -motivation-employee-engagement.

Parrish, D. 2017. "Technology Changes Everything: Digital Trends Shaping The Industrial Sector." SAP Blog, May 25. https://blogs.sap.com/2017/05/25/ technology-changes-everything-digital-trends-shaping-the-industrial-sector.

Pink, S., E. Ardèvol, and D. Lanzeni, eds. 2016. *Digital Materialities: Design and Anthropology.* London, UK: Bloomsbury.

Pink, S., H. Lingard, and J. Harley. 2016. "Digital Pedagogy for Safety: The Construction Site as a Collaborative Learning Environment." *Video Journal of Education and Pedagogy* 1(1): 5. https://link.springer.com/article/10.1186 /s40990-016-0007-y.

Pollock, R., A. Jefferson, and C. Wick. 2015. *The Six Disciplines of Breakthrough Learning: How to Turn Learning and Development Into Business Results,* 3rd ed. Hoboken, NJ: John Wiley & Sons.

Prieto, L.P., Y. Dimitriadis, and J.I. Asensio-Pérez. 2014. "Orchestrating Evaluation of Complex Educational Technologies: A Case Study of a CSCL System." *Qualitative Research in Education* 3(2): 175–205. www.researchgate.net /publication/307824802_An_Orchestrating_Evaluation_of_Complex _Educational_Technologies_a_Case_Study_of_a_CSCL_System/download.

Prieto, L.P., M. Dlab, I. Gutiérrez, M. Abdulwahed, and W. Balid. 2011. "Orchestrating Technology Enhanced Learning: A Literature Review and a Conceptual Framework." *International Journal of Technology Enhanced Learning* 3(6): 583–598. www.gsic.uva.es/~lprisan/Prieto2011_Orchestrating TELLiteratureReviewConceptualFramework.pdf.

Pushman, T. 2003. "A Short History of Character Sets." Gnomedia Codeworks, November 22. https://codeworks.gnomedia.com/2003/a-short-history-of -character-sets.

Qvortrup, A., and M. Wiberg. 2013. "Learning Between Means and Aims." Chap. 1 in *Dealing with Conceptualisations of Learning: Learning Between Means and Aims in Theory and Practice,* edited by A. Qvorturp and M. Wiberg. Rotterdam: Sense Publishers. www.sensepublishers.com/media/3166-dealing -with-conceptualisations-of-learning.pdf.

Ramstad, E. 2009. "Developmental Evaluation Framework for Innovation and Learning Networks: Integration of the Structure, Process and Outcomes." *Journal of Workplace Learning* 21(3): 181–197. https://doi.org/10.1108 /13665620910943924.

Recruiting.com. 2018. "The Case for Employment Branding." Recruiting.com blog. www.recruiting.com/blog/the-case-for-employment-branding.

Rees, M. 2018. *On the Future: Prospects for Humanity.* Princeton, NJ: Princeton University Press.

Ries, E. 2011. *The Lean Startup: How Today's Entrepreneurs Use Continuous Innovation to Create Radically Successful Businesses.* New York: Crown Business.

Rodrigues, I., and J. Gonzaga. 2015. *Empirical Studies on Fine-Grained Feature Dependencies.* Doctoral dissertation. Universidade Federal de Alagoas, Maceio, Brazil. www.repositorio.ufal.br/bitstream/riufal/1724/1/Empirical%20 studies%20on%20fine-grained%20feature%20dependencies.pdf.

Rollag, K., and J. Billsberry. 2012. "Technology as the Enabler of a New Wave of Active Learning." *Journal of Management Education* 36(6): 743–752. https://doi.org/10.1177/1052562912466220.

Rose, D. 2014. *Enchanted Objects: Design, Human Desire, and the Internet of Things.* New York: Scribner.

Rosenfeld, L., P. Morville, and J. Arango. 2015. *Information Architecture: For the Web and Beyond,* 4th ed. Sebastopol, CA: O'Reilly.

Rumelt, R. 2011. *Good Strategy Bad Strategy: The Difference and Why It Matters.* New York: Crown Business.

Russon, M.-A. 2018. "The Race to Make the World's Most Powerful Computer Ever." BBC, September 4. www.bbc.co.uk/news/business-45273584.

Sanjiv, K.R. 2016. "How VR and AR Will Be Training Tomorrow's Workforce." VentureBeat, February 21. https://venturebeat.com/2016/02/21/how-vr-and-ar-will-be-training-tomorrows-workforce.

Sawyer, R.K. 2014. "Introduction: The New Science of Learning." Chap. 1 in *The Cambridge Handbook of the Learning Sciences,* edited by R.K. Sawyer. Cambridge, UK: Cambridge University Press.

Schilling, D. 2013. "Knowledge Doubling Every 12 Months, Soon to be Every 12 Hours." Industry Tap, April 19. www.industrytap.com/knowledge-doubling -every-12-months-soon-to-be-every-12-hours/3950.

Schwab, K. 2018. "How to Design for Everyone, in 3 Steps." Fast Company, February 9. www.fastcompany.com/90160000/how-to-design-for-everyone-in-3-steps.

Schwab, K. 2017. *The Fourth Industrial Revolution.* New York: Currency.

Schwartz, E. 2010. "Finding Our Way with Digital Bread Crumbs." *MIT Technology Review*, August 18. www.technologyreview.com/s/420277/finding-our-way-with-digital-bread-crumbs.

Schwartz, M. 2016. *The Art of Business Value*. Portland: IT Revolution.

Segal, A. 2018. "When China Rules the Web: Technology in the Service of the State." *Foreign Affairs* 97(5): 10–18. www.foreignaffairs.com/articles/china/2018-08-13/when-china-rules-web.

Shaer, O., and E. Hornecker. 2009. "Tangible User Interfaces: Past, Present, and Future Directions." *Foundations and Trends in Human-Computer Interaction* 3(1–2): 1–137. www.researchgate.net/publication/220613480_Tangible_User_Interfaces_Past_Present_and_Future_Directions.

Shane, D. 2018. "Research Shows Users Are Leaving Facebook in Droves. Here's What It Means for You." Inc, September 11. www.inc.com/dakota-shane/research-shows-users-are-leaving-facebook-in-droves-heres-what-it-means-for-you.html.

Sharma, N. 2018. "Top 10 Learning and Development Trends for 2018." Elearning Industry, March 15. https://elearningindustry.com/top-learning-development-trends-2018.

Shirky, C. 2008. *Here Comes Everybody: The Power of Organizing Without Organizations*. New York: Penguin Press.

Shivayogi, P. 2013. "Vulnerable Population and Methods for Their Safeguard." *Perspectives on Clinical Research* 4(1): 53–57. www.ncbi.nlm.nih.gov/pmc/articles/PMC3601707.

Siadaty, M., D. Gasevic, J. Jovanovic, K. Pata, N. Milikic, T. Holocher-Ertl, … M. Hatala. 2012. "Self-Regulated Workplace Learning: A Pedagogical Framework and Semantic Web-Based Environment." *Journal of Educational Technology & Society* 15(4): 75. www.jstor.org/stable/jeductechsoci.15.4.75.

Siebel, T. 2017. "Why Digital Transformation Is Now on the CEO's Shoulders." *McKinsey Quarterly*, December. www.mckinsey.com/business-functions/digital-mckinsey/our-insights/why-digital-transformation-is-now-on-the-ceos-shoulders.

Simon, M. 2018. "It's Time to Talk About Robot Gender Stereotypes." Wired, October 3. www.wired.com/story/robot-gender-stereotypes.

Skiba, D. 2017. "The Potential of Blockchain in Education and Health Care." *Nursing Education Perspectives* 38(4): 220–221. https://journals.lww.com/neponline/Citation/2017/07000/The_Potential_of_Blockchain_in_Education_and.17.aspx

Snoeren, M.M., T.J. Niessen, and T.A. Abma. 2015. "Beyond Dichotomies: Towards a More Encompassing View of Learning." *Management Learning* 46(2): 137–155. https://doi.org/10.1177/1350507613504344.

Sourour, B. 2016). "The Code I'm Still Ashamed Of." Free Code Camp, November 16. https://medium.freecodecamp.org/the-code-im-still-ashamed-of-e4c021dff55e.

Stahl, B., J. Timmermans, and C. Flick. 2017. "Ethics of Emerging Information and Communication Technologies: On the Implementation of Responsible Research and Innovation." *Science and Public Policy* 44(3): 369–381. https://academic.oup.com/spp/article/44/3/369/2525576.

Stahl, G. 2004. "Building Collaborative Knowing: Elements of a Social Theory of CSCL." Chap. 3 in *What We Know About CSCL: And Implementing It in Higher Education,* edited by J.-W. Strijbos, P.A. Kirschner, and R.L. Martens. Boston: Kluwer. http://gerrystahl.net/cscl/papers/ch16.pdf.

Stahl, G. 2006. *Group Cognition: Computer Support for Building Collaborative Knowledge.* Cambridge, MA: MIT Press.

Standage, T. 2017. "A Toolkit for Predicting the Future." Medium, May 31. https://medium.economist.com/a-toolkit-for-predicting-the-future-2f24757d9699.

Stockard, J., T. Wood, C. Coughlin, and C. Khoury. 2018. "The Effectiveness of Direct Instruction Curricula: A Meta-Analysis of a Half Century of Research." *Review of Educational Research* 88(4). www.researchgate.net/publication/322332768.

Stone, I. 2012. *Upgrading Workforce Skills in Small Businesses: Reviewing International Policy and Experience.* Report for Workshop on "Skills Development for SMEs and Entrepreneurship." Copenhagen: OECD. www.oecd.org/cfe/leed/Skills%20Workshop%20Background%20report_Stone.pdf.

Strategic Foresight Initiative. 2011. "Technological Development and Dependency Long-term Trends and Drivers and Their Implications for Emergency Management." FEMA. www.fema.gov/pdf/about/programs/oppa/technology_dev_%20paper.pdf.

Strode, D.E. 2016. "A Dependency Taxonomy for Agile Software Development Projects." *Information Systems Frontiers* 18(1): 23–46. https://doi.org/10.1007/s10796-015-9574-1.

Suler, J. 2015. *Psychology of the Digital Age: Humans Become Electric.* Cambridge, UK: Cambridge University Press.

Sutherland, I. 1968. "A Head-Mounted Three Dimensional Display." In *Proceedings of the AFIPS Fall Joint Computer Conference* (295–302). Washington, D.C. www.cise.ufl.edu/research/lok/teaching/ve-s07/papers/sutherland-headmount.pdf

Sward, D. 2006. *Measuring the Business Value of Information Technology Practical Strategies for IT and Business Managers.* Hillsboro, OR: Intel Press.

Szabo, P. 2017. *User Experience Mapping: Enhance UX With User Story Map, Journey Map and Diagrams.* Birmingham, UK: Packt Publishing.

Talentedge. 2015. "Digital Learning Anywhere With 'Direct to Device' Technology." Talentedge video, February 11. www.youtube.com/watch?v=7ImBjipZH3Y.

Tallon, L. 2008. "Introduction: Mobile, Digital, and Personal." In *Digital Technologies and the Museum Experience: Handheld Guides and Other Media*. New York: Rowman & Littlefield.

Tapscott, D., and A. Tapscott. 2016. *Blockchain Revolution: How the Technology Behind Bitcoin Is Changing Money, Business, and the World*. New York: Portfolio/Penguin.

Tapscott, D., and A. Tapscott. 2017. "The Blockchain Revolution and Higher Education." *Educause Review,* March 13. https://er.educause.edu/articles /2017/3/the-blockchain-revolution-and-higher-education.

Taylor, D. 2017. *Learning Technologies in the Workplace: How to Successfully Implement Learning Technologies in Organizations*. London: Kogan Page.

Taylor, K. 2017. "40 of the Biggest Scandals in Uber's History." *Business Insider,* November 24. www.businessinsider.com/uber-company-scandals-and -controversies-2017-11.

Thaler, R., and C. Sunstein. 2009. *Nudge: Improving Decisions About Health, Wealth, and Happiness*. New York: Penguin Books.

The Eventful Group. 2018. "3 Trends That Will Shape Your L&D Strategy in 2018." www.techfestconf.com/ld/aus/blog/blog/learning-development/3 -trends-that-will-shape-your-ld-strategy-in-2018.

The Pitcher. 2015. "Entrepreneurship Skill Set Boost: When IoT Meets eLearning." The Pitcher. https://thepitcher.org/entrepreneurship-skill-set-boost-iot-meets -elearning.

The Week. 2018. "Amazon Workers Across Europe Go on Strike." *The Week,* July 17. www.theweek.co.uk/95089/amazon-workers-across-europe-go-on-strike.

Thornton, S. 2018. "A Guide to Chicago's Array of Things Initiative." Data Smart, January 2. https://datasmart.ash.harvard.edu/news/article/a-guide-to -chicagos-array-of-things-initiative-1190.

Toffler, A., and H. Toffler. 1970. *Future Shock*. New York: Random House.

Tozman, R. 2012. *Learning on Demand: How the Evolution of the Web Is Shaping the Future of Learning*. Alexandria, VA: ASTD Press.

Tretiakov, A., Kinshuk, and T. Tretiakov. 2003. "Designing Multimedia Support for Situated Learning." *The 3rd IEEE International Conference on Advanced Learning Technologies Conference Proceedings*. https://pdfs .semanticscholar.org/e5b5/7d8db27fff67e0668054a5c3c6435bd5c501.pdf.

UAE. 2018. "Smart City University to Provide Digital Skills Development." UAE Government News, April 24. www.itp.net/617018-smart-city-university-to -provide-digital-skills-development.

Udell, C. 2012. *Learning Everywhere: How Mobile Content Strategies are Transforming Training.* Alexandria, VA: ASTD Press.

Veix, J. 2018. "Exploring the Digital Ruins of 'Second Life.'" Digg, June 5. http://digg.com/2018/second-life-in-2018.

Vey, K., T. Fandel-Meyer, J.S. Zipp, and C. Schneider. 2017. "Learning & Development in Times of Digital Transformation: Facilitating a Culture of Change and Innovation." *International Journal of Advanced Corporate Learning* 10(1): 22. https://doi.org/10.3991/ijac.v10i1.6334.

Vincent, J. 2016. "Twitter Taught Microsoft's AI Chatbot to Be a Racist Asshole in Less Than a Day." The Verge, March 24. www.theverge.com/2016/3/24/11297050/tay-microsoft-chatbot-racist.

Vygotsky, L. 1978. *Mind in Society.* Cambridge, MA: Harvard University Press.

Wachter-Boettcher, S. 2017. *Technically Wrong: Sexist Apps, Biased Algorithms, and Other Threats of Toxic Tech.* New York: W.W. Norton.

Walker, K. 2006. "A Method for Creating Collaborative Mobile Learning Trails." Presented at the Kaleidoscope Convergence Workshop, Amsterdam, Netherlands: Les cahiers du laboratoire Leibniz. http://citeseerx.ist.psu.edu/viewdoc/download?doi=10.1.1.584.3086&rep=rep1&type=pdf.

Wallace-Wells, D. 2017. "The Uninhabitable Earth: Famine, Economic Collapse, a Sun That Cooks Us—What Climate Change Could Wreak—Sooner Than You Think." *New York Magazine,* July. http://nymag.com/daily/intelligencer/2017/07/climate-change-earth-too-hot-for-humans.html.

Wallach, A. 2016. "Three Ways to Plan for the Very Long Term." TED Talk, TEDxMidAtlantic, October. www.ted.com/talks/ari_wallach_3_ways_to_plan_for_the_very_long_term.

Walsh, B. 2013. "The Surprisingly Large Energy Footprint of the Digital Economy." *TIME,* August 14. http://science.time.com/2013/08/14/power-drain-the-digital-cloud-is-using-more-energy-than-you-think.

Webb, A. 2016. *The Signals Are Talking: Why Today's Fringe Is Tomorrow's Mainstream.* New York: Public Affairs.

Weinberger, D. 2014. *Too Big to Know: Rethinking Knowledge Now That the Facts Aren't the Facts, Experts Are Everywhere, and the Smartest Person in the Room Is the Room.* New York: Basic Books.

Wilen, T. 2018. *Digital Disruption: The Future of Work, Skills, Leadership, Education, and Careers in a Digital World.* New York: Peter Lang.

Williams, C. 2010. "Understanding the Essential Elements of Work-Based Learning and its Relevance to Everyday Clinical Practice." *Journal of Nursing Management* 18(6): 624–632. www.ncbi.nlm.nih.gov/pubmed/20840356.

Willingham, D. 2017. "Three Versions of Personalized Learning, Three Challenges." Daniel Willingham–Science and Education blog, November 14. www.danielwillingham.com/daniel-willingham-science-and-education-blog /three-versions-of-personalized-learning-three-challenges.

Wolf, M. 2018. *Reader, Come Home: The Reading Brain in a Digital World.* New York: HarperCollins.

Wood, D.J., J.S. Bruner, and G. Ross. 1976. "The Role of Tutoring in Problem Solving." *Journal of Child Psychiatry and Psychology* 17(2): 89–100. www.researchgate.net/publication/228039919_The_Role_of_Tutoring_in _Problem_Solving.

Woodill, G. 2010. *The Mobile Learning Edge: Tools and Technologies for Developing Your Teams.* New York: McGraw-Hill.

Woodill, G., C. Udell, and G. Stead. 2014. "Intertwingled Technologies: The Keys to The Emerging Enterprise Landscape." Whitepaper. Morton, IL: Float. https://gowithfloat.com/champions.

World Economic Forum. 2018. "Mastering a New Reality." Video recording. World Economic Forum, February 21. www.youtube.com/watch?time_ continue=163&v=a9OQLNvgf2Y.

Yao, M., A. Zhou, and M. Jia. 2018. *Applied Artificial Intelligence: A Handbook for Business Leaders.* San Francisco: Topbots.

Yin, C., B. Zhang, B. David, and Z. Xiong. 2015. "A Hierarchical Ontology Context Model for Work-Based Learning." *Frontiers of Computer Science* 9(3): 466–473. https://link.springer.com/article/10.1007/s11704-015-4200-4.

Yusoff, M., H. Zaman, and A. Ahmad. 2010. "Design A Situated Learning Environment Using Mixed Reality Technology - A Case Study." *International Journal of Computer and Information Engineering* 4(11): 1766–1771. https://waset.org/publications/15162/design-a-situated-learning-environment -using-mixed-reality-technology-a-case-study

ABOUT THE AUTHORS

 **Chad Udell** is the managing partner, strategy and new product development, at Float. There he leads his design and development teams to successful outcomes and award-winning work via a strong background in both disciplines and a singular focus on quality. He has worked with industry-leading Fortune 500 companies and government agencies to design and develop experiences for 20 years. Chad is recognized as an expert in mobile design and development, and he speaks regularly at national and international events and conferences on related topics. Chad is author of *Learning Everywhere: How Mobile Content Strategies Are Transforming Training* and co-editor and chapter author, with Gary Woodill, of *Mastering Mobile Learning: Tips and Techniques for Success.*

 **Gary Woodill** is a senior analyst with Float and CEO of i5 Research. He has been involved with computers in education since 1974, when he was introduced to the PLATO system for computer-assisted instruction in his master's studies. In the early 1990s, he co-founded an educational multimedia company that developed educational CD-ROMs for children and later designed an adaptable LMS. Gary has developed more than 60 online courses for various corporate clients. He has a doctorate in applied psychology from the University

of Toronto. Gary co-authored *Training and Collaboration With Virtual Worlds: How to Create Cost-Saving, Efficient and Engaging Programs,* and authored *The Mobile Learning Edge: Tools and Technologies for Developing Your Teams,* as well as numerous articles, research reports, and whitepapers on emerging learning technologies. He and Chad Udell co-edited and contributed to *Mastering Mobile Learning: Tips and Techniques for Success.*

INDEX